MAHATMA GANDHI IN THE BEGINNING OF TWENTY-FIRST CENTURY

MAHATMA GANDHI IN THE BEGINNING OF TWENTY-FIRST CENTURY

Editor

Dr. Ravindra Kumar

GYAN PUBLISHING HOUSE

New Delhi–110002

Mahatama Gandhi in the Beginning of
Twenty-First Century

Rs. 540

ISBN : 81-212-0898-X

Published in 2006 in India by
Gyan Publishing House
5, Ansari Road, Daryaganj
New Delhi-110 002

Phones-23282060, 23261060, Fax-23285914

Email : books@gyanbooks.com

Visit our Website at : http//www.gyanbooks.com

Laser type Setting by: Tact Computer Graphics, Delhi

Printed at: Salasar Imaging System, Delhi

Contents

Foreword 15
Introduction 17
List of Contributors 27

1. Mahatma Gandhi and Value Education: An Analysis. 31
   Ravindra Kumar
2. Gandhi and the World View: The South African Experiences. 41
   Vasant Kumar Bawa
3. Gandhi As a Critique of Violence in the World. 47
   Chaiwat Sta-anand
4. The Spinning–Wheel and the Seed: Gandhi's Legacy, Humanity's Hope. 53
   Vandana Shiva
5. Going Back to Gandhi [The Joy of Sacrifice and Service]. 71
   Subhash C. Kashyap
6. Mahatma Gandhi's Satyagraha. 75
   Karuna Kusalasaya
7. Gandhi and Burmese Democracy Movement. 79
   Tint Swe
8. Rama and Ramayana in the Life of Mahatma Gandhi. 83
   Lallan Prasad Vyas

9. Mahatma Gandhi on Non-Violence. 91
Asghar Ali Engineer

10. World Peace and Gandhism. 97
Babubhai Jashbhai Patel

11. Non-Violent Political Approach Towards Establishing Peaceful Co-Existence. 103
Shahidul Haque Munshi

12. The Bhagvad-Gita and its Influence on Gandhi. 109
Poonam Lakhanpal and *Anjula Rajvanshi*

13. Conflict Resolution and Peace Possibilities in the Gandhian Perspective. 121
Surinder K. Shukla

14. Tolstoy and Gandhi and their Legacy Today. 133
Christian Bartolf

15. Inspiration of Mahatma Gandhi: Source, Application and Effects. 139
Sachin Bathla

16. Nuclear Weapons, Gandhi's Birthday, and the Nuremberg Principles. 159
John Scales Avery

17. Gandhi and Nordic Countries. 181
Holger Terp

18. Gandhism, Optimism and the Gandhians. 185
Thomas Weber

19. Some Thoughts on Civil-Disobedience: My Duties and Responsibilities. 201
Jeff Knaebel

20. Mahatma Gandhi and His Inherent Love for Unity. 237

Mrinalini Sarabhai

21. Gandhian Institutions and Unfinished Work of Ba and Bapu: Some Reflections. 239

Rama Rauta

22. Gandhi, Non-Violence and Future of Mankind. 243

C.S. Dharmadhikari

23. Gandhi, Philosophy and Islam. 255

I. Khan

24. Understanding the Status of Women Through the Eyes of Gandhi. 285

Faridah Noor Mohammad Noor

25. Culture of Peace: Relevance of Gandhian Concept in the Twenty-First Century. 293

C. Naseema

26. Understanding the Present World Order: Perspectives of Gandhi and Russell. 301

R.K. Kothari

27. Peace, Non-Violence and Democracy in Burma: Voices from India of Buddha and Gandhi. 317

Sulak Sivaraksa

28. Problems Before Present Education: Some Remedial Suggestions Through Gandhian Approach. 321

Ravindra Kumar

Glossary of Indian Terms 331

Index 333

Seven Deadly Sins According to Mahatma Gandhi

1. Politics without principles
2. Pleasure without conscience
3. Wealth without work
4. Knowledge without character
5. Commerce without morality
6. Science without humanity
7. Worship without sacrifice

Abbreviations

A. I. C. C.	:	All India Congress Committee
C. C. S. U.	:	Chaudhary Charan Singh University
C. T. B. T.	:	Comprehensive Test Ban Treaty
H. E.	:	Hydro-Electric
I. C. C.	:	International Criminal Court
N. L. D.	:	National League for Democracy
P. G.	[:	Post Graduate
W. T. O.	:	World Trade Organization

Foreword

I feel honoured to write a Foreword to Dr. Ravindra Kumar's work entitled, **Mahatma Gandhi in the Beginning of Twenty-First Century.**

Not only India but for the whole world Mahatma Gandhi and his teachings have greater relevance today than ever before. The atmosphere of competition, conflict and fear which we see all over the world, the diminution of values in life and the problems having cropped up vividly cannot be eradicated without following the non-violent pathway shown by Mahatma Gandhi. There is no alternative to non-violence. The whole human history is within our purview. Whenever polities were under clutches of violence, tacitly or expressively, they could not get anything except doom and disaster to their citizens. Their own peace was fully shattered due to this doom and others were also badly affected. It is in this regard that in accordance with philosophy of Mahatma Gandhi, non-violence should be admitted as invariable part of our life and it is on the basis of this dictum that polities, especially democracies, must also operate.

Dr. Ravindra Kumar is a renowned Gandhian scholar and thinker. Through this remarkable volume he has rendered a great service to the academic-world and humanity to understand various aspects of non-violent Gandhian philosophy. I extend my best wishes to Dr. Ravindra Kumar and wish very success of this work.

Dr. Sein Win
Prime Minister
National Coalition Government of the
Union of Burma

Introduction

It was in 1969 that I had an opportunity to discuss a little about Mahatma Gandhi with my teacher for the first time. What conversation I had about is now lost in the abyss of time. But later I always wondered – why an international political leader like Gandhi was addressed as ***Mahatma***, an honorific frequently used for a spiritually elevated soul. To find an answer, I think it is essential to review his life not in parts, but as a whole.

Gandhi, affectionately called ***Bapu***, was a great leader endowed with a spiritual yearning for truth. The quintessence of his philosophy of life was the realization of ***Satya*** [truth] and ***Ahinsa*** [non- violence]. His purpose of life was as he once said, ***"To achieve self- realization, to see God face to face, to attain Moksha [Salvation]."*** But his approach was different from that of other seekers.

Gandhi received good ***Samskaras*** [pre-disposition] by virtue of his birth in a religious ***Vaishnava*** family of Gujarat, particularly from his mother who left an indelible impression of her saintliness on his tender mind. He imbibed truthfulness from the characteristics of the hero of the play ***'Harishchandra'***. He wondered, ***"Why should not we be truthful like Harishchandra?"*** The question haunted him day and night. King Harishchandra became the ideal hero of his dream and the paragon of truth. He so inspired him as to remain truthful all through his life even under trying circumstances and stand firm on his convictions.

Gandhi's endeavours for self-realization were through strict observance of truth. He moulded his actions on the basis of truth, only the truth that he perceived within. The word truth ordinarily connotes not to tell lies. But for Gandhi it implied much more Even hiding the truth from someone was deemed as untruth by him. He considered that the narrow implication of the term had belied its magnitude. Defining truth he writes, ***"The root of 'Satya' [truth] lies in 'Sat."***

Sat means the 'Being' and ***Satya*** – the feeling of the 'Being'. Everything is perishable except ***'Sat'***. Therefore, the true name of God is ***'Sat'***, thereby implying ***Satya*** [Truth] so, instead of saying '***God is Truth***', it is better to say ***'Truth is God'***. A question may now arise whether the realization of 'Truth' and the realization of 'Self' were one and the same for him or the two entities. We get the answer from ***Maharshi*** Raman:

"What is Satya except 'Self'? Satya is that which is made of Sat. Again Sat is nothing but Self. So Gandhiji's Satya is only the Self."

It is now clear, what Gandhi meant by Truth was in fact the realization of Self. He writes:

"What I meant to achieve – what I have been striving and pining to achieve these thirty years – is self-realization, to see God face to face, to attain Moksha [salvation]."

How to realize God is a complicate question. The realization of God can be attained by purity of mind and heart and ***Sadhana*** [constant practice]. The ***Shrimadbhagvad-Gita***, the dialogue between Lord Krishna and Arjuna in the epic ***Mahabharata***, is regarded as a sacred Hindu scripture and an infallible guide of daily practice. Lord Krishna tells about four paths of God-realization. They are the service and sacrifice [***Karma Yoga***], devotion and self- surrender [***Bhakti Yoga***], concentration and meditation [***Raja Yoga***], discrimination and wisdom [***Jnana Yoga***]. There is no line of demarktion between one and another and one path does not exclude the others. A seeker can follow any of them according to his/ her temperament. Ultimately they all lead to one goal - the realization of God.

Gandhi held the ***Bhagvad-Gita*** in high esteem. He writes:

"Those who will meditate on Gita will derive fresh joy and new meanings from it everyday. There is no single spiritual tangle which the Gita cannot unravel."

He found answer to the above question in ***Gita–Vairagya*** [non- attachment] or ***Abhyas Yoga*** [practice]. ***Vairagya*** means total indifference to worldly things and concentration only on the Absolute. Lord Krishna says in the ***Gita***:

"***Fix thy mind on Me only, place thy intellect in Me; then thou shalt no doubt live in Me alone hereafter.***" [Chapter XII: ***Shloka*** - 8]

And further says he, ***"If thou art not able to fix thy mind steadily on Me, then by Yoga of constant Practice [Abhyas Yoga] do thou seek to reach Me".*** [Ibid: 9]

Gandhi was born to serve humanity. He was a practical man; he chose the path of practice and the path of renunciation of the fruits of action. Absolute faith in God and surrender to His Will became his object of observance [***Niyam***] and the constant thought of the truth - practice [***Abhyas Yoga***]. His mind was always occupied with truth in all walks of life - personal, social or political.

Gandhi was a seeker and introspection was the method of his ***Sadhana***. He writes:

"I have gone through deep introspection, searched myself through and through, and examined and analyzed every psychological situation."

The study of *the* ***Gita*** and the process of self-introspection brought him face to face with the true meaning of ***ahimsa*** [Non- Violence] – no violence in thought, speech and act. He came to the conclusion that the realization of truth was impossible without adherence to the supreme conduct of man–***ahimsa***. In his opinion ***Satya*** and ***ahimsa*** were so inter- mingled as the two sides of a coin. For the achievement of one or the other, complete control over the senses of action [***Karmendriya***] and those of perception [***Jnanendriya***] is essential. Lord Krishna also says in the ***Gita***:

"Control Raga- dvesha [attachment–malevolence], obstructions on spiritual path; Do your duty well. Control desire and anger – the enemies of wisdom. Master first the senses. Kill this enemy - desire by restraining the self by Self and by knowing Him who is superior to intellect". [Chapter III: **Shloka** 37 – 43]

Truth and ***ahimsa*** appear to be at the same level as a pair truth– ***ahimsa***, yet Gandhi regarded ***ahimsa*** as means [***Sadhana***] and truth as the ultimate goal [***Sadhya***]. It is said ***ahimsa*** is the super-most religion [***ahimsa parmodharmah***], truth for Gandhi was the Almighty God. He, therefore, strived for and adhered to perfect truth in thought, speech and act all through his life and thereby achieved the realization of Self. It is most likely that he practiced also ***Kriya Yoga*** as was initiated in by ***Paramahansa*** Yogananda, who visited him in ***Wardha Ashram*** in 1935. Although lean and frail in appearance, he was strong in body and mind and glowed with spiritual health.

Gandhi once admitted that he had little knowledge of religions even of Hinduism, yet he believed, like every Hindu, in God, in rebirth and salvation. He had a broad perception of Hinduism. In this perspective he says:

"I believe Hinduism is not an exclusive religion. In it there is room for the worship of all the prophets of the world. It is not a missionary religion in the ordinary sense of the term. It has no doubt absorbed many tribes in its fold, but the absorption has been of an evolutionary, imperceptible character. Hinduism tells each man to worship God according to his own faith or dharma and so live at peace with all religions."

So, he regarded all religions with ***Samabhaav*** [equitability]. He perceived no religion was superior or inferior. He had studied about all religions of the world and came to the conclusion as he says:

"I believe the Bible, the Koran, and the Zend–Avesta to be as divinely inspired as the Vedas."

He even tried in his mind to unify the teachings of the ***Gita***, Sermon on the Mount and the Light of Asia and found renunciation in ***Gita*** as ***'the greatest philosophy of all religions'***.

Gandhi said:

"Nothing delights me as much as the music of the Gita or the Ramayana by Tulsidas."

It will, therefore, not be out of context if we consider here the influence of the ***Ramayana*** on him. The ***Ramayana*** is an epic like Milton's

'Paradise Lost'-a grand story, of a grand Man, in a grand style. But unlike ***'Paradise Lost'***, the ***Ramayana*** is a sacred scripture of Hindus. Therein, Tulsidas has portrayed the persona magnum, Rama, as an incarnation of Vishnu as well as a model human being with high moral values to serve as example for common man. Frank Whaling writes:

"Rama has remained a symbol of dharma, human relationship and kingship; for others he has been a symbol of 'Brahman' or a symbol of the loving Lord."

In his childhood, the repetition of the ***Ramanaam*** [Rama's name] suggested to him to ward off his fear of ghosts and spirits became an infallible guide for him later in life. Gandhi was highly impressed with the characteristics of Rama. Gandhi's heart was the permanent abode of Rama who was endowed with the attributes of ***Brahman.*** Rama's obedience, ready submission to the vows of his father, his love for his subject, protection to the weak, and equanimity to all beings he met during his exile, left deep impressions on Gandhi's mind and heart. But what impressed him most was Rama's way of administration–***Ramarajya,*** in which justice prevailed and the voice of the low of the lowest was given due regard. In fact, he regarded ***Ramarajya*** as the true model of democracy.

In introduction to his autobiography, Gandhi has written:

"My experiments in the political field are now known. But I should certainly like to narrate my experiments in the spiritual field, which are known only to me and from which I have derived such power as I possess for working in the political field."

Indeed, he relentlessly pursued truth all through his life and achieved self-realization.

It is an anomaly that he is remembered and evaluated only for his political achievements. Little attention has been paid to the spiritual force within him from which he derived power to work in personal, social and political fields. According to ***Maharshi*** Raman, ***Adhyatmik Shakti*** [spiritual force] was working within him [Gandhi] and leading him on. He always listened to his inner voice and took decisions accordingly. His inner- self prompted him to serve the wounded in Boer War and Zulu rebellion in South Africa. He was always in front line and fearlessly led people in ***Satyagraha*** and Non-Cooperation movements. Undaunted he walked unarmed without any protection through the riot- hit areas at the time of partition of India, giving message of faith, love and peace.

Gandhi was a ***yogi***- householder living amidst people. He was a ***Nishkam Karmayogi*** with no aspiration for any recognition or reward. He had limited his desires and needs to the bare minimum. Whatever he did, he did with right intention, right spirit and conviction, and worked for the benefit of others, irrespective of caste, creed or religion. Notwithstanding the power he wielded over the Congress party and the masses, he never aspired for or accepted any kind of office. Had his name been proposed as the first Governor-General of independent India in recognition of his services to the nation, I am sure, none would have opposed it but he himself. He was such a great and magnanimous person. Rabindranath Tagore, a poet and visionary, recognized his greatness and spirituality and called him ***Mahatma***, an attribute he aptly deserved.

Lord Krishna says to Arjuna in the ***Gita***:

"Whenever righteousness declines and unrighteousness becomes powerful then I myself come to birth." [Chapter IV – 7].

If we turn to the pages of the history of the world, it is evident that there have descended super- beings whenever the righteousness or ethical values are on decline to guide people on to the righteous path. The Indian soil is credited with the birth of many a super-being or the lofty spiritual personages who inspired people to forsake the evils of materialism that cause suffering, dissatisfaction and misery and to follow the path of spiritualism. Rational explanations of Mahatma Gandhi's thoughts and acts will certainly place him in history in line with Lord Mahavira, Gautama Buddha and Jesus Christ. Gandhi stood for truth, ***ahimsa***, compassion and service all through his life. 'To serve humanity is the service of God' was the principle of his life. He was a social saviour of the oppressed and down-trodden people and fought for their right of equality and justice. It is not all; he was the political saviour of nations in political turmoil. The leaders of many subjugated races and countries drew inspiration from him for their rights. Like Jesus Christ, he was Forgiveness Personified. He had no feeling of malice towards anyone in his dying moments and breathed his last remembering his chosen deity ***'Rama'***. Paying a glowing tribute to Mahatma Gandhi, Albert Einstein has written:

"Generations to come, it may be, will scarcely believe that such one as this ever in flesh and blood walked upon the earth."

Today, we are passing through a crisis – a crisis of identification of values. The world is entrapped in gross materialism. Man has become so selfish as to have utter disregard for others whether an individual or a society or a nation. Scientists are trying with each other to play the role of the Creator. It is high time to create a balance between materialism and spiritualism. In the chaotic circumstances prevailing all over the world today, we are looking for peace as elusive as the mirage in a desert. I think Mahatma Gandhi's life and his teachings can serve as beacon-lights to guide us and lead us to steady peace.

In this volume there is a collection of articles by eminent Gandhian scholars and subject-specialists from India and abroad who, through their valuable contributions, have thrown light on various aspects of Gandhian philosophy and thoughts and their relevance in the Twenty-First Century. I am sure this volume will add to the knowledge of those interested in Mahatma Gandhi's life, views and works.

I express my gratitude towards Professor John Scales Avery, Dr. Subhash C. Kashyap, Dr. Asghar Ali Engineer, Dr. Tint Swe, Dr. Vandana Shiva, Dr. Intakhab, Professor Dr. Farida Noor Mohammad Noor, Dr. Anjula Rajvanshi, Dr. Christian Bartolf, Justice Chandrashekhar Dharmadhikari, Mr. Sachin Bathla, Mr. Karuna Kusalasaya, Mrs. Mrinalini Sarabhai, Dr. Vasant Kumar Bawa, Professor Shahidul Huq Munshi, Mrs. Rama Rauta, Professor Chaiwat Sta-anand, Professor Dr. C. Naseema, Mr. Babubhai J. Patel, Mr. Lallan Prasad Vyas, Mr. Holger Terp, Dr. Surinder K. Shukla, Professor Thomas Weber, Dr. R.K. Kothari, Dr. Poonam Lakhanpal, Mr. Sulak Sivaraksa, and Mr. Jeff Knaebel for their articles incorporated in this volume. I am thankful to Mr. Sachin Arora, Mrs. Megha Arora, Mr. Mrinal Khurana, Mr. Manoj Kumar 'Manoj' and all those who have extended their help in preparing the manuscript of this volume. Especially, I express my gratitude towards Mrs. Kamlesh Ravindra Kumar and Ms. Aneeta Vijayakar, who not only pointed out some errors in the manuscript but made useful suggestions for designing this book.

Meerut [India]
January 30, 2006 **-Ravindra Kumar**

List of Contributors

1. *Dr. Ravindra Kumar* is the Former Vice-Chancellor of CCS University of Meerut [India].
2. *Dr. Vasant Kumar Bawa* is a well-known scholar and peace worker from Hyderabad, India.
3. *Professor Dr. Chaiwat Sta-anand* is the Director, Peace Information Centre, Foundation for Democracy and Development Studies, Faculty of Political Science, Thammasat University, Bangkok, Thailand.
4. The Right Livelihood Award winner *Dr. Vandana Shiva* is the Chief of NAVDANYA, New Delhi, India.
5. Universally renowned constitutional expert *Dr. Subhash C. Kashyap* has served the *Lok Sabha* [House of the People of Indian Parliament] as its Secretary-General.
6. Born in Thailand in 1920, *Dr. Karuna Kusalasaya* studied Hindi and Samskrit at Varanasi and Allahabad and later joined Visva Barati University of Santiniketan founded by Rabindranath Tagore. He stayed in India between 1933 and 1945 and, hence, had witnessed the Indian Freedom Movement under the unique leadership of Mahatma Gandhi. Dr. Kusalasaya is an eminent scholar who apart from Mahatma Gandhi's autobiography- "My Experiments with Truth" also translated Tagore's "Gitanjali" and Nehru's "Discovery of India" into Thai language.

7. *Dr. Tint Swe* is a Member of Parliament [NLD], of Burma [Myanmar].
8. *Mr. Lallan Prasad Vyas* is the International Chairman of the I. R. C.
9. *Dr. Asghar Ali Engineer*, an eminent scholar of Islamic Studies is one of the renowned human rights activitists. Also he is the Chairman of the Centre for Study of Society and Secularism in Mumbai, India.
10. *Mr. Babubhai Jashbhai Patel*, a leading freedom fighter and an eminent Gandhian was the Chief Minister of the Gujarat State between 1975 and 1979.
11. *Professor Dr. Shahidul Haq Munshi* is the head of the department of political scince at Dhaka University, Bangladesh.
12. Dr. Anjula Rajvanshi is an Assistant Professor at the R. G. [P. G.] College, affiliated to CCS University of Meerut, India.
13. *Dr. S. K. Shukla* is an Associate Professor at the Pol. Sc. Dept. of P.U., Chandigarh [India].
14. *Dr. Christian Bartolf* is the Chairman of Gandhi Information Centre, Berlin, Germany.
15. *Mr. Sachin Bathla* is a cultural anthropologist.
16. Renowned scholar and scientist *Professor Dr. John Scales Avery* is working at the University of Copenhagen, Denmark.
17. *Mr. Holger Terp* is the Editor of Danish Peace Academy, Denmark.
18. *Dr. Thomas Weber* is a renowned political scientist and professor from Australia.
19. *Mr. Jeff Knaebel* is a renowned peace worker and Gandhian from the U.S.A.
20. Well-known social worker *Mrs. Mrinalini Sarabhai* is an eminent figure in the field of performing

arts. She is the wife of eminent scienist Vikram Sarabhai and the Chief of the Darpana Academy of Performing Arts, Ahmedabad, India.

21. *Ms. Rama Rauta* is the President, National Women's Organization, Pune, India.
22. *Mr. C. S. Dharmadhikari*, a Former Judge of the Bombay High Court is one of the leading Gandhians. He is the Chairman of the Institute of Gandhian Studies, Wardha, India.
23. *Dr. I. Khan*, a known Scholar and educationist from JMI, India.
24. *Professor Dr. Faridah Noor Mohammad Noor* is the Deputy Director at the Centre for Civilisational Dialogue, University of Malaya, Kuala Lumpur, Malaysia.
25. *Professor C. Naseema* is the head of the Department of Education at the University of Calicut, Kerala [India].
26. *Dr. R. K. Kothari* is an Assistant Professor in Political Science at the Vidyasagar University, West Bengal.
27. Universally renowned peace-maker and the Right Livelihood Award winner *Mr. Sulak Sivaraksa* is the Chief of the SPD Institute in Bangkok, Thailand.
28. *Dr. Poonam Lakhanpal* is an Associate Professor at the R.G. (P.G.) College, affiliated to the University of Meerut, India.

1

Mahatma Gandhi and Value Education: An Analysis

Ravindra Kumar

Mahatma Gandhi's name requires no introduction because of his invaluable contribution to the national liberation movement of India. It was he, who, by awakening *crores* of people on the strength of non-violent activities, engaging them to an action, challenging the mighty empire of the world, ultimately threw the yoke of slavery. Those who believed that not a single country in the world history had achieved its freedom except by violent means, the action of Mahatma Gandhi compelled them to re-think and also to change their attitude. His reputation as a true nationalist as well as an internationalist shines like sun itself, but in the academic sense of term, he is not considered a great scholar or an educationist. We have not been enlightened by his views on education or on the problems relating to it, through any particular book written by him. Even there is no special research article available, which could have given us a glimpse of his ideas or suggestions on education system, except his occasional articles on the future of education in India written in a very simple and light manner. The same thing applies to the views he expressed on the subject now and then.

Despite this fact, the few articles that Mahatma Gandhi has written in the simplest manner, and the views he expressed on education as a common man are of utmost importance; they provide us a guide line to proceed towards value education. Not only this, if we apply them even in the modern perspective, they can, definitely, give a new dimension to our educational system.

Mahatma Gandhi once Said:

"Education means all-round drawing out of the best in child and man – body, mind and spirit."

As such, education becomes the basis of personality development on all dimensions – moral, mental and emotional. Therefore, we can say that in the long run education forms the foundation on which the castles of peace and prosperity can be built. Since ancient times, it is said ***Sa Vidyaya Vimuktaye***, which means that with education we finally attain salvation. This small ***Samskrit*** phrase essentially contains the thought and essence of Value Education that is relevant in all perspectives. This very concept, when applied to the simple but refined approach of Mahatma Gandhi, can provide us with a new dimension of educational development. As such, while analyzing the views of Mahatma Gandhi, we can observe his views under two main points:

(A) Morality and Ethics

Moral and ethical knowledge is the first point on which Mahatma Gandhi's concept of value education is based. Any education system that lacks these two cannot be termed as good. The reason behind such a thought is that, without morality and without ethics, no student, in real sense, can be considered to be healthy in mental and physical terms, because for it, self-control and good character is essential. A person, who is not a moralist and who does not differentiate between right and wrong, cannot rise to the essential level of a true student. Then, the attainment of spiritual growth that has been described by Mahatma Gandhi, as an essential part of education, can only be gained through morality and ethics. Seeing it through another viewpoint also proves the same thing because when we consider education as a means of attaining salvation and also as a support on the pathway to liberation, then we cannot differentiate it from Spiritualism.

Mahatma Gandhi laid down some rules for students so as to ensure that morality and righteousness always be considered as an essential and undifferentiable part of education so that every student shall gain in terms of knowledge and spirituality. He said that on one hand where students should gain education under the strict regimen of high morals, self-control and right thinking, on the other they would also be expected to provide service to the society in general. This includes their respect towards mother, father, teachers and elders, affection towards younger, following of social traditions and constant awareness towards their duties and responsibilities.

In order to strengthen morality and ethics in students, Mahatma Gandhi advocated the introduction of religious education. This kind of education brings the values of forbearance, tolerance and reverence in one's character. And in turn, these values are an indivisible part of ethics. Explaining the importance and need of religious education, Mahatma Gandhi writes in the 'Young India' of 6th of December 1923:

"A curriculum of religious instructions should include a study of the tenets of faiths other than one's own. For this purpose the students should be trained to cultivate the habit of understanding and appreciating the doctrine of various great religions of the world in a spirit of reverence and broad minded tolerance."[1]

Mahatma Gandhi calls upon all teachers to impart proper education of morality and ethics to students both at school and college levels. In this regard suggesting some guidelines for teachers, he says that it is the duty of teachers to develop high morals and strong character of their students. If teachers fail to do so, it means that they depart from their social and national responsibilities and as such they are also insincere towards their noble profession. He said that a teacher should lay an example, to be followed, before society and students. This can only be done when he himself leads his life with high standards of morality and strong character. An ideal teacher should be free from any addiction. He needs to be polite and should set an ideal example of simple living and high thinking. He should also remember that wasting time is a sin; therefore, he should be aware of his duties towards students and society. Moreover, he should have a good reputation in the society. Therefore, it is the foremost duty of students, as well as of teachers to make it certain that moral and ethical knowledge continues to be the integral part of the education process. By doing so, they can contribute in the development of Value Education.

(B) *Buniyadi* [Basic], Job-oriented or Technical Education

Another important point of Mahatma Gandhi's value education is basic or technical education.

No matter if the word ***buniyadi*** [or basic], which Mahatma Gandhi used during the 3rd and 4th decade of 20th century, meant the knowledge or education that could help rural people in promotion of village handicrafts or to establish cottage industries, the ultimate purpose behind his attempt was to make young men and women self-reliant in the economic field.

Even in modern perspective, his idea of ***buniyadi*** or basic education is well-worthy and it has no clash with the concept of today's job-oriented or technical education.

In fact, Mahatma Gandhi wants to prepare a student for technical knowledge right from the days of his primary level of education. In this regard, his logic is not only important but adaptable; it can prove to be a mile stone in the direction of value education. I myself, too, have the same kind of view point already elaborated in one of my articles entitled, ***'Education in the Twenty-First Century: Problems and Expectations'***, written in 1997 for the Golden Jubilee Souvenir of the Gauhati University, Assam.[2]

It is not so that Mahatma Gandhi has not talked of all-round or complete education on different occasions. He definitely spoke of imparting education based on curriculum; he, more or less wrote about graduate and post graduate levels of education. Not only this, as I have just discussed, he laid emphasis on moral and ethical knowledge, which is helpful for character building and for the physical and mental development of a student since the very beginning of his education. He clearly believed that without a healthy body, mind could not be developed fully. But even after that he, without any hesitation, said that until and unless education makes a young man or woman self-reliant, it is of no value.

It is but obvious that when a child starts his formal education, he enters at primary level and, step by step, at an age of twenty or twenty-two, he graduates from a University. And after so many years, if he does not find a necessary goal or if he lacks a direction to begin with his career, then what could be the use of such education. What is the use of the degree for him that he has in his hand?

Reality lies in the fact that after obtaining a degree the students should definitely have a clear direction for their future; they should have no doubt towards their future goal. They should be full of self-confidence. Side by side, they should be self-dependent and capable to tackle unavoidable day to day problems. They must not be worried for a suitable job.

But in reality, these days we see that our younger generation is directionless. Our youths are diverted and a feeling of helplessness and dejection is prevailing on them. According to a survey, there are millions of men and women who, even after completing their studies at graduation, post graduation and doctorate levels, fail to seek an employment of their choice. Is it not a failure of our social and educational system?

Even after spending the golden years of one's life in attaining higher education, our youths are not self-dependant. As such how would they be able to get rid of their day to day problems and how would they contribute to their society and the nation? Therefore, it is a challenge not only before the youths of this country but also before the educationists, scholars and those in the government.

To tackle this problematic challenge, Mahatma Gandhi's views can be of great support. In this reference, he has given us his golden words that there is a need of result-oriented education. He said that every child has some special qualities that can also be termed as inherited traits of personality, so at the very primary level, a student's quality and worth should be identified by his teacher. A student should gain education according to curriculum and moral guidance and as such also improve his physical strength. But the teacher should watch and identify his quality that could be of help in his later life.

For that purpose it is necessary that after completing studies to a certain level, he must, in addition to above three kind of education-general [according to syllabi], moral and physical- be provided facilities to gain technical knowledge in accordance with the special trait that has already been identified in his personality by his teacher. Since by nature he has interest in that knowledge, he will easily gain it; he will become an adept in that. Now, when he completes his study up to graduate level and with this extra knowledge comes out of a college or university, he would have a direction. As such, even if he does not get a private or government job, he would manage to get through some sort of self-employment on the basis of his technical knowledge. At least, then, his education would be considered as result-oriented.

This indeed is Mahatma Gandhi's view-point pertaining to Value Education if applied in a wider perspective. Its worth lies in the fact that education should necessarily be helpful in employment and its foundations should be laid on morality and ethics. We all who are concerned with it need to think over it deeply. We have to apply Mahatma Gandhi's ideas according to present circumstances of our country and also as the demand of time. I can again say that Mahatma Gandhi's unique and refined views about value education are not only important but are worth applying not only in India but also in the rest of the world.

References

1. In this regard further he pointed out, ***"This if properly done would help to give them a spiritual assurance and a better appreciation of their own religion...There is one rule, however, which should always be kept in mind while studying all great religions and that is, that one should study them only through the writings of known votaries of the respective religions."***
2. In my article I have mentioned two examples to clarify my view-point. Firstly, when I was a student of sixth or seventh class two men came to my school to demonstrate how to make Lifebuoy soap. The Principal ordered and all students assembled in playground. Both of them taught how to make the soap and then went away. Next day, a student of our school brought such an exquisite Lifebuoy soap of his own making that it surpassed even the soap of a company. The boy went to the Principal and presented the same to him. He praised the student very much. This definitely stimulated the courage of the student. The Principal presented this work of student before all in the school and asked to derive inspiration from that. This further inspired that student. The boy had become interested in soap making. He was virtuous. Accordingly, he continued to make Lifebuoy soap off and on at his home by *ghee*. The father of the boy was very angry at this. He used to come to the Principal so often to say, ***"You invited the persons who told how to make soap indigenously. My son has been constantly increasing the household expenses."*** The father did not encourage his son. Even then, the son continued to take interest in the soap-making. Today, he is approximately 40 or 42 years of age and is a

Manager at a soap manufacturing company of international repute. The soap of this company is popular all over the world for its remarkable quality. The son had to wait for 30 years to achieve a place but he did praise-worthy job because of his virtue, interest and capability. He could have achieved this distinction within 15 or 20 years in case he had encouragement from his father. The second example relates to the period of my higher education. There was a girl-student in our college. Her father was an ordinary farmer but was immensely interested in sugarcane and resultant products. He had gained considerable knowledge of these. His daughter-the student of this very accord also- took keen interest in performance relating to agriculture. The student passed B. Sc. in first division. Now, her father wished her to be a candidate at Civil Service and to go for M. A. by faculty change. The girl did not want this but respecting her father's wishes, she changed the faculty and passed M. A. securing third division. She was, now, under rebellion against her father. She further studied hard for two years and passed M. Sc. [Ag.] obtaining first division. Thereafter, she undertook research assignment and today she happens to be an eminent scientist of the country. It is a fact that the girl had to waste quite a significant time of two years but she presented a good example before others as per her virtue, interest and capability. An inspiration by her father at prior stage could have been much better for her.

2

Gandhi and the World View: The South African Experience

Vasant Kumar Bawa

"I do not want my house to be walled in on all sides and my windows to be stuffed. I want the cultures of all lands to be blown about my house as freely as possible. But I refuse to live in other people's houses as an interloper, a beggar or a slave ......" [Young India, 1-6-1921, p. 170]

"It took Britain half the resources of the planet to reach the level of prosperity it has achieved. How many planets will India and China require?"

Mohandas was born on 2nd October 1869 in Porbander, Gujarat, the son of Karamchand Gandhi, the ***Dewan*** [Prime Minister] of a small Indian state ruled by a ***Maharaja***. In 1876 the family moved to Rajkot where his father served as a court official and then as ***Dewan*** of that state. Mohandas showed little promise as a child and a youth, passing the matriculation examination of the University of Bombay in December 1887 with barely 40 per cent of the total marks. In September 1888 he left college at the end of the first term and sailed for England to study law and qualify for the bar. He passed the final Bar examination in January 1891, and stayed on in London for a few months to complete his terms.

After his return to India, Gandhi spent two years in unsuccessful attempts to establish himself as a lawyer. He was then invited to go to Natal in South Africa to help a senior counsel in a big civil suit filed by a Gujarati Muslim businessman. A major turning-point in his life occurred a week after his arrival in May 1893, when he was thrown out of a train at Pietermaritzburg station because of his race, although he had a valid first class ticket. This incident triggered off his decision to take up public service on behalf of India and Indians against British rule, a desire that had lain latent in him for some years. At the age of 24 he was transformed from a shy, retiring small-town lawyer into an adviser of the Indian community. [C.N. Patel, Mahatma Gandhi in his Gujarati Writings, New Delhi, ***Sahitya Akademi*** 1981, p. 3].

The idea of staying on in South Africa as equal citizens was new to Indians, who had come there either as indentured labourers or as businessmen with the desire to make money. In June 1884 Gandhi accepted the request of the Indian merchant community to lead their struggle against discriminatory treatment in South Africa, although he was about to leave for India.

The implications of the South African struggle for the development of Gandhi's personality and his world-view were profound. Gandhi was going through an intellectual crisis. He had not only to lead a struggle of Indians against discriminatory policies and exploitation by powerful vested interests – he had also to mould the Indians, widely known as ***"coolies",*** into a community. Their local and religious identities had to be merged into a new and overarching national identity. That such a task could be achieved in twenty years for about 100,000 Indians of different linguistic groups and religious persuasions, is a tribute to Gandhi's achievement as a leader of men. ***"For twelve years .... the struggle was along the recognized constitutional lines of public meetings, letters to newspapers, petitions and memorials to authorities and similar methods of educating public opinion."***

When he realized that the British response to Indian voluntary service in the Boer War of 1899-1900 and the Zulu rebellion of Natal in 1906 was ***"an even more humiliating racial law than any in the past, Gandhi in a creative flash of inspiration thought of resisting the law by disobeying it."***

A meeting of Indians in Johannesburg in September 1906 gave definite shape to the non-violent method of resistance, later called ***Satyagraha.***[C.N.Patel,op.cit., p. 6). On three occasions, in 1908, 1911 and 1912, the Transvaal or the South African government failed to honour the agreement arrived at with the Indians. In September 1913 ***Satyagraha*** was revived on a mass scale, involving thousands of indentured Indian labourers... ***"Three months later the Government agreed to appoint a commission to look into the grievances. A settlement was reached in June 1914 and Gandhi returned to India after a short trip to England."*** [p. 7]

For the time being at least the right of Indians to stay in South Africa without discriminatory restrictions had been ensured. This gave rise to the hope that much larger struggle could be taken up on similar lines in India.

The South African struggle acquired for Gandhi almost a spiritual significance. He did not try in his own mind to distinguish between his religious quest and his political activity. The world-view which Gandhi had evolved during the struggle was eclectic, but had an essential unity about it. He had been introduced to the ***Bhagvad-Gita*** and the Christian scriptures, including the Sermon on the Mount, in England. He did not see any basic contradiction between them. In June 1903 he started publishing the weekly ***Indian Opinion*** in two languages, Gujarati and English. It soon became the instrument of his ideas as well as the mouthpiece of the Indian struggle in South Africa. His work as a writer was intimately linked with his life work.

Gandhi had published a summary of the ***Apology of Plato*** in ***Indian Opinion*** before ***Sarvodaya*** was written. He saw Unto This Last as an expansion of Socrates ideas as found in Plato's work. [p. 2]. In his conclusion, he pointed out that although Natal enjoyed ***Swaraj*** or self-government, ***"her Swaraj stinks in our nostrils, for she crushes the negroes and oppresses the Indian. If by some chance the Negroes and the Indians left Natal, its white men would fight among themselves and bring about their own destruction..."***

He rejected the idea that ***Swaraj*** really means self-control. Only he is capable of self-control who observes the rules of morality, does not cheat or give up truth, and does his duty to his parents, wife and children, servants and neighbours..... A state enjoys ***Swaraj*** if it can boast of a large number of such good citizens. He rejected the immorality of British rule in India, but equally denied that ***Swaraj*** could be attained by the sin of killing Englishmen, as some misguided Indians did, rejoicing in bomb-throwing. He felt that ***"Europeans pounce upon new territories like crows upon a piece of meat. I am inclined to think that this is due to their mass-production factories".*** He went on to say that ***"India must indeed have Swaraj but she must have it by righteous methods. Our Swaraj must be real Swaraj, which cannot be***

attained by either violence or industrialization... If even Indian sticks to truth, Swaraj will come to us of its own accord". [Ruskin, *Unto This Last: A Paraphrase by M. K. Gandhi*; [translated from the Gujarati by Valji Govindji Desai] Ahmedabad: Navajivan Publishing House, 1964, pp. 41-44].

In ***Hind Swaraj***, Gandhi urged educated Indian youth to reject the false ideal of nationalism borrowed from the west, to give up the idea of adopting an imitated version of the English Parliament, and to reject the modern industrial system. He saw Parliament as having been captured by powerful vested interests and the industrial system as being the embodiment of materialism, which was the cause of colonial exploitation and war. He also rejected the widespread impression that British rule had brought blessings in the form of internal peace, the rule of law, railways and machinery. He argued that voting rights and law courts were being misused by powerful vested interests, and this same calamity would befall India if the British were removed by force. Non-violence was to him not just a convenient instrument with which to get rid of the British, but an article of faith. He rejected the railways and the industrial system, not because they were British or foreign, but because they were exploitative by their nature. The industrial system had given rise to the armaments industry, he felt. He saw an intimate connection between ends and means, and would never agree that wrong means could lead to good ends.

It is significant that by the end of his stay in South Africa, Gandhi's world view had been almost completely formed. He is said to have read over eighty books during his first year there. He was not, however primarily a thinker, but an activist. In this respect he differed radically from all the

Western thinkers who influenced him.His intellectual quest was supportive of his search for a faith and a political ideology, and may never have taken place if he had not been involved in the South African resistance movement. we have now to see how his views of the world were expressed during the rest of his life, the influences his thinking had on other Indian leaders, and his differences with them. If he could brave the derision of Gokhale's comments on ***Hind Swaraj***, and hold to his views, his views on global developments during the twenties, thirties, and forties were almost as controversial.

3

Gandhi As a Critique of Violence in the World

Chaiwat Sta-anand

Gandhi on "Nonviolence and World Crisis"

Members of the International Missionary Conference in Tambaram near Madras met Gandhi at Sevagram in December 1938 and confronted him with the question:

"How can humanity be saved from the impending international crisis that threatens to plunge it into an orgy of hate and violence?"

The issues raised at that meeting include: how nonviolence would work in the cases of a minority [the Jews], international warfare [China's ordeal against the Japanese], the nature of modern warfare that has become mechanical and ruthless dictatorship such as Hitler and Mussolini.

Gandhi's answers are related to the workings of nonviolence in contemporary world. I would reformulate his answers to them into 4 concepts. They are[1]:

1. Avoid passivity, emphasize active nonviolence; [Nonviolence is not passivity in any shape and form, it is most active force in the world];
2. Quantitative no cooperation with his invaders: [If 200 million Chinese won't bend their knee to the Japanese, Japan would become China's slave.

He quoted Shelley's *The Mask of Anarchy*

I with folded arms and steady yees,
And little fear, and less surprise,
Look upon them as they slay
Till their rage has died away

3. The human heart exists. In answering how can nonviolence combat aerial warfare, seeing that there are no personal contacts? Gandhi replied that ***"behind the death dealing bomb there is the human hand that releases it, and behind that still is the human heart that sets the hand in motion";***
4. Possibility of Redemption. What about Hitler? ***"Belief in non-violence is based on the assumption that human nature in its essence is one and therefore unfailingly responds to the advances of love ... They would recognize the superiority of nonviolent resistance over any display of violence that they may be capable of putting forth".***

He was asked what his motive was:

"The things that lead us to do what we do are: Purely religious.... I could not be leading a religious life unless I identified myself with the whole of mankind, and that I could not do unless I took part in politics... [The thing that moves Gandhi is] love of the people [not the cause]. Cause without people is a dead thing. Love of the people brought the problem of untouchability early into my life".

The World Today

Apart from the September attack in 2001, 2 wars and numerous violence, let's look at the world: Fact in early C21 : In the US alone, there were more than 450 hate groups in 1997-1998, with more than 100 neo-Nazi groups. In Mesa, Arizona, a man was convicted and found guilty of attempted murder yesterday in slaying of a Sikh who prosecutors said was gunned down on Sept. 15, 2001 attacks because he was mistaken for an Arab. The killer names is Frank Silva Rogue and the victim was Balbir Singh Sodhi.[2]

Fact: At 7.42 A.M. on February 27, 2002, Sabarmati Express pulled into the train station at Godhra, a small town in Gujarat, West India. Something happened in the Muslim neighborhood which ended in two carriages burned, firefighting efforts hampered and 58 passengers died mostly women and children. During the next few weeks, because the state allowed revenge killings instead of taking legal actions against those responsible, over a thousand lives were lost; over 100,000 Muslims were pushed into the state refugee camps with very little support.

Experiment

Prime Ministerial Order 187/2546: Managing Conflicts with Non-violence Policy: The World's most unique experiment!

Signed on September 1, 2003, this Prime Minister Order stipulates that conflicts in Thai society will not decrease due to changes in social behaviors, which in turn resulted from economic crisis, problem in natural resources allocation and management, mega projects, lack of trust between the people and the state, as well as constitutional changes in Thai society, all this takes place in the context of global changes where violence increasingly becomes arbiter of human affairs.

Objective: Appropriate mode of managing conflicts is the key to desirable social and political changes.

3 Principles

1. Norm in Conflict Management: Adhere to nonviolence as the only just way to deal with conflict which will ensure sustainable peace. This begins with the state and state agencies first;

2. Attitudes governing nonviolence: reduction of prejudice and no hatred to those who are different, no enemy but fellow beings facing lives of sufferings together; and
3. Atmosphere conducive to creative solution: based on the assumption that differences in opinions and cultures are foundations of power of Thai society.

Gandhian Influence on Prime Minister Order 187/2546 [2003]: Non-violence for Gandhi is the Way and that it presupposes self-suffering and no-hatred.

Critique

Three decades ago, the late Kenneth Boulding tried to apprehend Gandhi's failure. His main thesis is that nonviolence is only effective when aligned with truth. But truth in the modern world is so complex that it can no longer be perceived by common sense or by mystical insights. Thus when truth is rejected and illusion clouds judgment, nonviolence will consequently be rejected.[3]

Truth? : But Hindu-Muslim violence is neither endemic nor widespread in India. Rioting is heavily concentrated in a handful of towns. From 1950-1995 rural India accounted for a mere 4% of all deaths in Hindu-Muslim riots. Within urban India itself, 8 cities accounted for 46% of all deaths. These cities have about 6% of India's total population. In comparing 6 Indian cities, Ashutosh Varshney found that pre-existing local institutions of civic engagement: Political Parties, business associations, trade unions; professional association of teachers, students and lawyers, Ngo's reading and film clubs especially if they are mass-based as in South India explain why some cities remain peaceful. These are more prevalent in South and East politics– North and West.[4]

A couple of days after independence in 1947, a Sikh named Bhan Singh attacked a Muslim camp in Meharbanpura, and was killed in the attack. His son, Harbans Singh, a head constable at Jhabbal in the Khem Karan area, found a helpless young Muslim woman, Nawab Bibi, whose immediate family had been murdered. She was left without any relatives. The Sikhs gave her shelter. In early 1949, Nawab Bibi was taken away by some Pakistani Officials. Harbans Singh tried to look for her at the border and else where without success. He then took a Muslim name, Barkat Ali, and managed to cross the border into Pakistan. In Lahore, Barkat Ali, alias Harbans Singh, the son of Bhan Singh, who was killed by the Muslims, managed to find Nawab Bibi, Muslim women whose entire family was killed by the Sikhs. Although Indian newspaper which reported this story did not say if they lived happily ever after, following Ashis Nandy, I would say that "But frankly, I would like to believe that they do."[5]

References

1. M.K. Gandhi, *Non-Violence in Peace and War, Volume-I* [Ahmedabad: Navajivan, 1948] pp. 169-176.
2. *Bangkok Post*, October 2, 2003.
3. Kenneth E. Boulding, "Why Did Gandhi Fail?" in G. Ramachandran and T. K. Mahadevan [Edited], *Gandhi: His Relevance for Our Time,* [Berkeley: World Without War Council, 1971], pp. 129-134.
4. Ashutosh Varshney, "Understanding Gujarat Violence," *Items & Issues,* Vol. 4 No. 1 [Winter 2002-2003], pp. 1-5.
5. Chaiwat Sta-anand, "Crossing the Enemy's Line: Helping the Others in Violent Situations Through Non-violent Action", *Peace Research*, Vol. 33, No. 2 [2001], p. 111.

4

The Spinning-Wheel and the Seed: Gandhi's Legacy, Humanity's Hope

Vandana Shiva

Gandhi lives–as a perennial source of inspiration and political innovation to defend our freedoms. Globalisation as a project is a plan to extinguish all freedoms of people through the total control of trade, technology and property rights. The freedoms of rivers to flow and organisms to evolve, of farmers to save seeds and grow crops, of consumers to be free to choose what they eat and know how their food is produced. These fundamental freedoms of all species and ordinary humans are being robbed in the name of "free trade" or globalisation.

Globalisation is often presented as a process of new interconnections between societies. However, if it is geographical, it is about the global reach of giant corporations – not about a global joining of the hearts of people worldwide. But the real project of globalisation is colonization and commodification of the very resources and processes that give us life – our biodiversity, our food and our water.

Over the past two decades, my ideas and actions to defend life's freedom and diversity have come from Gandhi. Without his legacy it would be impossible to even imagine a response to the totalitarianism built into the project of owning life, owning seeds, owning water. Patents on life and the new biotechnologies are today's tools of imperialism, and they are a core part of the global ***"constitution"*** called the W.T.O rules of free trade in the form of Trade Related Intellectual Property Rights [TRIPS]. The phrase ***"Trade Related"*** had to be forcefully linked to intellectual property precisely because intellectual property has no place in a trade treaty and patents should not have been extended to cover life forms as they were under Act 273[b] of TRIPS which forces countries to patent life forms, in particular micro-organisms and genetically engineered plants and animals. These rules and laws were made by and for corporations. As a Monsanto spokesperson stated about the drafting of TRIPS ***"We were the patient, the diagnostician, the physician".***

Patents of life are a total control system. They allow corporations to claim ownership over life forms – micro-organisms, plants, animals. They allow corporations to define the acts of saving and sharing seeds as ***"intellectual property crimes".*** And they allow the crime of bio-piracy – the theft of traditional knowledge and bio-piracy to be treated as a right.

A patent is an exclusive right to own, make, sell, produce and use a patented product. A patent on seed implies that a farmer saving seed is an ***"intellectual property thief".*** But it means more. A system in which seed has become a corporate monopoly, a system in which a few companies control the seed supply is in effect a system of slavery for farmers. Where the freedom of seed disappears, the freedom of farmers disappears.

That is why, in 1987, when I first came to know about GATT and TRIPS and Patents on life, I searched for ways to defend the freedom of biodiversity and the freedom of peasants. And Gandhi's spinning wheel inspired dedicating my life to saving seeds to save small farmers and protect life.

Spinning Freedom

It was to regenerate livelihoods in India that Gandhi thought of the spinning wheel as a symbol of liberation and a tool for development. Power driven mills were the model of development in that period of early industrialization. However, the hunger of mills for raw material and markets was the reason for a new poverty, created by the destruction of livelihoods either by diverting land and biomass from local subsistence to the factory, or by displacing local production through the market.

Gandhi had said, ***"Anything that millions can do together becomes charged with unique power."*** The spinning wheel had become a symbol of such power. ***"The wheel as such is lifeless, but when I invest it with symbolism, it becomes a living thing for me."***

When Gandhi described the ***Charkha*** in 1908, the ***Hind Swaraj*** as a panacea for the growing pauperism of India, he had never seen a spinning wheel. Even in 1915, when he returned to India from South Africa, he had not actually seen a spinning wheel. But he saw an essential element of freedom from colonialism in discarding the use of mill woven cloth. He set up handlooms in the ***Satyagraha Ashram*** at Sabarmati, but could not find a spinning wheel or a spinner, who were normally women. In 1917, Gandhi's disciple Gangaben Majumdar started a search for the spinning wheel, and found one in Vijapur in the Baroda State. Quite a few people there had spinning wheels in their homes, but had long since consigned them to the lofts as useless lumbers. They now pulled them out, and soon Vijapur ***Khadi*** gained a name for itself. And ***Khadi*** and the spinning wheel rapidly became the symbol for India's independence movement.

The spinning wheel symbolized a technology that conserves resources, people's livelihoods and people's control over their livelihoods. In contrast to the imperialism of the British textile industry, the ***Charkha*** was decentred and labours generating, not labour displacing. It needed people's hands and minds, instead of treating them as surplus, or as mere inputs into an industrial process. This critical mixture of decentralization, livelihood generation, resource conservation and strengthening of self-reliance were essential to undo the waste of centralization, livelihood destruction, resource depletion and creation of economic and political dependence that had been engendered by the industrialization associated with colonialism.

Gandhi's spinning wheel is a challenge to notions of progress and obsolescence that arise from absolutism and false universalism in concepts of science and technology development. Obsolescence and waste are social constructs that have both a political and ecological component. Politically, the notion of obsolescence gets rid of people's control over their lives and livelihoods by defining productive work as unproductive and removing people's control over production in the name of progress. It would rather waste hands than waste time. Ecologically, too obsolescence destroys the regenerative capacity of nature by substituting manufactured uniformity in place of nature's diversity. This induced dispensability of poorer people on the one hand and diversity on the other constitutes of the political ecology of technological development guided by narrow and reductionist notions of productivity. Parochial notions of productivity, perceived as universal, rob people of control over their means of reproducing life and rob nature of her capacity to regenerate diversity.

Ecological erosion and destruction of livelihoods are linked to one another. Displacement of diversity and displacement of people's sources of sustenance both arise from a view of development and growth based on uniformity created through centralized control. In this process of control, reductionist science and technology act as handmaidens for economically powerful interests. The struggle between the factory and the spinning wheel continues as new technologies emerge.

As seeds are genetically engineered and patented, a crisis is being engineered for farmers and farming. And the seed becomes the ***charkha*** of today. That is why I started ***Navdanya.***

Diversity and Freedom

The Green Revolution was an exemplar of the deliberate destruction of diversity. The new biotechnologies, are repeating and deepening these tendencies, rather than reversing them.

Further, the new technologies in combination with patent monopolies being pushed through intellectual property rights regimes in GATT and other trade platforms as well as the biodiversity convention are threatening to transform the diversity of life forms into mere raw material for industrial production, and limitless profits. They are simultaneously threatening the regenerative freedom of diverse species, and the free and sustainable economy of small peasants and producers, which is based on nature's diversity and its utilization.

The seed, for example, reproduces itself and multiples. Farmers use seed both as grain as well as for the next year's crop. Seed is free, both in the ecological sense of reproducing itself, as well as in the economic sense of reproducing the farmers' livelihood.

This seed freedom is however a major obstacle for seed corporations. If the market for seed has to be created, the seed has to be transformed materially, so that reproducibility is blocked and its status has to be changed legally, so that instead of being the common property of farming communities, it becomes the patented private property of Seed Corporation.

As my involvement in these issues grew, the seed started to take shape as the site and symbol of freedom in the age of manipulation and monopoly of life in its diversity. Ethically and ecologically, unrestrained biotechnology development gives new tools for manipulation; patents offer new tools for monopoly ownership of that which is by its very nature free. I thought of Gandhi's Spinning Wheel, which had become such an important symbol of freedom, not because it was big and powerful, but because it was small and could become alive as a sign of resistance and creativity in smallest of huts and poorest of families. In smallness lay its power.

The seed too is small. It embodies diversity. It embodies the freedom to stay alive. And seed is still the common property of small farmers in India. Seed freedom goes far beyond freedom for the farmer from corporations. It indicates freedom of diverse cultures from centralized control. In the seed, ecological issues could combine with social justice. I could see that it was the seed that could play the role of Gandhi's spinning wheel in this period of re-colonization through **"free-trade".**

In spite of many blocks and pressures, I launched a national programme to save seed diversity in farmers' fields in cooperation with the movements I have been working with over many years. We call it ***Navdanya***, which literally means nine seeds and is a beautiful symbol of the richness of diversity.

Ours was not the first seed conservation programme. Genetic resources have always been collected for breeding. The risks for breeding towards uniformity led to the emergence of government gene banks in the 1970s. However, while gene banks collect biodiversity from farmers' fields, they do not conserve it through and with farmers. Instead, diversity flows from farmers' fields to gene banks and then on to corporate breeders, but is systematically eroded at the source. The farmers then become mere consumers of corporate seed, which in the future will also have IPR protection, thus forcing farmers to buy seed every year. This excludes the farmer from playing the critical role of conserver of genetic diversity and innovator in the utilization and development of seed. It robs farmers of their rights to their biological and intellectual heritage. It also separates conservation from production, and scientists from farmers. We wanted to build a programme in which farmers and scientists relate horizontally rather than vertically, in which conservation of biodiversity and production of food go hand in hand, and in which farmers' knowledge is strengthened, not robbed.

While the fundamental changes we are working towards can only be achieved in the long-term, at the small scale level, ***Navdanya*** has already had major impact in the villages in which we work. Realizing that our small efforts in the conservation of indigenous seed diversity are not enough, we have also joined hands with the farmers' movement to urgently mobilize public opinion against the emerging threat of multinational corporations gaining monopoly control on all life through the new biotechnologies and intellectual property rights.

In 1991, I started to contact the farmers' organisations, to alert them on the new trends, to work with them on protecting farmers' rights to freely conserve use, exchange and modify the seeds. In February 1992, we organised a national conference on GATT and Agriculture with the ***Karnataka Rajya Ryota Sangha*** [KRRS]. In October 1992, at a massive farmers' rally in Hospet organised by the KRRS, the Seed ***Satyagraha*** was launched following Gandhi's politics of ***Satyagraha*** as a fight for truth based on non-cooperation with unjust regimes. In March 1993, we held a nationally rally in Delhi at the historic Red Fort under the leadership of the national farmers organisations, the **Bharatiya Kisan** Union. Independence Day 15th August, 1993 was celebrated with farmers asserting their 'Collective Intellectual Property Rights' [***Samuhik Gyan Sanad***]. On 2nd October, 1993, one year of the seed ***Satyagraha*** was celebrated in Bangalore with a gathering of 500,000 farmers. We also had farmers from other Third World countries as well as scientists who work on farmers' rights and sustainable agriculture in an expression of solidarity. The internationalization of the Seed ***Satyagraha*** within one year has given the word globalisation a new meaning. From representing global markets as in the parlance of free trade proponents, it has come to mean from us the globalisation of people's resistance to centralized control over all aspects of their life.

The native seed has become a system of resistance against monocultures and monopoly rights. The shift from uniformity to diversity respects the rights of all species and is sustainable. Diversity is also a political imperative because uniformity goes hand in hand with centralization, while diversity demands de-centred control. Diversity as a way of thought and a way of life is what is needed to go beyond the impoverished monocultures of the mind.

For us, protecting native seeds is more than conservation of raw material for the biotechnology industry. The diverse seeds now being pushed to extinction carry within them seeds of other ways of thinking about nature, and other ways of producing for our needs. Uniformity and diversity are not just patterns of land use; they are ways of thinking and ways of living.

Conservation of diversity is, above all, the commitment to let alternatives flourish in society and nature, in economic systems and in knowledge systems. Cultivating and conserving diversity is no luxury in our times. It is a survival imperative, and the pre-condition for the freedom of all, the big and the small. In diversity, the smallest has a place and significance. Allowing the small to flourish is to me the real test of freedom – in the life of an individual, the life of an organisation, the life of a society, and the life of this planet. It is this connection between diversity, de-centredness and democracy, which has guided my ideas and actions, at the local as well as the global level.

Seed Saving: Our Ethical Duty, Our Human Right

Seed is the first link in the food chain. In ***Samskrit, Bija***, the seed, mcans the source of life. Saving seed is our duty, sharing seed is our culture.

Patents on seeds and genetic resources rob us of our birth right to derive our livelihoods by transforming seed saving and seed sharing into ***"intellectual property crimes".*** This is an assault on our culture, our human rights and our very survival.

Seed patents and seed monopolies are also becoming a major source of seed insecurity and food security. As seed is transformed from the common property of peasant communities into the private property of giant corporations like Monsanto, a number of associated transformations take place.

As seed saving is prevented by patents as well as by the engineering of seed with non-renewable traits, seed has to be bought for every planting season by poor peasants. A free resource available on farm becomes a commodity to which farmers are forced to by every year. This increases poverty and leads to indebtedness. As debts increase and become unpayable., farmers are compelled to sell kidneys or even commit suicide. More than 25,000 peasants in India have taken their lives since 1997 when the practice of seed saving was transformed under globalisation pressures and multinational seed corporations started to take control of the seed supply. Seed saving gives farmers life. Seed monopolies rob farmers of life.

The shift from farm saved seed to corporate monopolies of the seed supply is also a shift from biodiversity to monocultures in agriculture. The District of Warangal in Andhra Pradesh used to grow diverse legumes, millets, oilseeds. Seed monopolies created crop monocultures of cotton, leading to disappearance of millions of nature's evolution and farmers breeding.

Monocultures and uniformity increase the risks of crop failure as diverse seeds adapted to diverse ecosystems are replaced by rushed introduction of unadapted and often untested seeds into the market. When Monsanto first introduced Bt Cotton in India in 2002, the farmers lost Rs. 1 billion due to crop failure. Instead of 1,500 kg / acre as promised by the company, the harvest was as low as 200 kg. Instead of increased incomes of Rs. 10,000/ acre, farmers ran into losses of Rs. 6400/acre.

In the state of Bihar, when farm saved corn seed was displaced by Monsanto's hybrid corn, the entire crop failed creating Rs. 4 billion losses and hence increased poverty for desperately poor farmers.

Poor peasants of the South cannot survive seed monopolies. That is why the case of Percy Schmeiser will decide the fate not just of one Canadian farmer but billions of peasants. The unjust and unethical case brought by Monsanto against Percy is a double crime against farmers. Firstly by creating and enforcing illegitimate patent rights to seed, it robs us of our human right and human duty to be seed savers. Secondly, it rewards the polluter with enhanced property rights and profits. The principle of ***"pollute pays"*** has been transformed into the ***"polluter gets paid"*** principle.

This perverse jurisprudence must be corrected for the sake of all farmers, and all species. Farmers' freedoms must come before corporate monopoly. Farmers' survival must come before corporate greed. Percy's future is our future. Percy's seed freedom is our freedom. Percy's rights as a farmer are symbolic of the human rights of all farmers.

The Suicide Economy of Corporate Globalisation

While the government spends millions on advertisements saying ***"India Shinning"***, a large part of India is dying. The Indian peasantry, the largest body of surviving small farmers in the world, today faces a crisis of extinction.

Two thirds of India makes its living from the land. The earth is the most generous employer in this country of a billion that has farmed this land for more than 5000 years.

However, as farming is delinked from the earth, the soil, the biodiversity, the climate and linked to global corporations and global markets, and the generosity of the earth is replaced by the greed of corporations, the viability of small farmers and small farms is destroyed. Farmer's suicides are the most tragic and dramatic symptom of the crisis of survival faced by Indian peasants.

1997 witnessed the first emergence of farm suicides in India. Rapid increase in indebtedness was at the root of farmers taking their lives. Debt is a reflection of a negative economy, a loosing economy. Two factors have transformed the positive economy of agriculture into a negative economy for peasants–the rising costs of production and the falling prices of farm commodities. Both these factors are rooted in the policies of trade liberalization and corporate globalisation.

In 1998, the World Bank's structural adjustment policies forced India to open up its seed sector to global corporations like Cargill and Monsanto, Syhgenta. The global corporations changed the input economy overnight. Farm saved seeds were replaced by corporate seeds, which needed fertilizers and pesticides and could not be saved.

And the crisis of suicides shows how the survival of small farmers is incompatible with the seed monopolies of global corporations.

The second pressure Indian farmers are facing is the dramatic fall in prices of farm produce as a result of free trade policies of the W.T.O. The WTO rules for trade in agriculture are in essence rules for dumping. They have allowed an increase in agribusiness subsidies while preventing countries from protecting their farmers from the dumping of artificially cheap produce. High subsidies of $ 400 billion combined with forced removal of import restrictions is a ready-made recipe for farmers' suicides. Global prices have dropped from $ 216 / ton in 1995 to $ 133 / ton in 2001 for wheat, $ 98.2 / ton in 1995 to $ 49.1 / ton in 2001 for cotton, $ 273 / ton in 1995 to $ 178 / ton for soyabean. This reduction to half the price is not due to a doubling in productivity but due to an increase in subsidies and an increase in market monopolies controlled by a handful of agribusiness corporations.

Thus the Government on the United States of America pays $ 193 per ton to U.S. Soya farmers, which artificially lowers the price of soya. Due to removal of Quantitative Restrictions and lowering of tariffs, cheap soya has destroyed the livelihoods of coconut growers, mustard farmers, producers of sesame, groundnut and soya.

Similarly, cotton producers in the U. S. are given a subsidy of $ 4 billion annually to 25000 cotton producers. This has brought the cotton prices down artificially, allowing the U.S. to capture world markets which were earlier accessible to poor African countries such as Burkina Faso, Benin and Mali. The subsidy of $ 230 per acre in the U. S. is genocidal for the African farmers. African cotton farmers are loosing $ 250 million every year. That is why small African countries walked out of the Cancun negotiations, leading to the collapse of the W. T. O. ministerial.

The rigged prices of globally traded agriculture commodities are stealing incomes from poor peasants of the south. Analysis carried out by the Research Foundation for Science, Technology and Ecology shows that due to falling farm prices, Indian peasants are loosing $ 26 billion or Rs. 1. 2 trillion annually. This is a burden their poverty does not allow them to bear. Hence, the epidemic of farmers' suicide.

India was among the countries that questioned the unfair rules of W. T. O. in agriculture and led the G-22 alliance along with Brazil and China. India with other southern countries addressed the need to safeguard the livelihoods of small farmers from the injustice of free trade based on high subsidies and dumping. Yet at the domestic level, official agencies in India are in deep denial of any links between free trade and farmers' survival.

An example of this denial is a Government of Karnataka report on ***"Farmers suicide in Karnataka –A scientific analysis".*** The report while claiming to be ***"scientific",*** makes unscientific reductionist claims that the farmers suicides have only psychological causes, not economic ones, and identifies alcoholism as the root cause of suicides. Therefore, instead of proposing changes in agricultural policy, the report recommends that farmers require boosting up their self respect [**swabhiman**] and self-reliance [***swavalambam***]. And ironically, its recommendations for farmers' self-reliance are changes in the Karnataka Land Reforms Act to allow larger land holdings and leasing. These are steps towards the further decimation of small farmers who have been protected by land ***"ceilings"*** [an upper limit on land ownership] and policies that only allow peasants and agriculturalists to own agricultural land [part of the land to the tiller policies of the Devraj Urs government].

While the ***"expert committee"*** report identified ***"alcoholism"*** as the main cause for suicides, the figures of this ***"scientific"*** claim are inconsistent and do not reflect the survey. On page 10, the report states in one place that 68 percent of the suicide victims were alcoholics. Five lines later it states that 17 percent were ***"alcohol and illicit drinkers".*** It also states that the majority of suicide victims were small and marginal farmers and the majority had high levels of indebtedness. Yet debt is not identified as a factor leading to suicide. On page 32 of the report it is stated that of the 105 cases studied among the 3544 suicides which had occurred in five districts during 2000 – 2001, 93 had debts, 54 percent victims had borrowed from private sources and money lenders. More than 90% suicide victims were in debt. Yet a table on page 63 has mysteriously reduced debt as a reason for suicide to 2.6%, and equally mysteriously, ***"suicide victims having a bad habit"*** has emerged as the primary cause of farmers' suicides.

The government is desperate to delink farm suicides from economic processes linked to globalisation such as rise in indebtedness and increased frequency of crop failure due to higher ecologic vulnerability arising from climate change and drought and higher economic risks due to introduction of untested and unadopted seeds. This is evident in recommendation no. 4.3.24.3: ***"The government should launch prosecution on the responsible persons involved in misleading the public and government by providing false information about farmers' suicide as crop failure or indebtedness"*** [page 113 of expert committee report].

However, farmers' suicides cannot be delinked from indebtedness and the economic distress small farmers are facing. Indebtedness is not new. Farmers have always organised for freedom from debt. In the nineteenth century the so call ***"Deccan Riots"*** were farmers' protests against the debt trap into which they had been pushed to supply cheap cotton to the textile mills in Britain. In the eighties they formed peasant organisations to fight for debt relief from public debt linked to Green Revolution inputs. However, under globalisation, the farmer is loosing her / his social, cultural, economic identity as a producer. A farmer is now a ***"consumer"*** of costly seeds and costly chemicals sold by powerful global corporations through powerful landlords and money lenders locally. This combination is leading to corporate feudalism, the most inhumane, brutal and exploitative convergence of global corporate capitalism and local feudalism, in the face of which the farmer as an individual victim feels helpless.

The bureaucratic and technocratic systems of the state are coming to the rescue of the dominant economic interests by blaming the victim.

It is necessary to stop this war against small farmers. It is necessary to re-write the rules of trade in agriculture. It is necessary to change our paradigms of food production. Feeding humanity should not depend on the extinction of farmers and extinction of species. Another agriculture is possible and necessary–an agriculture that protects farmers' livelihoods, the earth and its biodiversity and public health.

From the Suicide Economy to Living Economics

Gandhi's creative vision of ***Swadeshi, Swaraj, Satyagraha*** and ***Sarvodaya*** inspires us to build living economies and living democracies. In his legacy we find hope, we find freedom, we find our own creativity. Gandhi's philosophy is a living philosophy both because it is not dead and because when it informs our actions, they become charged with life. Only through Gandhi do we begin, with constructive action and turn it into our best resistance. Our seed saving is a resistance to seed monopolies and seed patents. And when our government begins to implement TRIPS as it has done through three amendments of our Patent Act and the creation of new plant variety legislation, we remember Gandhi's words:

"As long as the superstition that people should obey unjust laws exists, so long will slavery exist".

And we renew our commitment to the ***Bija Satyagraha***. Like Mahatma Gandhi started the Salt ***Satyagraha*** to protest against the colonization of salt by the Salt Laws imposed by the British Empire, people's movement in India are committed to the ***Bija Satyagraha*** based on non-cooperation with unjust and immoral IPR laws being imposed on MNCs' and the rich countries. These laws are:

- The protection of plant varieties and farmers rights act which establishes MNC's monopoly over seeds, makes Indian farmers bio-serfs and robs them of their age old freedoms to save, exchange and sell seeds;
- The amended patent act which allows seeds, plants, animals, genes and all life forms to be patented and indigenous knowledge to be pirated; and
- The biodiversity act which gives free access to our genetic wealth and indigenous knowledge to bio-pirates within and outside India.

As genetic pollution threatens are biodiversity and globalisation threatens are farmers, we create living economies and living democracies based on ***Swadeshi*** and ***Swaraj***. Just as the seed has the potential to germinate and evolve and renew itself perennially, Gandhi's legacy has the potential to germinate, evolve, and renew our actions and strategies for freedom appropriate to our times and context.

From the seed, our ***Swadeshi*** efforts have grown to organic farming or ***jaiv kheti,*** fair and just trade, and ***Swadeshi*** in the form of biodiversity conservation has evolved organically into the ***Swaraj*** of ***Jaiv Panchayat*** or living democracy, resting on the resistance of ***Satyagraha***–non-cooperation with immoral, unjust laws that force patenting of life.

Gandhi's legacy lives, and gives us hope to shape ever new instruments to keep life in its diversity and integrity free. Gandhi's legacy carries the seeds for the freedoms of humans and all species. Gandhi's legacy is humanity's hope.

5

Going Back to Gandhi: The Joy of Sacrifice and Service

Subhash C. Kashyap

The most striking development of our times has been the digitalization of information leading to the building of info highways and super ways, e-mail and e-commerce, Internet, Cyber Cafes, multi-media and the rest.

Information however is not knowledge and even knowledge is far from being wisdom. Not all the knowledge in the world can give us the power to discern and discriminate between good and evil and to choose the right course of action when faced with a moral dilemma.

It calls for wisdom which comes from insight born of profound experience, intuition and repeated reflections on depths and heights of the soul normally inaccessible to ordinary processes of cognition and communication.

In today's scenario, our objectives are largely centered on material wants and sensory pleasures. Each one is for self, for fulfilling personal needs and working to enjoy life and extracting the maximum possible pleasure from it.

All religions extol sacrifice but today, we are not prepared to suffer for a cause beyond self-interest or to sacrifice for others. It is difficult to find persons who want to better the world around or ameliorate the sufferings of fellow human beings. Higher values and qualities of character are not in demand.

We face the debris of our dreams of old. Competitive consumerism, hedonism, stark materialism and unabashed possessivism have become the yardsticks of respect in society.

There is no alternative to going back to Gandhi. Gandhi talked of ***Asteya, Aparigraha*** and trusteeship. But today, for fear of being dubbed non-secular, we do not even talk of the old ideals of ***Aparigraha, Asteya and Santosham*** or of minimization of wants. Since everything around seems rotten, we tend to withdraw into shells of privatism and make selfishness the only virtue. The goals become making big money quick, achieving status and living well.

Nations which lose their vision perish. Societies which fail to transmit to their children their heritage, the quintessence of the accumulated wisdom of centuries and a system of values are relegated to debris. The rubble and the shambles of history and the stories of dead civilizations are a mute testimony to many such fallen stars.

Thousands of years ago, our common ancestors who incidentally were neither Hindus, nor Muslims, nor Christians, asked of themselves a question: Who am I, where did I come from, what is the aim of life, what heights of excellence can a man achieve?

It must be a cause for great concern and anguish that we are gradually getting cut off from the basic truths of our sublime past. Many of us are not even aware, for example, of the vast reservoir of knowledge in **Vedas** and ***Upanishads*** and in our old traditions.

The **Upanishads** represent world's highest philosophy ever developed anywhere. If we get to know them we can really be proud of this heritage left by our ancestors. These works of wisdom do not belong to any particular religion, community or group; they are the common heritage of every Indian, in fact of humanity.

The ***Upanishads*** teach us that there is no high or low. Every member of society has his own place of pride and honour because behind his individuality is his soul, his ***Atman***– eternal, infinite and immortal.

The human personality owes its creative energy and the spirit of oneness and equality to the ***Atman***. How can such knowledge be non-secular? It only awakens the consciousness of the oneness of family, neighbourhood, society, nation and humanity at large. In every other man, the individual sees himself. He feels the pain and sorrow of every other human being as his own.

Our nation can rise to great heights if we decide to give her our best but she will fall if we remain anxious only to take out the maximum for ourselves.

But today, we are anxious only to take and to stress our rights. We forget that rights are related to functions and are given only in return for some duties to be performed. Rights are conferred on individual citizens not only for their own development but also for social good. As the Declaration of Universal Rights puts it:

"Everyone has duties to the community in which alone the free and full development of his personality is possible."

Gandhi wrote to Huxley:

"I learned from my illiterate but wise mother that all rights to be deserved and preserved come from duty well done. Thus the very right to live accrues to us when we do the duty of citizenship of the world. From this one fundamental statement, perhaps it is easy enough to define duties of man and woman and correlate every right to some corresponding duty to be first performed. Every other right can be shown to be usurpation hardly worth fighting for."

What is needed is a new beginning. Each individual can begin with himself once he realizes that real happiness comes from giving and sharing and not from taking and grabbing, it resides not in ***bhog*** or enjoyment but in ***tyag*** or sacrifice. As the ***Isopanishad*** says, one should enjoy only through sacrifice. ***[Tena Tyaktena Bhunjitha].***

Here, there is a conflict between the two value systems. Is the world to be seen as a global market where everything is bought and sold and there is free competition or as a family **[*Vasudhaiva Kutumbakam*]** where there is compassion and caring for each other! The market eliminates while the family protects the weak member.

Social inequalities and tensions will keep multiplying unless we seek respite in spiritual wisdom and its quintessential of equality, unity and integrity of all humanity. The ***Atman*** or ***Jyoti*** which is within each one of us is the inexhaustible reservoir of energy and power. To recognize the 'I' or the ***Atman*** inside the physical body is the highest wisdom.

6
Mahatma Gandhi's Satyagraha

Karuna Kusalasaya

As far as I remember, the word ***Satyagraha*** first came into use and practice in South Africa where Mahatma Gandhi launched a crusade against apartheid. ***Satyagraha*** is a combination of two ***Samskrit*** words, namely, ***Satya*** meaning truth and ***Agraha*** with means hold on, determination or strong attachment. The words in combination, therefore, mean ***'hold on or attachment to truth'***.

In our Royal Institute Thai to Thai language the word ***Satyagraha*** is defined as follows:

"Application of truth in pursuit of social justice employing civil disobedience or passive resistance against unjust law or orders but without the use of force."

I personally feel that this definition of ***Satyagraha*** is right to the point.

The word ***Satyagraha*** was first used in the Thai language more than five decades ago, and the credit for doing so, as far as I can remember, goes to an Indian ***Sanyasi***, by name ***Swami*** Satyanand Puri of the Ramakrishna Order, Calcutta. Many among us, whose age is over half a century, must have heard the name of this once famous scholar and intellectual from India.

At this stage I would like to say a few words on the not-too-often heard of story of this remarkable Hindu monk.

Swami Satyanand Puri, ***Vedantapradip***, M. A., came to Thailand as long ago as in 1931, at the recommendation of Noble Prize Laureate Rabindranath Tagore and Dr. Kalidas Nag, the famous savant of gone-by Bengal. Both Gurudeva and Dr. Nag visited Thailand [then known as Siam] in 1927 as official quests of the Royal Thai Government. Having learnt at first hand from Tagore about the close cultural ties between India and Thailand, and above all, at the suggestion of the poet[1] himself, the ***Swami*** set out for Thailand, strongly determined to work for the strengthening of the cultural links between the two countries. And, within a couple of years after his arrival in Bangkok, ***Swami*** Satyanand Puri, with his erudition in Oriental Learning succeeded in winning admiration and respect from contemporary Thai scholars and men-of-letters. The ***Swami*** started publishing a periodical ***'Voice of the East'*** and founded the Thai-Bharat Cultural Lodge which remains active till today. Among the several books in Thai authored by the ***Swami***, one was ***'Mahatma Gandhi who Revolutionized India'***. In this, perhaps, the very first book on Gandhi in the Thai language, the word ***Satyagraha*** was introduced to the Thai reading public which I have just mentioned.

Swami Satyanand Puri, himself a staunch nationalist, succumbed to death in an aero plane crash on his way to Japan in the beginning of the Greater East Asia War.

Now let me return to my subject Mahatma Gandhi's ***Satyagraha***.

You all of course have heard of the word ***Ahimsa*** so often used by the ***Mahatma*** in his campaign for India's freedom.

Ahimsa, another word from ***Samskrit***, stands for non-violence. This word, in Gandhi's usage, usually appeared side by side with the words ***Satya***, e.g. ***Satya*** and ***Ahimsa***.

Ahimsa, as employed in ***Satyagraha*** and according to the Mahatma's definition, did not simply mean non-violence in the physical plane. More than that, it does embrace non-violence in the mental plane as well. Such teaching, indeed, is very hard to put into practice, don't you think so? For an ordinary being like myself, I humbly admit that lesson, though very noble, is really hard to practice.

Those who had witnessed the world famous award winning movie 'Gandhi' shown across the world about a decade ago, will recollect that the long line ***Satyagrahis*** [***Satyagraha*** fighter], under the leadership of Mahatma Gandhi, while moving towards the sea shore at Dandi defying the British Government salt making law, behaved in a very orderly and non-violent way, despite provocative and threatening manner on the part of police forces deployed at the scene. Such was the impact of Gandhi's influence and direction.

"A true Satyagrahi must be able to stand trial and tribunals in order to fulfill his mission", often emphasized the Mahatma.

Another important issue, I am often asked by my compatriots is whether ***Satyagraha*** as taught by Mahatma Gandhi and tested in India, could be employed successfully elsewhere? I say in reply that personally I am doubtful because of various factors such as situations, circumstances, motives etc.

Lastly, I would say a few words about ***Satyagraha*** in Action that I witnessed in India during my student days.

As already said I was a student in India [Uttar Pradesh, Bihar and Bengal] during the crucial years then was the way the Indian people, men and women, young and old, rich and poor, irrespective of castes and creeds, sacrificed their all for the freedom of their Beloved Motherland. I saw with my own eyes, long lines of ordinary Indian women folks; draped in their customary saries shy looking yet defiant and very spirited. They took to the streets, yelling out patriotic slogans ***Bharat Mata Kee Jai*** [Victory to Motherland] and ***Vande Mataram*** [Homage to Mother India]. Even today, after a lapse of more than half a century, the scene is vivid in my memory.

I hope I have been able to give you, both in theory and practice, not too bad a picture of Mahatma Gandhi's ***Satyagraha*** which enabled India regain her long lost freedom.

Reference

1. Rabindranath Tagore.

7

Gandhi and Burmese Democracy Movement

Tint Swe

The people of Burma [Myanmar] have been familiar with Gandhi at the same time the Indians did. Through 40 odd years of civil war Gandhi was only in the school text books in Burma, he became not only icon but also his practice was followed in the pro-democracy struggle in 1988 onward. Civil disobedience and all forms of protest by entire people brought down the 26-year old Burmese Socialist Program Party regime. When mass uprising was brutally crushed by the current rulers, energetic student folks resorted to arms struggle. Some of them are still engaging at the time of this writing.

As the protesters were allowed to vote in the election in 1990, it was not surprising that Aung San Suu Kyi's party decisively won. Her party, the National League for Democracy [NLD] while Aung San Suu Kyi was placed under the first house-arrest, chose a historic Gandhi Hall on ***Boaungkyaw*** Street, Rangoon to hold a national convention in July 1990. It was an interesting coincidence that as Gandhi braved against British colonial rule the Burmese student Aung Kyaw sacrificed his life against the same colonist.

Aung San Suu Kyi took not only example but also courage from international icons and the first of which is Gandhi. She officially declared that NLD's struggle is non-violent. Her people inside Burma continued to dare to protest against the authorities. Therefore the total number of prisoners of conscience never came down below 1,500 marks throughout last 15 years. Over 200 elected MPs took part the call to convene the parliament and were detained in 1996. As protest went on even in the prisons and supplemented by inhuman brutality, the death in custody of political prisoners is more than a dozen including at least 3MPs.

Aung San Suu Kyi's motto in Gandhian way was ***"Not to say unjust is right and evil is not bad".*** She set the example herself by walking through calmly at gun point and the order to shoot. Her strict instruction to her all travel companions was not to strike back even being beaten or manhandled. Those who lost mind controls were sent back home.

It was active nonviolence theory and practice introduced in the exile struggle in later years. Those students became the practitioners. India-based Burmese groups have more opportunities to learn and gain support from Indian Gandhian champions. The most senior living follower of Mahatma Gandhi like Nirmala Deshpande becomes indispensable source of energy. It becomes that an Indian leader would say, ***"I come here for Burmese cause because of two women: Daw Aung San Suu Kyi and Nirmala Deshpande".***

Likewise Gandhi Peace foundation is occasional partner. The World Peace Movement Trust [lead by Dr. Ravindra Kumar] and other non-violent and peace organizations are key supporters. The Burmese group becomes a member of recently constituted Non-violent Peace- Force.

How just it is, the Burmese struggle has been over a decade. Being their beloved leader detained again and again, the people infrequently look for the outside help – practical help. Unfortunately the United Nations seems toothless in case of Burma as paper resolutions of 12 consecutive years did not work. The staunch crusader of human rights America has no big business interest in such a small nation. No new investment in Burma came too late and too less as millions of oil sector investment has been already in. The European Union needs for consensus which calls for a long process and reaches less strong common position. The natural neighbors, ASEAN block countries tied their own hands. Both India and China may not risk changing their supports. Chinese shows no sign of change from tremendous support to the regime. Similarly India's awesome engagement policy depends on the battle between morality question and interest theory among the Indian politicians. Will new government in Delhi adopt fresh approach?

As a result Burmese people cannot expect much from outside. They have to rely on themselves. The will has already been there – see 1988 uprising and 1990 election result. What they do need is the way. The way must be in line with active nonviolence augmented by moral as well as possible maximum support from outside.

Since last month NLD has launched signature campaign for the release of Aung San Suu Kyi and reopening of the party offices. Do outsiders see any raison d'être of closure of a legally existing party office closed down after hundreds of NLD members massacred by the authorities during a political tour? Who knows if Daw Suu was not detained she may lead a Salt March like protest rally.

Anyhow the signature campaign of NLD is significant. Moreover the victims of forced labour are making legal complaints knowing that judiciary system is completely partial. In May 2004, the regime resumed 8-year old near dead national convention in which NLD and key ethnic political parties did not participate. Since then NLD, instead of dialogue, claimed that convening of the Parliament was the way out. Will over 200 MPs risk the detention again? The people won't sit idle. All indications call for people mobilization. Will Gandhi's India see the right time to do something then? Will Gandhi prevail in Burma?

8

Rama and Ramayana in the Life of Mahatma Gandhi

Lallan Prasad Vyas

The world knows of India's perpetual adherence to the principle of peace, non-violence and truth since ancient times. The great name of Mahatma Gandhi is known in this connection; he inspired and influenced the contemporary world history by becoming as a living symbol of these great Indian values. Now, the time has come to know further as to who influenced and inspired Gandhiji to reach such Himalayan heights...it was none other than Shri Rama...the unparalleled hero of ***Ramayana***, a perfect man with all the greatest possible human qualities and to many including Gandhiji, a direct and full manifestation of Supreme God, the Creator of the universe. Gandhiji had become one with Rama, the last two words ***"Hey Rama"*** uttered by him just before his last breath after receiving the assassin's bullets; provide the strongest proof of his lifelong faith in Ram. He used to recite the name ***"Rama"*** within his heart with every breath-a fact admitted by him on couple of occasions under some compelling circumstances.

Once a devotee famous for propagation of the name of Rama by taking pledges from others in writing to the effect that they would henceforth write or recite daily, certain fixed numbers of ***Ramanaam***. On his insistence to Gandhiji for a pledge he said:

"There passed hardly a moment when I do not remember Ram."

On other occasion, he was provoked to say:

"Though he can not tear open the chest and show Shri Ram in his heart but he was sure to recite the Ram Naam as his last words, even in event of being shot by somebody and if it does not happen then tell the world that Gandhi was just a show-man and not Mahatma."

But he was a Mahatma [Great Soul]-a-fact proved beyond doubt, His utterance of last two words ***"Hey Rama"*** was in fact, the mirror of his life. The said prophecy came out of his very strong inner conviction which was the result of his equally strong emotional attachment with the Tulsi Das' ***Ramayana "Ram Charit Manas"*** since childhood.

Ram is Truth

Mahatma Gandhi had experienced that very divinity in his life which had always been part and parcel of the name Rama and the ***Ramayana***. He used to call it magic or miracle in worldly sense. But in reality it was far beyond that. He did not find any heart. He said that people go to any extent to care physical body to cure physical diseases knowing well that this body had a definite end-still they do not bother about the need for cure of spiritual illness. If it is done sincerely then it favourably affects on physical illness also. Here the relevance of ***Ramanaam*** comes in the picture, which ultimately aims at disciplining the life.

He described ***Ramanaam*** as a most valued treasure which never decreases even after spending from it to any extent. ***Vedic*** scriptures like ***Upanishad*** say:

"Full is always full. If full is taken away from the full it still remain full."

"Purnam-.adah purnam id-am purnat purnam-ucyate,

purnasya purnam-adaya purnam-purnamevaiash-ishyate"

Concept of Ramarajya

Mahatma Gandhi was much fascinated by the concept of ***Ramarajya*** [Kingdom of Rama] as described in the ***Ramayana***. That was the reason; he was tempted to see a film ***"Ramarajya"*** for the first time in his life. In fact, ***Ramarajya*** became his dream for the independent India as he himself wrote in ***"Hind Swarajya"*** long before India became free. As mentioned earlier the ***"Ramcharit Manas"*** of Saint Tulsi Das had lasting influence on Mahatma's mind. The great saint poet writes in his four-century old classic that because of Rama being a most ideal and spiritual-minded king, there was no disease either physical or inflicted by nature or God. All men having love for each other and they were doing their duties according to the teachings of ***Vedas***. The ***Ramayana*** describes:

"DAIHIK DAIVIK BHAUTIK TAPA
RAMRAJ KACHUHI NAHI VYAPA"

Nature become so merciful in ***Ramarajya*** that cows used to provide milk as desired:

"MAN BHAOTO DHENU PAI SRAVAHI"

Sea while remaining within limits used to throw valuable pearls to the shore:

"SAGAR NIJ MARJADA RAHIN
DARAHI RATNA TATANHI PAI LAHARIN"

Clouds used to rain on demand

"MANGE VARID DEHI JAL RAMCHANDRA KE RAJ"

In this context ***Ramayana*** conveys the message that if any system or order that takes into consideration the spiritual or the human values and keeps them uppermost, then not only the whole environment becomes congenial but the nature also showers grace all round. Human relations obviously take a better turn. Society looks like a vast family-a great concept based on ***"Vasudhaiva Kutumbakama"***-the world, a family.

Unfortunately, the dream of ***Ramarajya*** which has always been a dream of Indian mind could not be realized in post independent India. The country, in spite of having many great personalities adorning its glorious history, could neither be able to produce a king like Rama nor was an ideal brother like Bharata during this modern age known for its power hungry and power-grabbing politicians in every corner of the world and for that matter India is also no exception. Nevertheless, the only consolation we could derive from the fact that since India had produced the greatest symbol of sacrifice in the names of Rama and Bharata in the past, it ignites the hope for the future also. The basis of the ***dharma*** in India since ancient past had been self-sacrifice and not greed for power.

Gandhiji, scantily clad Mahatma, who himself tried to set an example of selflessness and sacrifice, had won the hearts of millions of millions not only in India but throughout the world. Even being a top leader of the Congress which became party in power just after the Britishers left, he refused to become part of the power structure in any way. On the other hand, when on 15th August, 1947, India was celebrating its independence day with all pomp and show, Mahatma Gandhi was thousands of miles away from the well illuminated national capital, in the interior of disturbed Noakhali area of West Bengal making all efforts for communal peace. Therefore, we could very well derive a conclusion that Mahatma Gandhi by his sheer ***sadhana*** [spiritual practice], ***swadhyaya*** [self study] and sacrifice [renunciation] became a symbol of Rama himself in furtherance of the virtues attached to Rama.

Ram is Kalpa Tree

In fact, many of the realized saints and seers of India since ancient time saw in ***Ramanaam*** or

Ramayana, a ***KALPA-VRIKSHA***, the mythological tree of heaven which unfailingly fulfills what ever is prayed for. But, because of illusory influence of the ***Maya*** most of them pray for worldly accomplishment. Like a petty street beggar, who cannot think for great things except at the most for some more money, clothing and shelter even on being asked by a king. But Mahatma Gandhi was none of them. On coming in contact with the divine ***Ramanaam***, Mahatma Gandhi thought of and fought for the greatest possible thing of his time-independence of his own great country from the worst foreign rule. Ultimately, the impossible happened in 1947 which also paved the way for the independence of many other countries of Asia, Africa and even South America. Whatever happened in his life, big or small, he took that as a wish of Rama. So was the freedom of India for him.

It would not be out of place to mention here that though on the social plane he pleaded for a truth that Rama, Allah, God or Buddha all was one and the same. But for individual meditation or the concentration, only Rama was there in his heart. The true seekers or the devotees, who know some thing of this spiritual process in the sphere of ***bhakti*** [devotion], would definitely be able to understand and agree that for higher spiritual attainments one particular form and the name of God are essential.

The famous ***bhajan***, a prayer to Rama- ***"Raghupati Raghav Raja Rama, Patit Pawan Sita Rama"*** became more like a national song during the freedom struggle lead by him than a mere ***bhajan*** and used to be sung not only during his daily prayer but on the occasions of various annual sessions of Indian National Congress also. Once the weave with a handloom in his early life he was brought up by a Muslim weaver couple though believed to have a ***Brahmin*** origin.

After the death of Mahatma Gandhi, a highly realized saint of Ayodhya-***Paramhansa*** Rama Mangal Das whom I had also an opportunity to meet, authorized a person to decode the book and get it published during nineties of the last century. Then the mystery of Kabir's rebirth as Mahatma Gandhi was known to most of us. Now it is up to the people to believe it or not. But there is one truth beyond doubt that many great souls used to come back on the earth to fulfill their unfinished mission. Even Lord Buddha had admitted in certain ***Jatak*** stories that he himself was Rama ***Pandit*** in his previous incarnation.

So far as Mahatma Gandhi is concerned, he had many similarities with saint Kabir. Firstly, both by their absolute devotion and complete dedication became one with Ram. For them Rama was manifestation of Supreme Godhead. Secondly, both were fearless in expressing their views with great conviction. They became symbol of Hindu-Muslim unity. Thirdly, both became weavers-one with handloom and other with ***Charkha***. Fourthly, the love for humanity and the love for God were supreme for both of them. Truth and love became solid foundation for Ahimsa [non-violence] of Mahatma Gandhi while Kabir said in a couplet:

"POTHI PARHI PARHI JAG MUWA, PANDIT BHAYA NA KOYE

DHAI AAKHAR PREM KA PARHAI SO PANDIT HOYE"

Meaning thereby:

People died after reading and reading huge volumes but none of them became Pandit [scholar] in the real sense. He who reads only two and a half letters of love becomes ***Pandit*** in reality. [The Hindi word ***Prem*** may be considered as having two and half letters.]

We often hear-it is truth that prevails. Now after knowing Mahatma Gandhi and Saint Kabir we may add that it is also the love that prevails. The philosophy of Lord Buddha broadly endorses this view.

I am sure, all of us agree that Mahatma Gandhi was greatest contribution from India i.e. Bharat to the world humanity-of course after Lord Buddha.

9

Mahatma Gandhi on Non-Violence

Asghar Ali Engineer

Mahatma Gandhi and non-violence have become integral to each other and one cannot think of Gandhi without non-violence and non-violence without Gandhi in our own times. Gandhi's concept of non-violence is very comprehensive and seminal. As we know violence has many forms, it could be physical or psychological, it could be individual or institutional and it could be obvious or subtle. To refrain from physical violence is not enough, one has to pledge oneself even to avoid any thought of violence.

All founders of great religion have exhorted us to avoid violence and have stressed need for peace. It is not Buddhism and Christianity alone, even Islam's central emphasis is on peace and non-violence. The Qur'an expounds it in its verse 5:32 which says that ***"..whoever kills a person, unless it be for manslaughter or for mischief in the land, it is as though he had killed entire humanity. And whoever saves the life, it is as though he has saved entire humanity."***

But we find so much violence in the history of all religions precisely because religions soon after the death of their founders turn into huge establishments and the politics of controlling these institutions begin and violence ensue. And of course, religious doctrines are used to legitimise violence giving false impression about the doctrines themselves. Individual violence, though condemnable is not as dangerous as institutional violence and particularly state violence.

The kind of non-violence advocated by Mahatma Gandhi is based on cultivating a particular philosophical outlook and is integrally associated with truth. According to Gandhi God is Truth and Truth is God. Thus one cannot think of non-violence without being accompanied by truthfulness. Gandhiji believed in what he called ***Satyagraha***, i.e., insistence on truth.

Thus first of all one should be thoroughly convinced of truth of one's cause before launching any struggle for that. Without such deep rooted conviction one cannot consistently avoid violence in ones struggle. Gandhiji stressed purity of soul time and again. One is faced with crises in life, especially when you are struggling for a cause. When faced with such crises Gandhiji used to deeply reflect on the causes and would not take any decision unless he felt his soul is pure and without any malice.

It is not easy to practice such rigorous self-discipline for ordinary people, howsoever desirable. Nevertheless it should remain an ideal for us to be achieved. We see so much violence in the world today because we pursue not truth but our own desires and commit violence to achieve them. Similarly we see so much state violence as the politicians controlling the state try to pursue their own desire and to perpetuate their hold over the state.

Today America who wields absolute power has become perpetrator of greatest degree of violence in the world. Its sole pursuit is to control maximum resources of the world and commits unparalleled degree of violence to achieve that objective. It backs up Israel as through it, it wants to control Middle Eastern oil. Thus violence invariably results if one pursues desires rather than truth.

It is said that Gandiji was more of an anarchic. There is some truth in it. Pursuit of power always leads to violence. In order to be strictly non-violent, one has to keep away from pursuit of power. Any organised attempt by any institution results in coercion and coercion generates feeling of violence in its victim. Coercion itself is a form of violence. To enforce anything on anyone can and does result in violence.

Thus for rigorous practice of non-violence strict self-discipline is highly necessary. Gandhiji had practiced this strict self-discipline to a degree of perfection. If one accepts Truth through self-discipline no violence of any degree will be involved. Anything enforced from above, be it truth, involves violence. Thus non-violence has to be accompanied by strict self-discipline.

Also, freedom and absolute freedom, even to the degree of anarchy, is needed for creating condition for genuine non-violence. Absence of freedom leads to coercion and coercion leads to violence. Thus freedom of soul is very important for practicing non-violence. One should experience freedom deep into one's soul. These are some of the conditions for promoting non-violence. Needless to say these conditions are far from being prevalent in our conflict and violence torn world.

Also, there has to be absence of hatred for non-violence to prosper. We see that nationally and internationally certain minorities and nations are targeted for hate campaign and intense hatred is spread against these ethnic or religious communities or nations. And such hate campaigns are not without reason. There are powerful vested interests who try to fulfil their political and economic objectives through such campaigns. In India the ***Sangh Parivar*** uses hate campaign against Muslims and Christians to target Hindu votes and this often results in communal violence.

Internationally America is targeting Muslim nations, particularly in the Middle East, to establish its absolute hegemony in the region. Prof. Huntington of Harvard University wrote a book ***The Clash of Civilizations*** to promote hatred against Islam and Muslims in the west to achieve hat objective. With such impure self and selfish motives how can one promote peace and non-violence whatever the rhetoric. One cannot promote peace and non-violence with such impure motives. Hence, so much violence in our country and in our world today.

We are also experiencing retaliatory violence in the form of bomb explosions or what is called suicide bombing. When a dominant community or dominant power tries to enforce its hegemony coercively over a community or a people a section of it retaliates with violence again killing innocent people. We see so much violence today in Iraq today for the same reason. Palestine is another example. Suicide bombs wreak havoc. Chechens are also resorting to retaliatory violence.

There appears to be so much hatred in our country and in our world today. The ***Sangh Parivar*** not only hates Muslims and Christians but also those who sympathise with them. It was for this reason that Nathu Ram Godse assassinated the very embodiment of non-violence Mahatma Gandhi precisely because Gandhiji had sympathy for Muslim minority in India. They could not tolerate tolerance of Gandhi.

Suicide bombing should also be condemned though it is often resorted to by helpless people who are targets of powerful states. These suicide bombings also result in death and destruction and create further justification for state violence or violence by dominant communities. Can Gandhiji's concept of passive resistance help in such situations? I think so, if passive or non-violent resistance is based on deep conviction of truth and if motives are pure.

It will be very difficult for the victims of Israeli or American violence to agree to such a course. This course, though extremely difficult to follow as it requires rigorous self discipline and pursuit of truth, would be anytime much more fruitful than retaliatory violence. Retaliatory violence invites greater degree of violence from the dominant powers, instead of teaching them any lesson and thus the vicious circle of violence continues unabated.

Instead if Gandhian method of non-violent resistance is followed based on truth and purity of soul, it is bound to impact deeply on the mind and soul of aggressor, though not immediately. A non-violent resister has to have great patience. In fact truth and patience are quite integral to each other. One can hardly pursue the truth without inexhaustible amount of patience.

In fact retaliatory violence legitimises aggressive violence in the eyes of people. Also, violence ***'empowers'*** victims and they begin to behave with the sense of power, which is the root of evil. Thus ***'empowerment'*** of victims of violence through violence aggravates the situation. The victim in fact is not empowered through violence as he thinks. He, in turn, also becomes part of the same game and both aggressors and victims find justification in each other and become each other's mirror image.

If we have to see end of violence in our country and in our world, let us begin with our own region, our own area. Let us try to establish peace in our own place through ***Satyagraha*** for justice in our own area. Difficult though it is, it should not be impossible. We have to pursue non-violence with pure motives as any trace of impurity in our motives can beget violence. Only such honesty and purity can promote non-violence as any dishonesty is injustice to the other and any injustice sure prescription for violence.

We must distance ourselves from all unjust power structures to practice non-violence. Once we are sucked into blast of power, we can never liberate ourselves from it. That is why Gandhiji, with all his prestige kept his distance from state power after liberation of India from the British rule. Had he gone near state power, he would have done violence to his own purity of self. It was his streak of anarchy which saved him from testing the fruit of forbidden tree. He thus retained his paradise of peace and non-violence.

10
World Peace and Gandhism

Babubhai Jashbhai Patel

Mahatma Gandhi was described as the Father of the Nation in India. This was because he bestowed fatherly care on all problems of India. He was concerned with the problems of all the sectors of the society. He gave thought to hygiene, village uplift, employment, social security, mutual goodwill and brotherhood, population control, basic needs of the people, democracy, industrial relations, non-exploitative society, just social order, control over authoritarianism, etc.

His research of a fair social order and experiments with solving India's problems with minimum cost of time, money and energy, are equally helpful to people outside India also. His non-violent struggle for India's freedom provides a guideline to all countries placed in India's position of bondage. His success in securing India's freedom provides an alternative to violent struggle, points an alternative to destructive war involving tremendous loss of lives and property compared to his method involving minimum damage to life and property, and leaving least rancour and ill will behind. When the British rulers left India it was possible for Free India to offer the Governor Generalship of India to the last Viceroy of India who till then represented the British Crown. In a violent struggle this is unimaginable.

The world has tried the violent war method for ages to solve the world's problems. Every war becomes increasingly destructive. Hiroshima and Nagasaki could be annihilated in no time during the Second World War. Next war is likely to be far more destructive. The ruthless wars ultimately and in negotiations and dictation of terms by the conquerors on the vanquished, leaving a tremendous trail of bad blood, eternal enmity and spirit of vengeance. The Gandhian method believes in exchange of views, negotiations, arbitration, etc. If all these fail it would resort to peaceful resistance of evil and non-co-operation with the conquerors, trying to change the heart of the oppressor through self suffering without ill will. This is a more effective and less destructive process, leading to a permanent solution rather than a temporary forced peace.

The Gandhian approach is based on goodwill, self denial, self suffering, leaving only sweet memories of the struggle and no trace of bitterness. It some times takes more time than the violent method. But taking into consideration the aftermath, it appears to be a much better alternative.

Under the Gandhian struggle even women, children and elderly persons could participate as in the freedom movement of India which involved millions of people including women, children, farmers and labourers.

Gandhi's method was employed in the industrial dispute between textile workers and mill owners of Ahmedabad in 1918. It ended in the betterment of the lot of the workers and evolution of the method of discussion, conciliation, arbitration or adjudication for the solving of industrial disputes with resorting to strikes, hooliganism, destruction, bad blood and loss of wages and production. This method can fruitfully be employed the world over to resolve industrial disputes and similar differences of opinion in various spheres.

The unfair recovery of land revenue in spite of failure of crops and the unconscionable, unfair, steep rise and enhancement of land revenue could be resisted by farmers in 1918 and 1928 in Kaira and Bardoli without causing any damage to public property, only on the strength of the determination and readiness to suffer loss of land or property in order to resist unfair administrative pressure.

One has to understand Gandhi's philosophy to appreciate his method of dealing with problems. His concept of a social order based on the motto of service and brotherhood is the corner stone of his philosophy. If one feels that he is a TRUSTEE of everything that he possesses including his wealth, economic and political power, and hid physical as well as intellectual faculties, he will never be covetous and desirous of unlawful gains. He will be content with what the society endows him with.

He will accept the theory of being content with the minimum that the society can afford to give to him and at the same time keen to contribute his maximum to the society. With this approach greed will have no place in the social order. Exploitation will be out of question. With the approach of economic and frugal style of life there will be easy availability of basic needs and no shortages and therefore, no black money or black marketing. There will be a healthy economy.

The world over civilization is based on increase of wants, higher standard of life, minimum physical labour, unending desire for creature comforts, leading to ever unsatisfied greed resulting in the desire to corner more and more of money and wealth by any means fair or foul. This leads to a temptation to give a go-bye to ethical values, as well as social responsibility and resort to violence and conflict to secure more than one's legitimate due. Therein lies the root of social chaos. Gandhian approach leaves no room for such decaying social order. His method would lead to a healthy, contented society based on the foundation of love, mutual help, goodwill and development of the principle of service above self.

Gandhi believed in practicing before preaching. He was the son of a Chief Minister of an Indian State. He was a barrister by education. Yet, he chose to lead the life of the simplest of his countrymen. When he established a colony for himself and his colleagues he got constructed ordinary hutments to live in. There was no electric power in the colony. Water had to be fetched from wells. Diet was simple without spices. Everyone including Gandhi himself was not averse to manual labour, cleansing of latrines, cooking, cleaning of utensils and clothes and maintaining the economic standard of life of the humblest of India's villagers. That is why Gandhi was able to communicate his ideas of simple living and high thinking to some of the intellectually and economically tallest of living Indians of his times.

The Western world felt like switching over to animal power for cultivation and depending on organic manure instead of chemical fertilizers. The idea of 'Small is Beautiful' is getting more and more acceptable. Gandhi's theory of equal wages to a barber and a barrister has evoked thoughtful response. China utilizes agricultural waste and animal dung for generating gas to meet the cooking and lighting needs of two thirds of its rural households.

If Gandhi's approach to health and hygiene is accepted the world would be able to meet its growing need, through the available natural resources whereof wastage of any sort will be avoided. Growing population could be checked by his approach to family planning.

In 1981 fifty three Nobel Prize winners of the world had declared that the solution to world's problems lies in the Gandhian approach which would lead to an end of strife, warfare, unhealthy rivalry and several evils that are eating into the vitals of human existence.

Gopal Krishna Gokhale a leading Liberal National Leader of India paid very glowing tribute to Gandhi at the session of the Indian National Congress in 1909 in the following words:

"Fellow delegates, after the immortal part which Mr. Gandhi has played in this affair I must say it will no be possible for any Indian, at any time, here or in any other assembly of Indians to mention his name without deep emotion and pride [here the huge gathering rose to its feet and accorded three hearty and most enthusiastic cheers to Mr. Gandhi]. Gentlemen, it is one of the privileges of my life that I know Mr. Gandhi intimately and I can tell you that a purer, a Nobler, a braver and a more EXALTED SPIRIT has never moved on this earth [cheers and loud applause]. Mr. Gandhi is one of those men, who, living an austerely simple life themselves and devoted to all the highest principles of love to their fellow being and to truth and justice, touch the eyes of the weaker brethren as with magic and give them a new vision. He is a man who may be well described as a man among men, a hero among heroes, a patriot among patriots, and we may well say that in him Indian humanity at the present time has really reached its highest watermark."

Our present day world is fortunate that we had this Gandhi in our midst only a few years back. His preaching and practice have left a rich legacy for us which if it is digested by the world we would have a peaceful, lovable, healthy, contented world.

11
Non-Violent Political Approach Towards Establishing Peaceful Co-Existence

Shahidul Haque Munshi

History has been analyzed in two ways. The school of capitalists expounded history according to subjective point of view. This point deals with the subjective analysis of anything and being of the world. It only discusses the eternal clash between goodness of God and badness of evil. This subjectivity fails properly to find out the reasons of devotion towards God and hatred towards evil. It only gives an emotional explanation of historical evolution, which is not scientifically accurate. But it is true from both schools' points of view [***Capitalists' School & Socialists' School***] that history is the cosmic struggle between the goodness of God and badness of evil. It is the school of socialists that analysed history from the objective point of view. According to them, history fights for just demand against exploitation. Just demand represents goodness of God and exploitation stands for badness of evil.

The homogeneous Indians were deprived of their rightful demands as soon as they were invaded by the outsiders. The external enemies under different pseudonymous titles subjugated the Indians up to the 15th August, 1947. The native Indians fought before their present independence against many illegal foreign rulers under the leadership of many great persons.

The last hero, who fought for the goodness of God against the badness of evil is Mahatma Gandhi, a charismatic leader, without any doubt. From the capitalistic angle he struggled for the goodness of God that represented the rightful demand of the homogeneous Indians clarified from the socialistic point of view. Leaving the sweetness of advocacy of South Africa, this great leader came to his birthplace India with an ambition to establish the goodness of God or the just demand of the Indians through non-violent political approach. There are two ways to change the political system. One is constitutional way and the other is revolutionary process.

Mahatma Gandhi being a philanthropist supported the constitutional process to oust the British rulers in the then Indian subcontinent. No aggressive approach he showed or encouraged to oust the Britishers from the Indian sub-continent with the help of peaceful non-cooperation following non-violent political process he established the legal rights of the homogeneous Indians.

His non-violent political approach is non-communal, that fights for the legal rights of every Indian irrespective of every caste and creed. The political concept of this great charismatic leader is quite different from other contemporaneous great leaders. He may be compared with the finest charismatic leader Nelson Mandela.But in perspective of state administration he is greater than Nelson Mandela. He kept himself quite untouched out of the falsified hallucination of state administration other than giving suggestion to the party members being the shadow head of the party and state. He was found totally very simple hi his life style, which he applied also in his thinking and thought. Complication he didn't like, at all. Avoiding complexity in every sphere of life, he established the greatness and goodness of simplicity in Indian politics. It is he, who supported many non-Hindus for being their leaders in the Indian National Congress. This shows his non-communal political approach towards establishing the peace and co-existence through out the Indian subcontinent. He believed in the importance of the three paradigms to establish peaceful co-existence through out the world. For India, he suggested these three paradigms as the pre conditions of peace and harmony. The three paradigms are tolerance, compromise and evaluation of others opinions. Because of tolerance and the power of sustenance he never turned aggressive in any sphere of his political career.

He suggested his party activists to be tolerant and that's why, he persuaded the non-violent political approach in the arena of the then sub continent. Peaceful negotiation he preferred always. That's why, he compromised, many a time, with the evil forces or the antagonistic forces to lessen illogical commotion. Because of his compromising tendency he easily left the golden chair of the Independent India for his beloved disciples. This wonderful quality has made his immortal and quite transfigured before the political exponents and analysts. He never criticized others' opinions. He evaluated others opinions with due honour. It is he, who never harassed any Muslim political leaders, who at that time wanted Pakistan, to be a separate independent territory. But he logically strove to make them convince for a united Indian sub continent. But when they [Muslims] got obstinate, he compromised with them and let them form a separate independent state for their own. Who will do like this in this age of global political crisis? Theological leader Jesus

Christ, the holified soul, did something like this. He also preached the goodness of tolerance and non-violent approaches. Really his approaches are very fruitful for establishing peace globally. Those, who explode bombardment today illogically in different places of the world threatening others sovereignty and independence can avoid perpetrating this if they follow the great political ideals and principles of the Charismatic leader Mahatma Gandhi. To nullify the possibility of Clashes of Civilizations [According to S. P. Huntington] we globally should follow his principles of tolerance, negotiation and evaluation of others opinions. What he did monthly in his political and a political life was putting emphasis on the others opinions. This world is full of crisis only become others opinions are not truly evaluated. If others opinions are emphasised, that's to say, it people's opinions are evaluated, there will be no crisis in the world other than peace and harmony. Mahatma Gandhi fought for peace and harmony in the logical sequences, which resulted in the independence of the two nations- India and Pakistan. Without Mahatma Gandhi, there would be no birth of these two states. It must be admitted by all those, who are conscious wholly, soully and ritually. He never believed in Jingoism. According to him, it brings destruction for the believer and the supporters. He disliked parochialism because, according to him it resists the tempo of development and reformation. In the real sense of the term, in this age of global crisis, we need to welcome the non-violent political approaches of this great leader to mitigate global political restlessness. His treat political ideals that are tolerance, negotiation and evaluation others opinions, should be translated into reality for global peace and tranquillity. Before its implementation everybody concerned should be made ready to accept its challenges as well as goodness, otherwise, it will ruin the motto of global peace. We need to be sure of the fact that God Himself will be riffraff if he mixes with them directly without making them understand that He is God himself.

So, the doctrine Mahatma Gandhi can be a great success for establishing global peace and tranquillity if it is clearly and distinctly preached by all those, who understand it truly for all those, who don't understand it truly. If the buzzards once are made realizing about the utility of Gandhi's doctrine of global peaceful co-existence, they will take part in the long march of peace and tranquillity as well as prosperity throwing their spirit of evilism in the holified river Gangas. The spirit of Gandhi's political indoctrination may be poeticised in the following way:

"Non violence is peaceful journey, Towards the establishment of harmony."

For the people world wide, It fights for peaceful tide:

With the help of tolerance,
Creating fructified clearance,
It applies compromise,
For making every one wine,
Supporting evaluation of others opinions,
Turning all divided unions,
Into a singular one,
Preventing peace from the wane,
Making people ready,
For their being hardy,
Against parochialism,
Against dogmatism.

Only for humanism we should be all above cynicism.

For a seen never clouded,
For a people never goaded,
For a globe never flooded,
For a flow of peace never blooded,
By badness of evil,
Goodness of God Gandhism will reveal.

12

The Bhagvad-Gita and its Influence on Mahatma Gandhi

Poonam Lakhanpal and Anjula Rajvanshi

The ***Shrimadbhagvad Gita***, known to be a great Hindu epic, is also a unique work of Indian Philosophy. In fact, four ***Vedas*** and 108 ***Upanishads*** are not much easy to understand by common men. But the ***Gita*** griped in comparatively simple language can be understood easily.

The ***Gita*** is a dialogue [***samvad***] between Lord Krishna and Arjuna in the battle of Kurukshetra. It is not only a teaching process; it's a right way to learn the techniques of ***Karma*** and ***Dharma***. Lord Krishna removed various confusions of Arjuna by his dialogues [***Samvads***], which are collectively known as the ***Gita***.

Basically, the ***Gita*** is a symbol of humanity, truth and non-violence. The ***Gita*** is not a treatise for reading only, it is a work of good learning, living a practical life and performing the jobs properly. It is capable of changing our life style as also the viewpoint of thinking. Side by side, it teaches us how to Live and let live?

Essence of the *Gita*

The ***Gita*** has been composed for those who want to be clear about their work and worship, want to gain spiritual strength or to be enlightened and also to gain knowledge of reality.

After going deep into the ***Gita,*** we well understand all the three concepts—***Karmayoga***, ***Bhaktiyoga*** and ***Jnanayoga***. These three concepts are very important and necessary parts of our life. Accordingly these three types of behaviour, there are three types of virtues in this world-***Satoguna***, ***Rajoguna*** and ***Tamoguna***. If these three virtues are not in a balancing position then the world seems to stand on the door of destruction. By these three virtues, we can see the diversity of human nature.

As said already, the ***Gita*** is not an ordinary treatise to be studied only, it is a work for learning and understanding. A man who maintains harmony and works to assimilate on among these three virtues, can come closer to these three concepts- ***Karma***, ***Bhakti*** and ***Jnana***. The ***Gita*** has been divided into eighteen chapters. I am giving here a brief summary of these chapters.

In first chapter, there is the ***'Vishada of Arjuna'***. When Arjuna inspected the rival forces, there he found all relatives and friends. Seeing those persons, Arjuna suddenly felt surged and he refused to fight.

In second chapter, Krishna counsels Arjuna not to give over the mere destruction of transient bodies because ***'Atma'*** [the soul] can never die. Just see these two shlokas:

"Na jayte mriyate va kadachinnayam, Nayam bhootva bhavita va na bhooyha. Ajo nityah shashvtoyam purarno,Na hanyae hanaymane shareere." [20]

"Vedavinashinam nityam ya enmajmavyyam, Katham sa purushah partha kam ghatyati hanti kam." [21]

Meaning thereby: He is not born, nor does he die; nor having been, ceases he anymore to be;

unborn, perpetual, eternal and ancient, he is not slain when the body is slaughtered. Who knows him in destructible, perpetual, unborn, undiminishing, how can that man slay, ***O Partha!*** or cause to be slain?

In fact, this chapter is considered to be the essence of the ***Gita*** [***Gita ka Saar***].

In chapter third, All shlokas are full of the knowledge of ***Karma***. This chapter is known as the ***Karma Yoga***. Arjuna wants to be enlightened of his duties in present conditions in the battlefield of Kurukshetra by Lord Krishna. In his reply to Arjuna, Lord Krishna says:

"Niyatam kuru karma tvam karma jyayo hyakarmarnah Shareeryatrapi ch te na prasidhyedkarmarnah." [8]

Meaning thereby: Perform you right action, for action is superior to inaction, and inactive, even the maintenance of thy body would not be possible.

In chapter four, ***'Divya Jnana'***, Lord Krishna clarifies to his power and ***Maya*** to Arjuna and says:

"Yada—Yada hi dharmasya glanirbhavti Bhart, Abhyuthanamdharmsya tadamainam srijamyaham." [7]

"AritraPanaya sadhunam vinashaya ch dushkritam,Dharmsansthap narthaya sambhavani yuge-yuge." [8]

It means: Whenever there is decay of righteousness, O ***Bharata***, and there is exaltation of unrighteousness, then I myself come forth; For the protection of the good, for the destruction of evil-doers, for the sake of firmly establishing righteousness, I am born from age to age.

In chapter fifth, "***Karmayoga Krishnabhavnabhavit karma***", Lord Krishna solves the confusion of Arjuna about the renunciation of

karma and the action with bhaktiyoga. Krishna told to Arjuna about the real process of karma by twenty nine shlokas.

He says:

"Yogyukto vishudhatma vijitatma jitendriyah, Sarvbhootatambhootatma kurvannapi na lipyate." [7]

He who is harmonized by ***yoga,*** the selfpurified, self-ruled, the senses subdued, whose self in the self of all beings, although acting he is not affected.

In chapter sixth, ***"Dhyanayoga"***, Lord Krishna told about the process of victory on ***'Mann'*** [***atma***] and the real friend of a humanbeing through forty seven ***shlokas***.

In chapter seventh, ***Bhagvadgyana*** in eighth, ***Bhagvadprapti***; in nineth, ***Param guha jnana***; in tenth, ***Shree Bhagvan ka Eshvarya*** and in eleventh ***Viratroopa***, Krishna tells about the way of ***Bhagvadprapti*** and his virat roop in detail.

In chapter twelveth, ***"Bhaktiyoga'***, Lord Krishna tells to Arjuna, which type of persons he likes and why? In this regard, especially we can see these two ***shlokas:***

"Samah shatrau ch mitre ch tatha manapmanayoha, Sheetoshrnsukhaduhkheshu samah sangvivarjitha." [18]

"Tulynindastutimaurni santusto yen kenchita, Aniketha sthirmatibharktimanme priyo narah." [19]

Meaning thereby:

Alike to foe and friend, and also in fame and ignominy, alike in cold and heat, pleasures and pains, destitute of attachment. Taking equally praise and reproach, silent, wholly content with what cometh, homeless, firm in mind, full of devotion, that man is dear to me.

In chapter thirteen [***Prakrati, Purush Tatha Chetna***] and chapter fourteen [***Prakrati Ke Teen Gun***] show that a human being is totally dependent on Lord. In chapter fourteen Lord Krishna especially tells us about the three characteristics of nature-***Rajoguna, Tamoguna*** and ***Satoguna*** such as:

"Sattvatsamjayate gyanam rajaso Lobh ev ch,pramadmohau tamso bhavtogyannev ch." [17]

It means:

From Harmony wisdom is born, and greed from mobility, heedlessness and delusion from lack of wisdom.

In chapter fifteen, ***"Purushottama Yoga"***, and chapter sixteen ***"Daivi Tatha Aasuri Swabhav"***, Lord Krishna speaks of universal truth and the difference of good and bad behaviour of human being. The first, second and third ***shloka*** of chapter sixteen should be considered here:

"Abhayam sattavsanshudhigyanarjany-ogvyavas-thitiha, Danam damasch swadhyaystap aajarvam." [1]

"Ahimsa satyamkrodhstyaghashantir-peshunam, Daya bhooteshvloluptvam mardavam wheerchaplam." [2]

"Tejaha kshama dhritiha shauchmadroho natimanita, Bhavanti sampadam devimbhi-jatasya Bharat." [3]

To explain them:

Fearlessness, cleanness of life, steadfastness in the ***yoga*** of wisdom, almsgiving, self-restraint and sacrifice and study of the scripture, austerity and straightforwardness. Harmlessness, truth, absence of anger [wrath], renunciation, peacefulness, absence of crookedness, compassion to living beings, uncovetousness, mildness, modesty, absence of fickleness. Vigour, forgiveness, fortitude, purity, absence of envy and pride—these are his who with the divine properties, ***O Bharata!***

In the last two chapter of the ***Gita***, Lord Krishna speaks of the types of faith and renunciation. He speaks of three faith-***Satoguni, Rajoguni and Tamoguni***. By all this description I want to clearify the importance and relevance of the ***Gita*** in all time, all conditions and in every country. So, the ***Gita*** can never be an older and out of time matter for human beings.

Influence on Gandhi

Mohandas Karamchand Gandhi is known to be a great Mahatma. Subhas Chandra Bose called him the ***Father of the Indian Nation*** and ***Gurudev*** Rabindranath Tagore bestowed the title of the ***Mahatma*** upon Gandhi, who was a stern believer of humanity, a great supporter of justice for all and an apostle of place, truth and love. His work to humanity was as full and powerful as was of Jesus Christ or Lord Buddha or Lord Mahavira. In his broad vision he not only looked upon India but the world as a community.

In this context, Albert Einstein remark about Mahatma Gandhi is worth quoting here.

He says that he is such a leader of his countrymen who has not secured any help from outside power. He is such a rare politician whose success in not based upon any trick, even not upon the full knowledge of the technique. It all depends upon the reliable strength of his personality. He is such a victorious warrior who has ever discarded the use of force. He is such a wise and humble person who possesses tremendous determining power and has been firm to his ideals and who has entirely devoted all his energies for ameliorating and uplifting the forlorn condition of his countrymen. He has encountered the European tyranny and a sober and simple minded human being and for this he has kept himself upon the best level. It is just possible that the coming generations may not believe that a human being like Gandhi was ever physically present on this earth.

In fact, Mahatma Gandhi became popular neither for his physical strength nor for his wealth. He is known for his selfless work and fight for humanity. He was highly influenced by the ***Gita***. In his autobiography, he admits that he studied the ***Gita*** in foreign and ***"At that time I realized that 'the Bhagvad-Gita' is a precious epic. Slowly, my faith upon The Gita increased and now, I believe that the Gita to be the best epic for the knowledge of divine. In desperation, the Gita helped me very much."***

Gandhiji not only studied the ***Gita*** but he tried to bring its teachings totally in his daily behaviour. His starting was like a commonman but he became an unparalleled personality. He did all this by his faith on the ***Gita***. Many shlokas of the ***Gita*** can be fond in the chapters of his autobiography. Many of his articles which he wrote about peace and the way to achieve it, are influenced by the ***Gita*** to a great extent.

In his autobiography, he wrote that he was impressed by ***shloka*** 62 and 63 of the second chapter of the Gita which say:

"Dhyayto vishyanspunshasangasteshu-pjayta, Sangatsanjayte kaamha kamotkrodho-abhijayata." [62]

"Krodhadbhavati sammoha sammohatsmri-tivibhramha, Smritibhanshad buddhinasho Buddhinashat-pranshyati." [63]

Meaning thereby:

Man, musing on the objects of sense, conceives an attachment to these, from attachment arises desire; from desire anger comes forth.

From anger proceeds delusion; delusion confuses memory; from confused memory the destruction of Reason; from destruction of reason he perishes.

As Gandhiji tried to bring the ***Gita*** in his behaviour, especially he emphasized on Karmayoga in day-to-day practices, result of which was that he become a man of the era. It was the impact of the ***Gita***, Gandhiji won over his hunger, sleep and the difference of climate. Gandhiji was inspired by this ***shloka*** also:

"Karmaryevadhikarsti ma faleshu kadachn, Ma karmfalhetubhoormara te sangostavkarmrni. [47]

It means:

The business is with the action only, never with its fruits; so let not the fruit of action be your motive, nor be you to inaction attached.

Working according to the need of time and space, Gandhiji first of all tried to control himself and then he controlled others indirectly through his behaviour and idealism. This was the reason of his working capacity in every unfavourable climate and conditions. His love for the ***Gita*** can be seen in his autobiography in chapter ***Mrityu Shayya Par***, in which he mentions:

"Till morning, death did not come but I could not have the wish to live and then realizing that death is near, I tried to listen the Gita from my friends as long as possible."

Gandhiji did not associate the ***Gita's Bhaktiyoga*** with any religious, non-religious and idol-worship. In the chapter entitled ***Nirbal Ke Balram*** of his autobiography, he has written:

"In those days, I did not know about religion and God and that how it works with us."

He had great respect for his parents, elder brother and the ***Bhagvad-Gita***. His strong belief was that heartily worship is the supreme medicine. He has written in his autobiography:

"I have no doubt that heartily worship is the best treatment for purification of deteriorated mind and heart. But to gain this blessing, we should have complete courtesy."

Further Mahatma Gandhi explain his views:

"I have observed that when all hopes are shattered and we are just to give up things, then a help comes from somewhere. Prayer and worship are not delusions; but true as much as our eating and walking. It will be no bombast if I say that only this is true and everything else is false."

For those was wish to realise or meet God, Gandhiji has suggested out them to study second chapter of the ***Gita*** especially the ***shloka*** 59. He believed that the ***Gita*** prevents one from desperation. It has been mentioned in the said ***shloka***:

"Vishaya vinivartanteniraharsya dehinha, Rasvarg rasopyasaya parm drishtava nivartte."

To say:

The objects of sense, but not the relish for them, turn away from an abstemious dweller in the body; and ever relish turns away from him after the supreme is seen.

During his early studies, Gandhi lernt only from textbooks but later on, with the inspiration of the Gita and encouragement of his friends, he started gaining knowledge about other religions. By changing his life-style and reading more and more books, he tried to gain knowledge performing truth and non-violence. He also tried to acquire knowledge about the use of non-violence at a proper time and place, to make use of it for unity, harmony, religious tolerance and for value based politics etc. As a result, influence of the ***Gita*** can be clearly seen upon his views of cultute, education, patriotism, politics, religion, society and other matters related to day-to-day behaviours.

About education, he has written in his autobiography:

"I have always preferred education of heart, i.e. development of character."

He further wrote:

"In my opinion the existing system of education is defective, apart from its association with an utterly unjust Government in three most important matters: [1] It is based upon foreign culture to the almost entire exclusion of indigenous culture; [2] It ignores the culture of heart and the hand, and confines itself simply to the head; and [3] Real education is impossible through a foreign medium." [Ravindra Kumar, Gandhi and Gandhism, Meerut: WPMT, 2001, P. 71]

As Gandhiji assumes the ***Gita*** to be a teacher of universal education, hence his teachings were practical and not confined to books. His teachings had the influence of the ***Gita*** effect of which can be realized by the study of the various chapter of the ***Gita*** itself. Gandhiji as a universal human being, believed use of the ***Gita*** to be pleasant and beautiful, wherever it may be in social or personal life or in field of battle.

One should be clear about justice as well as about his duties in the every field of life by the studying of the ***Gita***. As Arjuna ultimately surrendered himself before Lord Krishna; someone should fulfil his duties properly and should not think for the results. Gandhiji expressed his views several times regarding duty and religion in his autobiography. He wrote:

"Duty [religion] means self-knowledge, the knowledge of spirit."

Gandhiji never supported narrow meaning of religion and this was all due to the influence of the ***Gita***. In fact he accepted:

"First of all, he understand the meaning of word "Trustee" from the Gita only".

Gandhiji as a believer of ***Sarvodaya***, considered the teachings of the ***Gita*** to be evergreen and welfaristic for all, each and everyone. He considered the ***Gita*** to be a source of great learning and pleasure. According to him, to see, understand and learn excellent union of duty, religion and politics, one should read the ***Gita.*** Winning and losing are the parts and parcel of politics but being afraid of this, one cannot give up his duty. That is why to turn down British rule, he launched ***Non Co-operation and Civil Disobedience Movement*** on the strength of non-violence. From ***shloka*** 38 of chapter second of the ***Gita*** we can judge the impact of it upon his views. It has been said in this ***shloka***:

"Sukhduhkhe same kritva Labha Labhau Jayajayau, Tato yudhaya yuysav neivam papmvapsyasi."

It means:

Taking as equal pleasure and pain, gain and loss, victory and defeat, gird those for the battle; thus you shall not in cure sin.

The Gita has highly influenced Gandhiji's eating, sleeping, working, knowledge, celibacy, wisdom and his daily routine. Especially on reading chapters second, forth and fifth of the ***Gita***, one can understand the influence of the ***Gita*** upon him.

As a bay in mother's womb acquires the attributes of his mother and after coming in this world, these attributes become his first identity; similarly, knowledge of the ***Gita*** became an identity of Gandhiji. The impact of the ***Gita*** can be seen in every act or action of Gandhiji whether it is the ***Salt Satyagraha*** [***Dandi March***], Quit India Movement or the Non-Cooperation Movement started in 1920.

As a unique statesman, patriotic and mass leader, protector of humanity, devotee of truth, supporter of non-violence, Gandhi did every work as an oblation. He always moved a step ahead after fixing his goal. Oblation is not a religious sacrifice, it is possible in every walk of life. If man takes his jobs as a battle and performs it as an oblation in his life, no hazard can persist in his path of success. Although, today, people do not accept Mahatma Gandhi completely, but following his footsteps, we can get rid of disorder, grouping, corruption and other problems up to some extent. Believing truth as best friend and the ***Gita*** as the best mother and teacher, Gandhiji himself became an inspiration for many. I hope a time will come when people will realize the importance of Gandhi and the ***Gita***, and will bring their teachings in their life.

Bibliography

Ravindra Kumar, Champaran to Quit India Movement, New Delhi, Mittal Publications, 2002.

M. K. Gandhi, Satya Ke Prayog Athva Aatmakatha, Navajivan, Ahmedabad, 1957, p. 58

Srimadbhagvad-Gita, Gorakhpur [G. P.]

Annie Besant and Bhagwandas, The Bhagwad-Gita, Delhi, Anmol, 1986.

13

Conflict Resolution and Peace Possibilities in the Gandhian Perspective

Surinder K. Shukla

Truth alone can resolve conflict. Peace can occur only in truthful environment. Fear, anger, hatred and cowardice lead to conflict and there can be no peace in such a situation. Gandhi exhorts upon the individual to base himself on truth and non-violence. The conflict at individual level must go before the conflict on a larger level can be resolved.

What is Truth? Gandhi identified two truths—one may be called the absolute Truth and, the other, relative Truth. The absolute Truth refers to the ultimate, absolute, and perfect ideals which can never be realised fully, given the imperfect nature of man.[1] The relative Truth refers to the immediate goals which are fully realizable.

But there is no conflict between the absolute Truth and the relative Truth. Through the relative truth, the absolute truth can be approached. The idea of the absolute truth is the pointer, the regulator, and the corrector of relative human truth.

Gandhi had a hypothesis, an assumption, and an intuition that the spirit or the essence of human unity—or God's existence—is present always and everywhere in all human hearts as well as it transcends the whole world and that it is supremely powerful. He proceeded to test the hypothesis everyday, and year after year. He stated his belief that truth and God are synonymous. He entitled his autobiography, ***"The Story of My Experiments with Truth."***[2]

Gandhi considered that truth in this world cannot be discovered except through non-violence. There will always be conflicts, great and small, in human affairs. The nuclear bomb has made it obvious that total war can no longer settle conflicts. And clearly no conflict can be ended in its inner reality by the alleged deterrence from the possession of nuclear weapons. In such a stalemate, the possibility of using non-violent resistance might be worth examining.[3]

At the first mention, the term ***"non-violent resistance"*** seems self-contradictory. How can any resistance be effective in this modern world unless it has backing up, of great strength, power, and weapons? Nevertheless there have been instances in history where great courage, deep conviction, and a fine cause have prevailed without violence, against armed might. Gandhi's struggle for freedom of India was one instance. He believed that unity can also be aroused, fruitfully and enduringly, by love and the desire for justice leading to resolution of conflict.

War or Peace?—exactly proportionate to the attainment of non-violence by each individual.

Gandhi believed that the way of the peace is the way of the Truth. Truthfulness is even more important than peacefulness. Indeed lying is the mother of violence. A truthful man, he continued, cannot long remain violent. He will perceive in the course of his search that he has no need to be violent, and he will further discover that so long as there is the slightest trace of violence in him, he will fail to find the truth he is searching for.

There is no half way between truth and non-violence on the one hand and untruth and violence on the other. Man may never be strong enough to be entirely non-violent in thought, word, and deed. But we must keep non-violence as our goal and make steady progress towards it. Gandhi believed that the attainment of freedom whether, for a man or for a nation or the world, must be in exact proportion to the attainment of non-violence by each.[4]

Theory and Practice of Non-violence

Gandhi gave the theory and practice of non-violence, practised it in his daily life and used it to resolve conflicts. In the method we are adopting in India, he said, fraud, deceit, lying and all the ugly brood of violence and untruth have absolutely no room.[5] Everything is done openly and above board, for truth hates secrecy. The more open you are the more truthful you are likely to be. There is no such thing as defeat and despair in the dictionary of a man who bases his life on Truth and Non-violence. And yet the method of non-violence is not in any shape or form a passive or inactive method. Truth and non-violence are perhaps the activist forces in the world. A man who uses regular weapons and is intent on destroying his enemies, does at least require some rest,Gandhi argued. He is therefore essentially inactive for some part in the twenty four hours. Not so in the case of the votary of truth and non-violence.

Mathematics of Non-violence

In a discourse, Gandhi explained to a professor of mathematics the working of non-violence which may be described as the mathematics of non-violence. The study of mathematics reassured the professor and in geometry he experienced for the first time the existence of a real world which is not visible to the bodily eye. The triangle he learned about in geometry was not a particular triangle that he himself might draw but the essence of all triangles.[6]

Gandhi employed the scientific method[7] in everyday life. Gandhi's application of the scientific method was in the realm of living forces. One feature of living forces is that all life responds to suitable stimuli. And growth depends on many repetitions of tiny and gentle stimuli. Gandhi recognised and practised this law. For one hundred and fifty years all his teaching and action consisted of many repetitions of gently loving stimuli to the spirit in the hearts of all men, including his opponents. He thus caused the seed of the spirit in the hearts of almost everyone, to sprout and grow and in many cases to govern their actions.

The question arises: does the exercise of non-violence have limits? Gandhi replied that the exercise of non-violence requires far greater bravery than that of swordsmanship. Cowardice is wholly inconsistent, he said, with non-violence. Non-violence presupposes the ability to strike. It is a conscious, deliberate restraint put upon one's desire for vengeance the sun does not wreak vengeance upon little children who throw dust at him. they only harm themselves in the act.[8] Gandhi said that individual conviction is the essence of carrying out non-violence.

Non-violence Based on Eternal Law of Love

Gandhi used the non-violent method by basing on the eternal law of love which is the single largest tool for resolving conflict. Gandhi argued that Jesus lived and died in vain if he did not teach us to regulate the whole of life by the eternal law of love.[9] He said that non-violence is not merely a personal virtue. It is also a social virtue to be largely cultivated like other virtues. Surely society is largely regulated by the expression of non-violence in its mutual dealings. What I ask for, he said, is an extension of it on a larger, national and international scale.

Non-violence is superior to violence because it is diametrically opposed to violence. Violence is needed for protection of external things whereas; non-violence is needed for protection of ***Atman*** for the protection of one's honour.

Non-violence cannot be learnt by staying at home. . . He who trembles when he sees two people fighting is not non-violent but a coward. A non-violent person will lay down his life in preventing such quarrels. This power was trained and utilised by Gandhi to foster the principle of non-violence in bringing about India's freedom without blood shed.

Violence Thrives on Counter-Violence

Gandhi believed that means are related to the end. Violence can only breed counter-violence. The vital problem connected with non-violence was that the mankind had all along tried to justify violence and war in terms of unavoidable self-defence. The rule was simple that the violence of the aggressor could only be defeated by superior violence of the defender.[10] This led to a mad race for armaments.

It may sound paradoxical but violence always thrives on counter-violence. Violence can never be ended with violence. Gandhi showed by practical experience, several times in his life, that violence can be countered by non-violence.[11]

Compromise and Trust, argued Gandhi, is the essence of non-violence. The power of non-violence is evident by the use of the twin concept of compromise and trust. Even if the opponent plays him false twenty times, the resister must be ready to trust him for the twenty-first time, for an implicit trust in human nature is the very essence of his creed. Compromise expresses a willingness to adjust to realities and avoid conflicts, even at the cost of sacrificing some position taken originally, howsoever, sound it may have been. In modern times compromise and trust are important weapons which can be employed with success in conflict resolution and bringing about peace in the world.

Modern Examples of Non-violent Resistance

There have been many instances of successful use of non-violent resistance in different countries and at different times. This has been analysed by Richard B. Gregg in his ***"The Power of Non-violence."***[12] Because the taste of historians inclines more towards politics and wars, these other events have received very little attention at their hands, and records of many of them have been lost. In some instances the non-violent resistance was by individuals, in other instances it took the form of a mass or corporate form. The latter form is rarer and perhaps more significant Gregg quotes few outstanding examples[13] to which the latest has been added at the end of the list:

Hungary	—	1867
South Africa	—	1906
India	—	Champaran, 1917
India	—	Vykom in the State of Travancore, 1925
India	—	Kotgarh near Shimla, 1921
India	—	Bardoli, 1928
India	—	Struggle for independence
Denmark	—	1940
Norway	—	1940
United States	—	Montgomery, 1956
South Africa	—	1994 Success of Anti-apartheid Policy of Nelson Mandela

Appreciating the use of non-violence at a larger level, Albert Einstein[14] said that in our age of moral decay Gandhi was the only statesman who represented that higher conception of human relations in the political sphere to which we must aspire with all our power. We must learn the difficult lesson that the future of mankind will be tolerable only when our course in world affairs as well in other matters is based on justice and law, rather that on the threat of naked power.

Similar ethos is echoed in N. Radhakrishnan's Gandhi: The Quest for Tolerance and Survival in which he notes with regret that India failed to project Gandhi who offered a healthy vision of life based on self-respect, self-help, non-exploitation, non-violence, and transcendental eco-friendly—in short, a definite alternative to the manipulative, violent, and exploitative world order.

Not much research was conducted on the issue of these till the middle of this century. Gandhi was the shining example of the twentieth century who employed peaceful methods for bringing about a larger Peace. In 1968, Willy Brandt gave a speech at a UNESCO Conference highlighting peaceful coexistence as the spirit of solidarity.[15] He said that peace is not merely the absence of war and violence, although we know that there are people that today would even be grateful for that. Peace demands freedom from oppression, from hunger, and from ignorance. Only under these conditions can men and people develop their capacities freely and responsibly.

In a world divided along the following lines of conflict, the Gandhian perspective of peace resolution is the only answer:

—Conflict of Religious interest;

—Conflict between Christian and non-Christian world, Islamic and non-Islamic, fundamentalist and modernists;

—Conflict of Economic interest—conflict between developed and less developed countries; and

—Conflict of Political interest—East and West relations and peaceful coexistence.

Gandhi showed the world the way in modern times to fight for peace in a most non-violent manner. Revolution without the use of violence was the method by which Gandhi brought about the liberation of India. It is my belief[16] that the problem of bringing peace to the world on a supranational basis will be solved only by employing Gandhi's method on a large scale.

This is more true in today's world where, according to Michael Brecher,[17] crisis, conflict, and war are intricately interrelated, both conceptually and empirically. All are characterised by mutual mistrust between adversaries, turmoil, tension, and hostility. Violence, the essential trait of war, is often. . . . present in crisis and conflict.

The world is standing today at the threshold of transformation which calls for new alternatives, fresh approach, and search for a new paradigm. In making our choice we must accept that we have just one future or no future at all. What is required is a new paradigm from which all will benefit.

In this context Gandhi's methodology of truth and non-violence based on love and cooperation rather than cut-throat competition has benign possibilities for the future. Most modern studies suffer from the major inadequacy of not viewing the relations from the standpoint of the less-developed countries.[18] Inadequacy of a proper paradigm can be removed by using the Gandhian perspective of conflict resolution which is most democratic.

Economic conflict is the major conflict in the modern world. Anurag Gangal[19] establishes in his book that the quest for a New International Economic Order has a lot to benefit from the Gandhian perspective as it is based on peace. According to Gandhi, non-violent crafts are those occupations which are fundamentally free from violence and which involve no exploitation or envy of others.[20]

Gandhi dreamt of a free India in which peace will prevail. Such realization was possible only when individuals are bound to each other by cords of love like the members of a family. Therefore anything that sets one individual against another is inimical to the realization of a non-violent socialism.

Gandhi said that if we want love and peace, we cannot have it by preaching hatred and strife, just as if we want water cooled, we cannot have it by placing it over fire. Gandhi therefore advocated the ideals of love, non-possession, and ***Brahmacharya*** or self-control. As a matter of fact, suggests Kumarappa,[21] the eleven vows of Gandhi's ***Ashram*** are essential for the establishment of a non-violent society. There are truth, love, ***Brahmacharya***, non-possession, non-stealing, bread labour and control of the palate, fearlessness, equality of religion, untouchablity, and ***Swadeshi***.

In the highly technically developed modern world of today which thrives on severe competition, it may not be possible to employ all the eleven vows of the ***Ashram*** to the hilt but the basic tenets of truth and love must be employed if the world has to survive.

Gandhi chose to resolve the conflict in his life and his times by the use of the tools of love and non-violence. ***"It is for India to show an example to the world by employing these tools once again if humanity has to survive-if children do not have to grow up before time,*** [22] ***if children have to be saved from the cult-throat competitions, if modern life has to be relieved of stress, and if the world has to be saved from the scourge of war."***

We need to focus on a Science of peace, not Military Science, in all earnest because more than war, we need peace.

References

1. Greek Philosopher Plato describes in his The Republic the ideal which is possible only in Heaven and towards which the mind's "inner eye" must be focussed in order to arrive at an image close to the perfect one.
2. Richard B. Gregg: The Power of Gandhi's Non-violence," in the Profiles of Gandhi [New York: IBC, 1960], p. 168.
3. Richard B. Gregg, The Power of Non-violence [Ahmedabad: Navajivan Publishing House, 1938], preface.
4. Young India, 20 May 1926.
5. **Ibid**, 31 December 1931.
6. Harijan, 20 March 1937.
7. Richard Gregg, Profiles of Gandhi, p. 168.
8. Young India, 12 August 1926.
9. Harijan, 17 January 1939.
10. **Ibid**, 1 September 1940.
11. **Ibid**, 30 March 1947.
12. Richard B. Gregg, The Power of Non-violence, 1938, pp. 3-39.
13. Ibid.
14. Albert Einstein, "On Peace and Gandhi" in Richard B. Gregg, Profiles in Gandhi, p. 100
15. Willy Brandt, "Peaceful Coexistence in the Spirit of Solidarity," Speech UNESCO Conference, 6 November 1968.
16. Albert Einstein, "On Peace and Gandhi," p. 100.
17. See "Crisis, Conflict, War: State of the Discipline," International Political Science Review, Vol. 17 [1996], No. 2.
18. J. Bandopadhyaya, North Over South: A non-Western Perspective of International Relations [New Delhi, 1982].
19. Anurag Gangal, New International Economic Order: Gandhian Perspective, New Delhi, 1985.

20. Harijan, 1 September 1940.
21. B. Kumarappa, Ed, Towards Non-violent Socialism [Ahmedabad: Navajivan Publishing House, 1951].
22. In Japan, children do not go out for vacation for fear of losing in class by missing out on Summer Schools during the holidays.

14

Tolstoy and Gandhi and their Legacy Today

Christian Bartolf

Tolstoy and Gandhi followed the principle of Non-violence in interpersonal and international relations between individuals and organisations. There are many aspects of Non-violence in today's life which could give us benefit in case we are prepared and willing to learn from Tolstoy and Gandhi. Four aspects of Non-violence according to Tolstoy and Gandhi are of utmost importance and meaning for us today:

1. Good Labour / Bread Labour;
2. Vegetarian / Vegan Ethics;
3. Pacifism / Antimilitarism; and
4. Trusteeship

If we summarize the ***"Gospel of Renunciation"*** according to Tolstoy and Gandhi, we find the following basic ideas for our future action:

- Creating empathy and compassion for the weakest whose lives are endangered;
- Identifying with the poorest to contribute to their/our social and moral uplift; and
- Emancipating society from all forces of violent fear and destruction.

Global emancipation will be only possible through the suppressed outcast [es] of society who follows Truth on the pathway of Non-violence. We should give an example!

During the preparation of my lecture on Tolstoy's and Gandhi's legacy for an international conference on ***"Nuclear weapons and Non-violence"*** in Copenhagen [Denmark], I recollected by heart the basic ideas of both of them with reference to Labour, Nature, Peace and Property.

1. Good Labour / Bread Labour: Tolstoy as well as Gandhi was influenced by the Christian writer Timofej Bondarev and his plea for Bread Labour and by John Ruskin and his plea for Good Labour. Both writers inspired Tolstoy and Gandhi tremendously. The Russian peasant writer Bondarev described the life as a peasant and gardener [agriculture and horticulture] as the ideal life. He recommended students and academics to spend one month per year as peasant or gardener, not in the city but in a village. The English writer John Ruskin emphasized the value of Good Labour which gives benefit to all mankind, most of all to the weakest and poorest of society. Both writers drew inspiration from the Gospels on Life and Teachings of Jesus Christ. Both writers were Christians whose message convinced Tolstoy and Gandhi.
2. Vegetarian / Vegan Ethics: Tolstoy became Vegetarian when he visited the slaughter-house in Tula [Russia] and observed the slaughtering of animals for meat production. He wrote an impressing essay on Vegetarian Ethics when he described ***"The First Step"*** on the fragile path to realize good principles and to reform the individual life: first to fast and to contemplate the essence and meaning of life, then to become Vegetarian and afterwards continue with new steps towards the ***"Gospel of Renunciation"***. Gandhi had been an ardent believer in the ideas of Vegetarian Ethics since his student days when

he became member of the London Vegetarian Society and when he met Henry Salt, the most important writer on the history and philosophy of Vegetarianism. During all his life, Gandhi made experiments with Vegetarian diets of various kinds: saltless diet, fruitarian diet, abstention from cow's milk etc. In addition, he made experiments with Nature Cure, inspired by Central European writers. Gandhi combined Vegetarian Ethics and Nature Cure. He struggled hard to observe the principles of Chastity and Renunciation in thought, word and deed. And we know, he frequently accused himself in failing, in being weak, not strong on his path of Non-violence – the same with Tolstoy who went almost desperate and insane. Both, Tolstoy and Gandhi, knew that they were not able to live up to their principles completely, but nevertheless continued their ***"Experiments with Truth"*** on the path of Non-violence.

3. Pacifism / Antimilitarism: Tolstoy and Gandhi advocated the abolition of the military, of military conscription and the military system! They were opposing any kind of war or civil war or military aggression, even the use of the military as means of defending the borders, the territory, the people or the democracy. Of course, Tolstoy and Gandhi learnt their lessons in their life: Tolstoy as a soldier in the Crimean War, Gandhi as a stretcher-bearer in the South African Boer War and the socalled Zulu Rebellion and in the First World War. Both, Tolstoy and Gandhi, became followers of the principle of Non-violence, pure and simple, and Pacifists who advocated the end of any war, the end of all wars. But both of them knew how immense the struggle would become to secure State action in the desired direction, because each would be afraid and distrustful of his neighbour. Tolstoy's active

support for conscientious objectors to military service, not only in Russia, but also in several other countries, was the basis for his sympathy and solidarity in his correspondence with young Gandhi in South Africa. Gandhi, in his later years, did not insist on imposing his own principles on his contemporaries, like e.g. Pandit Jawaharlal Nehru, but he kept his principles until his very last days when he wanted to actively reconcile the relations between India and Pakistan.

4. Trusteeship: Tolstoy and Gandhi believed in God and knew that their individual lives were given to them by God. They knew that they were trustees in all respects. Everything that was given to them was only lent to them. That meant: They were not forever the owners of their body, of their intellect, of their life. Their ideal was to live according to the principle that they should gain the confidence of the weakest and poorest of their fellow citizens by acting in such a non-violent way that would benefit to the welfare of all: *Sarvodaya*. And they knew that their relation to property would be the same: only for a certain period of time during which they fulfilled their duty for the benefit of all, not only for a majority, but for everyone, every human being. Trusteeship was, in principle, just another concept which they could find in the Christian Gospels. And they could apply this principle of Trusteeship to Democracy, Industry, Culture and Society. Of course, this principle was excluding brute force or violence against any owner or class of owners, but no owner deserved his wealth and possessions unless he realized his individual and social responsibilities to support and help everyone in the society, most of those entire outcasts without public voice and vote. That is why Tolstoy

wanted to become himself a peasant that is why Gandhi wanted to become himself a farmer and weaver that is why Tolstoy supported the Vegetarian Pacifist farmers and craftsmen of the Doukhobors that is why Gandhi supported the outcastes in his society, the socalled untouchable Dalits or Harijans.

If we summarize the ***"gospel of renunciation"*** according to Tolstoy and Gandhi, we find the following basic ideas for our future action:

- Creating empathy and compassion for the weakest whose lives are endangered;
- Identifying with the poorest to contribute to their/our social and moral uplift; and
- Emancipating society from all forces of violent fear and destruction.

Global emancipation will be only possible through the suppressed outcast (es) of society who follows Truth on the pathway of Non-violence. We should give an example!"

15

Inspiration of Mahatma Gandhi: Source, Application and Effects

Sachin Bathla

Sources of Inspiration could be personal and impersonal, individual and universal but the thing that counts is how much a person is under the sway of such inspirations and if such inspirations are worthy of inspiring or not. These days we see people getting inspired of things that are totally -fanatic-but Mahatma Gandhi was a man of distinguished thought process. He was a great judge of personalities. He was not only aware of the flaws of people around him but he was also a self-critic. He knew the several weaknesses of a human mind and always tried to win over them.

Source

As for the sources of inspiration, Mahatma Gandhi himself said:

"Three persons have left a deep impression my life and captivated me. Raj Chanderbhai by his living contact; Tolstoy by his book, The Kingdom of God is Within You; and Ruskin by his book Unto This Last."

Besides these three personalities, Gopal Krishna Gokhale, the ***Bhagvad-Gita*** and the Bible were life long sources of inspiration for Mahatma Gandhi.

Mahatma Gandhi's study of other religions had developed in him knowledge and acceptance of esoteric principles of all religions. He believed that all religions lead on one pathway to God. The man whom he acknowledged as being influential in this respect was Raj Chanderbhai. He was a deeply philosophical man who came closest to being Mahatma Gandhi's spiritual master. It was Raj Chanderbhai who assured Mahatma Gandhi that there was little formulated in other religions that were not to be found in Hinduism.

Leo Tolstoy, the well-known philosopher of Russia, was the only one with whom Mahatma Gandhi had some prolonged correspondence. Tolstoy and Mahatma Gandhi had quite similar religious beliefs and sought wisdom from similar sources such as- Buddha, Socrates, Mohammed, ***Upanishads*** and ***Bhagvad-Gita***. Both of them were not mere philosophers, but teachers of humanity who endeavoured hard to realistically apply what they preached.

Tolstoy himself had undergone a profound conversion to a personal form of Christian anarchism. Mahatma Gandhi described himself as Tolstoy's disciple in his letters to Tolstoy. Tolstoy admired the pivotal significance of success brought by the application of ***Satyagraha*** in South Africa. Tolstoy was the prophet of the latter half of the nineteenth century and Mahatma Gandhi of the first half of the twentieth century.

Mahatma Gandhi translated Tolstoy's ***'Letter to a Hindoo'*** that was written in 1908 in response to aggressive Indian nationalists and the two corresponded until Tolstoy's death in 1910. The letter by Tolstoy uses Hindu philosophy taken from the ***Vedas*** and sayings of the Hindu God Lord Krishna to present his view of that state of growing Indian nationalism. And while presenting a letter from Tolstoy for publication, Mahatma Gandhi wrote:

"To me, as a humble follower of that great teacher whom I have long looked upon as one of my guides, it is a matter of honour to be connected with the publication of his letter, especially as the one which is now being given to the world. When a man like Tolstoy, one of the clearest thinkers in the western world, one of the greatest writers, one who as a soldier had known what violence is and what it can do, condemns Japan for having blindly followed the law of modern science, falsely so-called and fears for that country 'the greatest calamities,' it is for us to pause and consider whether, in our impatience of English rule, we do not want to replace one evil by another and worse, India, which is the nursery of the great faiths of the world, will cease to be a nationalist India; whatever else she may become, when she goes through the process of civilization in the shape of reproduction on that sacred soil of gun factories and the hateful industrialization which has reduced people of Europe to a state of slavery, and all but stifled among them the best instincts which are the heritage of the human family."

These lines clearly show the admirations Mahatma Gandhi had in his heart for Tolstoy's philosophy and the nobility of his purpose. Finally Tolstoy's The Kingdom of God is within you' brought an overwhelming inspiration to Mahatma Gandhi. It left an abiding impression on Mahatma Gandhi by its emphasis on esoteric principles, independent thinking, profound morality, logic and truthfulness.

So Tolstoy's philosophy, stimulated Gandhi's search for truth and non-violence in his own religion. While appreciating Tolstoy's approach, Mahatma Gandhi also wrote:

"There is no doubt that there is nothing new in what Tolstoy preaches. But his presentation of the old truth is refreshingly forceful. His logic is unassailable. And above all he endeavours to practise what he preaches. He preaches to convince. He is sincere and earnest. He commands attention."

Ruskin, the English thinker, was also a powerful source of inspiration when Mahatma Gandhi himself described Ruskin's book, ***'Unto This Last'*** as 'the magic spell.' Mr. Polak, an intimate friend of Mahatma Gandhi, offered him Ruskin's book and he read it on his train journey from Johannesburg to Durban in South Africa. The book attracted Mahatma Gandhi so much that every teaching of the book appealed him instantaneously and Mahatma Gandhi paraphrased it into Gujarati as ***Sarvodaya*** [The welfare of all].

Other than that, ***'The Sermon on the Mount'*** strongly appealed him because of its activist philosophy. It was, however, the ***Bhagvad-Gita*** that supplied him the basis of his religious beliefs. In the ***Bhagvad-Gita***, Krishna, an incarnation of the Supreme God Vishnu, urges Arjuna to dispel doubts about his action against his own family members in the battle because his duty in life called upon him to take up his warrior duties. Krishna's message, that a man must not be diverted by distractions however great, from seeking truth about his position in relation to the scheme of things and thereby realise God, had a profound meaningful effect on Mahatma Gandhi: The ***Bhagvad Gita*** offered salvation through selfless action. Mahatma Gandhi's personal philosophy about duty and service combined with social justice coincided with this aspect of Hinduism. It made him an ardent social activist with religious justifications.

Application

1. At Tolstoy Farm

The settlement was called the Tolstoy Farm at the suggestion of Herman Kallenbach. Mahatma Gandhi stated in his letter to Tolstoy that the former worldly architect had gone through most of the experiences that Tolstoy had so graphically described in his work My Confession:

"No writing has so deeply touched Mr. Kallenbach as yours; and as a spur to further effort in living up to the ideals held before the world by you, he has taken the liberty, after consultation with me, of naming his farm after you."

The Tolstoy Farm offered him an opportunity to experiment with the implementation of his ideas. His challenge was greater because the settlement consisted of men, women, and children for short, long, and irregular intervals, who were Hindus, Muslims, Christians, Parsees, White or Indians, people who spoke one or more languages from among Gujarati, Hindi, Tamil, and English.

In running the settlement, Mahatma Gandhi worked for the achievement of prime goal in an individual's life. He emphasised on the concept of self-realisation that could come from the search for ***Satya*** [truth] in specific instances and Absolute Truth as an ultimate reality.

He believed that such training might be most fruitfully undertaken in the education of young children. He took such a hard task as he has also mentioned in his autobiography:

"Tolstoy Farm was a family in which I occupied the place of the father and that I should so far as possible shoulder the responsibility for the training of the young."

At Tolstoy Farm, in daily routine, there was a discipline followed by the residents purpose was to prevent the wastage of time and to make them feel that they were being constructively useful. Everybody was assigned a task for the morning. The contribution of work such as sweeping, scavenging and water fetching was seen to be invaluable to the psychological, social and moral well-being of an integrated community. Mahatma Gandhi's objective in this context was to inculcate the ideals of social service and citizenship through all the activities of children from the earlier formative years. While at 7 p.m. the residents assembled before Mahatma Gandhi who reviewed the day's events, pointing out problems and suggested ways of preventing their recurrence. The meeting ended with readings from books on religion and the singing of hymns.

Through different activities at Tolstoy Farm, Mahatma Gandhi hoped to cultivate in the residents virtues he held high in his own life. His presence at the Tolstoy Farm was felt everywhere, for he was, as Robert Payne states:

"The chief judge, the chief sanitary inspector, the chief teacher in the children's school, the chief baker and marmalade maker."

It was here that he experimented with and developed the technique of ***Satyagraha*** or Passive Resistance. The technique of non-violent resistance was successfully tried out since 1906 and brought unexpected success.

Tolstoy Farm also served as a laboratory for experimenting with problematic issues of diet, nature cure, harmonious living with nature, righteousness and self-restraint. It also proved to be a training ground for his leadership among the people of India.

While admitting the importance of Tolstoy Farm, Mahatma Gandhi wrote:

"I have serious doubts as to whether the struggle could have been prosecuted for eight years, whether we could have secured larger funds and whether thousands of men who participated in the last phase of the struggle would have borne their share of it, if there had been no Tolstoy Farm."

2. At Sabarmati Ashram

On his return from South Africa, Gandhiji selected Ahmedabad for three reasons. In his own words:

"Being a Gujarati, I will serve my country best through the use of Gujarati language. As Ahmedabad was the centre of handloom in early days, the work of spinning wheel [Charkha] could be done in a better way, I believed. Being the capital of Gujarat its wealthy persons will also make larger contribution, I hoped."

His first ashram was at Kochrab near Paldi, Ahmedabad. It was a bungalow of his friend Jivanlal Desai. This place had to be abandoned after two years in the wake of a plague epidemic. The choice now made was of a site on the bank of Sabarmati River. Pointing out the objective of the Ashram, Mahatma Gandhi wrote:

"To take training for the national service which is not contrary to universal well-being and constantly endeavouring for such national service is the aim of this Ashram."

Gradually -a few dwelling units were built and the ***Ashram*** soon became busy with different activities. The units were simple in style but very functional. This was the establishment of ***'Sabarmati Ashram.'*** Mahatma Gandhi also laid down certain principles that the dwellers of Sabarmati ***Ashram*** had to observe to realise ***Satya*** [truth]. These were Ahimsa [non-violence], ***Asteya*** [non-stealing, non-covetousness], ***Aparigraha*** [non-possession, non-acquisitiveness], and ***Brahmacharya*** [celibacy]. These were the principles that had been stressed in Hindu religious writings as being necessary for an individual's moral growth. At the ashram, women enjoyed full freedom and equal rights, there was complete religious tolerance, and caste distinctions were ignored.

Mahatma Gandhi had little faith in formal education presumably because it did not concern itself with the building of character. He wrote in 1914:

"That a child should learn that, in the struggle of life, it can easily conquer hate by love, untruth by truth, violence by self-sacrifice."

This is presumably what he had in mind when he stated later in his autobiography that education should concern itself with the ***"culture of the heart or the building of character"***. His goals in the education of the young minds were similar to his insistence upon what adults should strive towards in their lives.

Thus Mahatma Gandhi introduced a new system of learning. This system included both 'manual' and 'mental' training. Everyday the ashram children were expected to spend three hours in the morning duties that involved gardening, farming, shoemaking, or sewing clothes. Such works were counter balanced with a programme of lessons in geography, history, arithmetic and writings. Singing hymns and reading interesting stories were also included in the teaching. Mahatma Gandhi did not consider textbooks necessary. ***"Of textbooks,"*** he said, ***"I never felt the want."*** The ***"true textbook for the pupil was his teacher,"*** which in this case was Mahatma Gandhi. He used to feel that instruction based on the teacher's experience and convictions would carry more weight than the lifeless pages of a textbook.

Fasting was a matter of spiritual discipline and religious significance for Mahatma Gandhi. He believed that it helped the individual in attaining the ***"supremacy of the spirit over the flesh... the sincerest form of prayer".*** Mahatma Gandhi fasted on days of religious significance, Hindu as well as Muslim and urged others to do the same.

The first struggle that Mahatma Gandhi headed from ***Sabarmati Ashram*** was that of textile mill workers. On the third day of his fast the mill-owners came to terms. The establishment of Textile Labour Association was the far-reaching consequence of this encounter.

Effects

1. Emergence of the Philosophy of *Satyagraha*

Mahatma Gandhi defined Satyagraha as follows: ***"Its root meaning is holding on to truth, hence truth-force. I have also called it Love-force or Soul-force."*** Mahatma Gandhi advocated ***"self-suffering"*** as a means of protest against wrong. His philosophy of Satyagraha found its roots in the principles of Jainism and Christianity. Mahatma Gandhi believed if opponents' actions were wrong, then they could be made to amend their wrong practices through acts of love and non-violence. This was somewhat equivalent to ***'turning the other cheek'*** and ***'hate sin, not the sinner'*** in Western religions. Those who practiced Satyagraha came to be known as ***Satyagrahis. "If man-made laws are unfair,"*** Mahatma Gandhi wrote, the Satyagrahi ***"breaks them and quietly suffers the penalty for their breach."*** And the world knows that this philosophy went a long way in accomplishing tasks that were impossible at times.

2. Success in South Africa Through Satyagraha

During his stay in South Africa, Mahatma Gandhi experienced that the British had made rules to meet their own interests. The Indians, living there, were constant subject of British misbehaviour. Mahatma Gandhi decided to make the Indians aware of their rights.

Another important event that caused him to work in that direction was the Asiatic Law Amendment Ordinance of 1906. This law proposed that Indians and Chinese were to register their presence in the Transvaal, giving their fingerprints and carrying passes. The protest to the act united the two communities and they decided to oppose the Ordinance by peaceful methods.

Protestors got together at the Empire Theatre where Mahatma Gandhi spoke to the protestors, with the theme of ***"violence begets violence"*** and the philosophy of passive resistance was born. Protestors then marched through Johannesburg, were arrested and thrown into prison.

Transvaal Colonial Secretary Jan Smuts called Gandhi to his office and offered to repeal the law if Indians and Chinese registered voluntarily. Mahatma Gandhi was looked down upon by the community for agreeing to this and was termed a traitor and severely beaten. Meanwhile, the community registered under the law, but Smuts went back on his word - the new law was passed as the Transvaal Asiatic Registration Act of 1907. In response to this, Mahatma Gandhi encouraged his colleagues to burn their passes. Later, he made an appeal to the British and they put pressure on the Transvaal government, which eventually repealed the Act.

Tolstoy, in correspondence with Mahatma Gandhi, once wrote:

"Socialism, communism, anarchism, the Salvation Army, the growth of crime, unemployment among the population, the growth of the insane luxury of the rich and the

destitution of the poor, the terrible growth in the number of suicides-all these things are signs of this internal contradiction which ought to and must be solved- and of course, solved in the sense of recognizing the law of love and renouncing all violence. And so your work in the Transvaal, at the other end of the world as it seems to us, is the most central and most important of all tasks now being done in the world and not only Christian peoples, but peoples of the whole world will inevitably take part in it..."

3. Indian National Movement

Mahatma Gandhi returned to India in 1915. At that time he had a growing desire of doing something for the suffering Indians. To access his field of action, he first decided to study the situations prevailing over the Indian scenario. He established the Sabarmati ***Ashram*** in the year 1916 and it was here that he started to advocate the teachings of ***Satya*** [Truth] and ***Ahimsa*** [Non-violence].

It was in the year 1917 that, for the first time, Mahatma Gandhi got the opportunity to run a ***Satyagraha*** Movement at Champaran in Bihar followed by ***Satyagraha*** in Kaira in Gujarat, and it was also during this movement that Vallabhbhai Patel, later came to be known as the Sardar and the Ironman of India, came in close contact with Mahatma Gandhi.

A. Hindu-Muslim Unity and Rise of Nationalism

Mahatma Gandhi was a worshipper of Hindu-Muslim unity. He believed that India could win freedom if these two communities worked together. History is witness that several times in his life; he fasted to end some communal tension.

Mutual respect and tolerance between Hindus and Muslims assumed an important role in India.

Mahatma Gandhi mentioned that he taught the Tolstoy Farm residents against ***"infection of intolerance and to view one another's religions and customs with a light-hearted charity. They learnt how to live together like real brothers".*** And this was one reason that Mahatma Gandhi admitted his religious experiment as ***"among the sweetest reminiscences of the Tolstoy Farm..."*** Mahatma Gandhi respected various religious affiliations of the children so he stressed that the Christians should be instructed in the reading of the Bible, the Muslims in the Koran and the Parsees [Zoroastrians] in the Zend Avesta.

He encouraged common respect for all religions by asking the residents of his ashram to observe the fasts of each other. Even the non-Muslims joined the Muslims in their month of fasting during the ***Ramzan***.

Along with this, ***Satyagraha*** also worked to transform the masses in India. The simple people did not fully understand all the revolutionary dimensions and after-effects of ***Satyagraha*** but they realised that it was a new, justified and noble force. They understood the clear and simple terms in which Mahatma Gandhi explained ***Satyagraha*** as it was based upon truth and aimed against a clearly defined wrong.

Mahatma Gandhi himself believed that suffering must occur in order for a new world to arise. Thus he became free from his fear of suffering. Being free from this fear inspired him and his followers to begin a process of intentional suffering that was based on active non-violence. Such an action gave a meaning to the suffering and a confidence that the suffering would not be fruitless, because it was a part of ***Satyagraha*** and not of a suffering that came from hatred, resentment or revenge.

Mahatma Gandhi's quiet and resourceful simplicity, his boundless energy and his incredible staying power worked a great deal in uniting the Indians irrespective of their religion, caste and creed.

B. Non-Cooperation Movement

During the First World War, although Mahatma Gandhi raised his voice in support of the rights of farmers and labourers, still he had strong faith in the justice of the British. So during the war, he asked people to whole-heartedly support the British government. He believed that by doing so, the British would grant independence to the Indians. After the war, the British appreciated Mahatma Gandhi's efforts and conferred him with the title of ***'Kesar-e-Hind.'***

But within a year it became clear that the British had no intention to grant independence. They carried on with their exploiting economic policies and raised the prices of all those commodities that were essential for the Indians. During the course of war, several calamities hit Indian people but the British levied more and more taxes to meet their war expenses. Then the British enforced Rowlett Act to counter revolutionary activities. Under this act, the government had right to arrest any person without any legal proceeding. On the 6th of April an unprecedented strike was seen in many cities including Ahmedabad, at the call of Mahatma Gandhi against Rowlett Act. Later, after the inhumanly incident at Jalianwala Bagh, he openly and strongly criticized the British government and its policies.

In reality, before the enforcement of Rowlett Act, Mahatma Gandhi was hopeful from the British side. This was the reason that he helped them in recruiting soldiers earlier that year. But after this act, all his hopes were shattered. Now he had started thinking of the independence of India. He was shocked at the incident at Jalianwala Bagh, Amritsar on the 13th of April 1919.

Chirol has described the incident in following words:

"The panic stricken multitude broke at once but for ten consecutive minutes he [Michael O'Dyer] kept up a merciless fusillade in all 1650 rounds on that sea thing mass of humanity, caught like rats in a trap vainly rushing for the few narrow exits or lying flat on the/ground to escape the rain of bullets, which he personally directed to the points where the crowd was thickest targets, to use his own words, were good and then at the end of those ten minutes, having almost exhausted his ammunition he marched his men off by the way they came."

After this incident, a wave of frustration ran all over the Indian people. Mahatma Gandhi was much inspired to act on the mode of national independence. And this inspiration became more intense when the Hunter Commission submitted its investigation report on the Jalianwala Bagh incident. In its report it tried to shield the then deputy governor of Punjab, Michael O'Dyer even after his direct involvement in such an inhumanly cruelty.

Thus Mahatma Gandhi decided to start the Non-Cooperation Movement, which indeed was a first step in the direction of struggle against injustice and cruelty.

C. Dandi March and the Start of Civil Disobedience Movement

The Congress convention was due to be held at Lahore in the year 1929. This was the Punjab province and as such people began to recall the incidents of past atrocities of the year 1919 - Jalianwala Bagh, Rowlett Act. People also recalled the Non-Cooperation Movement, British suppression and the failure of movement. The social and political condition of India was worst than ever. Mahatma

Gandhi wrote a letter to the then Viceroy Lord Irwin and claimed the British responsible for such conditions. But there was no change in the government policies and thus people began to realise that without gaining independence, the conditions would not improve. After repeated demands, the British appointed a commission under the leadership of Sir John Simon to report on the needed reforms in Indian administration. But this commission did not include a single Indian so it was like a formal approach. This commission was strongly opposed.

Then the Indians, under the leadership of Pt. Motilal Nehru, submitted a report on the required reforms. All Indian political parties unanimously accepted this report. But the British refused to accept it Then a talk was held between Mahatma Gandhi and Lord Irwin. It also failed to provide a proper solution therefore Mahatma Gandhi finally put forward the resolution of 'Complete Independence.' After the acceptance of Congress, it was decided to start breaking government laws. On the eve of this, Mahatma Gandhi said:

"I wish that there should be no suspension or abandonment of the war that commences tomorrow morning or earlier, if I am arrested before that time. I shall eagerly await the news that ten batches are ready as soon as my batch is arrested. I believe there are men in India to complete the work begun by me. I have faith in the righteousness of our cause and the purity of our weapons. And where the means are clean, there God is undoubtedly present with His blessings. And where these three combine, there defeat is impossibility. A Satyagrahi, whether free or incarcerated, is ever victorious."

Thus the Civil Disobedience Movement was started on the 12th of March 1930 with the famous ***'Dandi March'*** and on the 6th of April, Mahatma Gandhi along with other marchers reached the sea-shore and started making salt from sea-water, thus breaking the law. This was the formal start of the

Movement. Thousands of arrests were made, the Viceroy decided it was a stalemate and he held talks with Gandhi, which resulted in the Salt Acts being interpreted more humanly and an agreement that Gandhi could represent Congress Party at the 1931 Round Table Conference in London. Although the Conference led nowhere but the Dandi salt march gave Indians self-respect and confidence that they could gain independence.

D. Quit India Movement

Civil Disobedience Movement ended without any effective results and Mahatma Gandhi detached himself of the political affairs for some time. During this period, the Act of 1935 was passed and elections were held in 11 provinces. Eight of the provinces witnessed the success of Indian National Congress. In the meantime Second World War began and the British government involved Indian forces in it. This was done without taking the newly elected provincial governments under confidence. To oppose such a decision all members of the Congress cabinets resigned and a constitutional deadlock developed between the British government and the Congress. To remove this deadlock, a mission under the leadership of Sir Cripps was sent to India in March 1942 but it failed.

During the course of World War, Japanese army reached the borders of India. It was feared if British lost the war, then India could go under the rule of some other power. As such Indians were under dismay regarding their future.

Mahatma Gandhi decided to awake the feeling of nationalism, on a new note, among the Indians. He declared that it was the time to ***'Do or Die.'*** The inspirational wave through his slogan soon ran across the country. Subhas Chandra Bose's inspirational speeches also provided support to Mahatma Gandhi's approach by inspiring Indians to take a final stand against the British. He said:

"Standing on the cross-roads of world history, I solemnly declare on behalf of all freedom loving Indians in India and abroad that we shall continue to fight British Imperialism till India is once again the mistress of her own destiny. The hour of India's salvation is at hand. India will now rise and break the chains of servitude that have bound her so long."

In August 1942, a session of Congress Working Committee was called at Bombay in which Mahatma Gandhi delivered his speech saying:

"God has vouchsafed to me a priceless gift in the weapon of Ahimsa. I and my Ahimsa [non-violence] are on our trail today. If in the present crisis, when the earth is being scorched by the flames of Himsa [violence] and crying for deliverance, I failed to make use of the God given talent, God will not forgive me and I shall be judged unwrongly of the great gift. I must act now. I may not hesitate and merely look on, when Russia and China are threatened."

Thus the Congress agreed on the proposal of Mahatma Gandhi to start the Quit India Movement.

The Muslim League did not take part in the movement; still this could not weaken Mahatma Gandhi's will. He kept on inspiring people but he was soon arrested and government chose violent means to suppress the movement.

4. Gaining Independence and Beyond:

Mahatma Gandhi was finally released in May 1944. After his release he tried to reach to an agreement with the Muslim League, but failed. Then in the year 1945 he participated in the Shimla

Conference after which the cabinet put forward the plan of partition. Mahatma Gandhi was not in favour of partition. He said:

"Even if the whole of India is in flames, it will not bring Pakistan and, Pakistan would be made on my dead-body."

Still Congress, which from the beginning stood for a united independent India, agreed to the partition of India, primarily because it felt that there was no other way to achieve freedom and prevent a further worsening of the situation. India became independent on the 15th of August 1947. A separate state of Pakistan comprising West Punjab, East Punjab, Sind and Northwest Frontier Province was formed. The Indian people after their century long struggle had usurped the British rule even though it happened through a course of tragedies.

Mahatma Gandhi was unhappy with the settlement because it divided India into two states - India and Pakistan - the first largely for Hindus, the second largely for Muslims. But even after the partition and the empathy for sufferings of migrated Indians, Mahatma Gandhi always taught the lesson of non-violence. He was moved by the account of any violent incident. At the start of 1948, when migrated Indians were struggling for their survival, an incident occurred at Delhi. Mahatma Gandhi reacted to it in the following words:

"There are some Muslim houses at a little distance from the Camp. About four or five hundred inmates of the Camp mostly women and children but also some men -rushed out of the Camp to take possession of the houses. I am told they did not indulge in any kind of violence. Some of the houses were vacant. The owners occupied some. They tried to take

possession even of the latter. All I can say is that is a matter of great shame for us. It is highly improper to go and occupy other people's houses. It is for the Government to find them shelter or whatever else their need. Today the Government is our own. But if we defy our own Government and defy the police and forcibly occupy houses the Government is not likely to continue for long."

Gandhi did his best to pacify the violence between Hindus and Muslims and his work achieved some success. But in 1948 he was shot and killed by a fellow Hindu who believed Gandhi was betraying the Hindus by working for reconciliation.

Albert Einstein said that Mahatma Gandhi's great contribution to our time was his determination to moralise politics. In his words:

"Generations to come, it may be, will scarcely believe that such a one as this ever in flesh and blood walked upon this earth."

Mahatma Gandhi was a pioneer in pointing the value of manual work along with intellectual work and in his progressive ideas about education. His concept of ***Satyagraha*** was not simply a strategy for opposing evil without using violence rather it was a whole way of reconstructing society, using love and striving for truth. In his words:

"To me, Truth is God and there is no way to find Truth except the way of non-violence."

He said that we could apply the same moral values to politics, business or industry as we do in private life. Love, truth, non-violence - all these ideals could be applied here and now to every aspect of life.

"It is perfectly possible," as Gandhi said, ***"for an individual to adopt this way of life without having to wait for others to do so."***

Thus we can see that under all circumstances, Mahatma Gandhi always preached of self-restraint, non-violence and empathy. To him these were the pathways to happiness and to God realisation. And today we need much to learn from his philosophy, if we wish to make this earth a calm and serene place to live on in undisturbed harmony.

References

1. Gandhi, M. K., An Autobiography or The Story of My Experiments with Truth, Navajivan, Ahmedabad, 1940.
2. Radhakrishnan, S. [Ed.]. Mahatma Gandhi: Essays and Reflections on His Life and Work, Jaico, Bombay, 1956.
3. Swan, Mahatma Gandhi: The South African Experience, Ravan, Johannesburg, 1985.
4. Kumar, Dr. Ravindra, Essays on Gandhism and Peace, Krishna Publications, Meerut, 1999.
5. Gandhi, M. K., Satyagraha in South Africa. Navajivan, Ahmedabad,1950.
6. Mosley, Leonard, The Last Days of the British Raj, Harcourt, Brace & World, New York, 1961.
7. Nehru, Jawaharlal, Mahatma Gandhi, Signet Press, Calcutta, 1949.

16

Nuclear Weapons, Gandhi's Birthday, and the Nuremberg Principles

John Scales Avery

Nuclear weapons, Gandhi's birthday and the Nüremberg Principles? What do these three things have to do with each other? Let us first look at them separately, and then explore the connection.

Nuclear Weapons

During the Cold War and especially during the Cuban Missile Crisis, the threat of a massive nuclear exchange between the two superpowers caused grave public concern. There was a danger that a third world war fought with nuclear weapons would not only cause hundreds of millions of civilian deaths in the combatant countries, but also, through fallout, additional millions of deaths and disabled persons in neutral countries.

It is understandable that when the Cold War ended, the general public received a sigh of relief and put the worrying subject of nuclear weapons out of their minds. However, the threat has not really gone away. Because of nuclear proliferation and because of the Bush Administration's policies, the danger of use of these weapons of mass destruction is greater now than ever before.

During the Cold War, a number of international treaties attempting to reduce the global nuclear peril had been achieved after much struggle. Among these, the 1968 Nuclear Non-Proliferation Treaty [NPT] has special importance. The NPT was designed to prevent the spread of nuclear weapons beyond the five nations that already had them; to provide assurance that ***"peaceful"*** nuclear activities of non-nuclear-weapon states would not be used to produce such weapons; to promote peaceful use of nuclear energy to the great extent, consistent with non-proliferation of nuclear weapons; and finally, to ensure that definite steps towards complete nuclear disarmament would be taken by all states, as well as steps towards comprehensive control of conventional armaments [Article VI].

The non-nuclear-weapon states insisted that Article VI be included in the treaty as a price for giving up their own ambitions. The full text of Article VI is as follows:

"Each of the Parties to the Treaty undertakes to pursue negotiations in good faith on effective measures relating to cessation of the nuclear arms race at an early date and to nuclear disarmament and on a Treaty on general and complete disarmament under strict international control."

The NPT has now been signed by 187 countries and has been in force as international law since 1970. However, Israel, India, Pakistan and Cuba have refused to sign and North Korea, after signing the treaty, withdrew from it in 1993. Israel began producing nuclear weapons in the late 1960's [with the help of technology provided by France and with the tacit approval of the United States] and the country is now believed to possess 100-150 of them, including neutron bombs. Israel's policy is one of ***"nuclear opacity"*** i.e., visibly possessing nuclear weapons while denying their existence.

India produced what it described as a ***"peaceful nuclear explosion"*** in 1974. By 1989 Indian scientists were making efforts to purify the lithium-6 isotope, a key component of the much more powerful thermonuclear bombs. In 1998, India conducted underground tests of nuclear weapons and is now believed to have roughly 60 warheads, constructed from Pu-239 produced in ***"peaceful"*** reactors.

Pakistan's efforts to obtain nuclear weapons were spurred by India's 1974 ***"peaceful nuclear explosion".*** Zulfiquar Ali Bhutto, who initiated Pakistan's program, first as Minister of Fuel, Power and Natural Resources and later as President and Prime Minister, declared:

"There is a Christian Bomb, a Jewish Bomb and a Hindu Bomb. There must be an Islamic Bomb! We will get it even if we have to starve - even if we have to eat grass!"

As early as 1970, the laboratory of Dr. Abdul Qadeer Khan, [a metallurgist who was to become Pakistan's leading nuclear bomb maker] had been able to obtain from a Dutch firm the high-speed ultra centrifuges needed for uranium enrichment. With unlimited financial support and freedom from auditing requirements, Dr. Khan purchased restricted items needed for nuclear weapon construction from companies in Europe and the United States. In the process, Dr. Khan became an extremely wealthy man. With additional help from China, Pakistan was ready to test five nuclear weapons in 1998.The Indian and Pakistani nuclear bomb tests, conducted in rapid succession, presented the world with the danger that these devastating bombs would be used in the conflict over Kashmir. Indeed, Pakistan announced that if a war broke out using conventional weapons, Pakistan's nuclear weapons would be used ***"at an early stage".*** Early in 2004, it was revealed that Dr. Khan had for years been selling nuclear secrets and equipment to Libya, Iran and North Korea. As more and more countries obtain nuclear weapons, it becomes increasingly likely that one of them will undergo a revolution, during the course of which nuclear weapons will fall into the hands of sub national organizations.

Article VIII of the Non-Proliferation Treaty provides for a conference to be held every five years to make sure that the NPT is operating as intended. In the 1995 NPT Review Conference, the lifetime of the treaty was extended indefinitely, despite the general dissatisfaction with the bad faith of the nuclear weapon states: They had dismantled some of their warheads but had taken no significant steps towards complete nuclear disarmament. The 2000 NPT Review Conference made it clear that the nuclear weapons states could not postpone indefinitely their commitment to nuclear disarmament by linking it to general and complete disarmament, since these are separate and independent goals of Article VI. The Final Document of the conference also contained 13 Practical Steps for Nuclear Disarmament, including ratification of a Comprehensive Test Ban Treaty [CTBT], negotiations on a Fissile Materials Cuto Treaty, the preservation and strengthening of the Anti-Ballistic Missile [ABM] Treaty, greater transparency with regard to nuclear arsenals, and making irreversibility a principle of nuclear reductions. Another review conference is scheduled for 2005, a year that marks the 60th anniversary of the destruction of Hiroshima and Nagasaki.

Rather than witnessing progress towards implementation of Article VI of the NPT, recent years have unfortunately shown us dangerous backward steps. The United States election of 2000 brought to power a group of neoconservatives who have since exhibited a general contempt for international laws, treaties and norms. In 2002, the Bush Administration published its Nuclear Posture Review paper; a document that totally undermines not only the Non-Proliferation Treaty but also the duly signed but not yet ratified Comprehensive Test Ban Treaty [CTBT].

The 2002 Nuclear Posture Review paper proposed that US nuclear weapons should target seven countries-Russia, China, Libya, Syria, Iraq, Iran and North Korea. Situations in which the weapons might be used included war in the Middle East, conflict between China and Taiwan, North Korean invasion of South Korea, or responding to ***"surprising military developments"***, a vague phrase that could include many things. Furthermore, the Bush Administration's 2002 paper called for the development of small and ***"usable"*** nuclear weapons, for example a ***"nuclear robust earth penetrator"*** that could be used to destroy deeply buried concrete bunkers. Such new nuclear weapons would need testing, and thus a program to develop them would undermine the CTBT. The development of low-yield nuclear weapons would trivialize and legitimize them, thus eroding the taboo that has prevented nuclear tragedies during the half century since the destruction of Hiroshima and Nagasaki.

There is a danger that the NPT will be seriously weakened by the Bush Administration's new policies. The signatories are already skeptical because of the nuclear weapon states' bad faith regarding their own promise of nuclear disarmament. They will now ask:

"If the nation with most conventional armaments, a nation whose military

expenditures exceed those of all others combined, feels that it needs more nuclear weapons to be secure, do we not need them as well?"

The danger of a new nuclear arms race provoked by the Bush Administration's policies is very real.

In addition to violating the NPT, the Bush Administration's Nuclear Posture Review paper also violates the advisory Opinion on Nuclear Weapons given in 1996 by the International Court of Justice in The Hague, a ruling that will be discussed in more detail below.

Flaws in the Concept of Nuclear Deterrence

Before discussing other defects in the concept of deterrence, it must be said very clearly that the idea of ***"massive nuclear retaliation"*** is completely unacceptable from an ethical point of view. The doctrine of retaliation, performed on a massive scale, violates not only the principles of common human decency and common sense, but also the ethical principles of every major religion.

The enormous and indiscriminate destruction produced by nuclear weapons formed the background for an historic 1996 decision by the International Court of Justice in The Hague. In response to questions put to it by W. H. O. and the U. N. General Assembly, the Court ruled:

"The threat and use of nuclear weapons would generally be contrary to the rules of international law applicable in armed conflict and particularly the principles and rules of humanitarian law."

The only possible exception to this general rule might be ***"an extreme circumstance of self-defence, in which the very survival of a state would be at stake".*** But the Court refused to say that even in this extreme circumstance, the threat or use of nuclear weapons would be legal. It left the exceptional case undecided. In addition, the Court added unanimously:

"There exists an obligation to pursue in good faith and bring to a conclusion negotiations leading to nuclear disarmament in all its aspects under strict international control."

Having said these important things, we can now turn to some of the other defects in the concept of nuclear deterrence. One important defect is that nuclear war may occur through accident or miscalculation-through technical defects or human failings. This possibility is made greater by the fact that despite the end of the Cold War, thousands of missiles carrying nuclear warheads are still kept on a ***"hair-trigger"*** state of alert with a quasi automatic reaction time measured in minutes. There is a constant danger that a nuclear war will be triggered by error in evaluating the signal on a radar screen. For example, the BBC reported recently that a group of scientists and military leaders are worried that a small asteroid entering the earth's atmosphere and exploding could trigger a nuclear war, if mistaken for a missile strike.

A number of prominent political and military figures [many of whom have ample knowledge of the system of deterrence, having been part of it] have expressed concern about the danger of accidental nuclear war. Colin S. Grey [Chairman, U. S. National Institute for Public Policy] expressed this concern as follows:

"The problem, indeed the enduring problem, is that we are resting our future upon a nuclear deterrence system concerning which we cannot tolerate even a single malfunction."

General Curtis E. LeMay [Founder and former Commander in Chief of the United States Strategic Air Command] has written:

"In my opinion a general war will grow through a series of political miscalculations and accidents rather than through any deliberate attack by either side."

Bruce G. Blair [Brookings Institute] has remarked:

"It is obvious that the rushed nature of the process, from warning to decision to action, risks causing a catastrophic mistake...This system is an accident waiting to happen."

Another serious failure of the concept of nuclear deterrence is that it does not take into account the possibility that atomic bombs may be used by terrorists. Indeed, the threat of nuclear terrorism has today become one of the most pressing dangers that the world faces, a danger that is particularly acute in the United States.

Since 1945, more than 3,000 metric tons [3,000,000 kilograms] of highly enriched uranium and plutonium have been produced - enough for several hundred thousand nuclear weapons. Of this, roughly a million kilograms are in Russia, inadequately guarded, in establishments where the technicians are poorly paid and vulnerable to the temptations of bribery. There is a continuing danger that these fissile materials will fall into the hands of terrorists, or organized criminals, or irresponsible governments. Also, an extensive black market for fissile materials, nuclear weapons components etc. has recently been revealed in connection with the confessions of Pakistan's bomb-maker, Dr. A. Q. Khan. Furthermore, if Pakistan's less-than-stable government should be overthrown, complete nuclear weapons could fall into the hands of terrorists.

On November 3, 2003, Mohamed El Baradei, Director General of the International Atomic Energy Agency, made a speech to the United Nations in which he called for:

"Limiting the processing of weapons-usable material [separated plutonium and high enriched uranium], in civilian nuclear programmes-as well as the production of new material, through reprocessing and enrichment-by agreeing to restrict, these operations to facilities exclusively under international control."

It is almost incredible, considering the dangers of nuclear proliferation and nuclear terrorism, that such restrictions were not imposed long ago. Nuclear reactors used for ***"peaceful"*** purposes unfortunately also generate fissionable isotopes of plutonium, neptunium and americium. Thus all nuclear reactors must be regarded as ambiguous in function and all must be put under strict international control. One might ask, in fact, whether globally widespread use of nuclear energy is worth the danger that it entails.

The Italian nuclear physicist Francesco Calogero, who has studied the matter closely, believes that terrorists could easily construct a simple gun type nuclear bomb if they were in possession of a critical mass of highly enriched uranium. In such a simple atomic bomb, two grapefruit-sized sub critical portions of HEU are placed at opposite ends of the barrel of an artillery piece and are driven together by means of a conventional explosive. Prof. Calogero estimates that the fatalities produced by the explosion of such a device in the center of a large city could be several hundred million.

In this dangerous situation, the only logical thing for the world to do is to get rid of both fissile materials and nuclear weapons as rapidly as possible. We must acknowledge that the idea of nuclear deterrence is a dangerous fallacy and acknowledge that the development of military systems based on nuclear weapons has been a terrible mistake, a false step that needs to be reversed. If the most prestigious of the nuclear weapons states can sincerely acknowledge their mistakes and begin to reverse them, nuclear weapons will seem less glamorous to countries like India, Pakistan, North Korea and Iran, where they now are symbols of national pride and modernism.

Gandhi and Non-violence

Let us now turn to Gandhi and non-violence.

Mohandas Karamchand Gandhi was born on October 2, 1869, in Porbander, India. His family belonged to the Hindu caste of shopkeepers. [In Gujarati ***"Gandhi"*** means ***"grocer"***.] However, the family had risen in status, and Gandhi's father, grandfather and uncle had all served as prime ministers of small principalities in western India.

In 1888, Gandhi sailed for England, where he spent three years studying law at the Inner Temple in London. Gandhi's exceptionally sweet and honest character won him many friends in England and he encountered no racial prejudice at all. However, when he traveled to Pretoria in South Africa a few years later, he experienced racism in its worst form. Although he was meticulously well dressed in an English frock coat and in possession of a first-class ticket, Gandhi was given the choice between traveling third class, or being thrown of the train. [He chose the second alternative.] Later in the journey he was beaten by a coach driver because he insisted on his right to sit as a passenger rather than taking a humiliating position on the footboard of the coach.

The legal case which had brought Gandhi to South Africa was a dispute between a wealthy Indian merchant, Dada Abdullah Seth and his relative, Seth Tyeb [who had refused to pay a debt of 40,000 pounds, in those days a huge sum]. Gandhi succeeded in reconciling these two relatives and he persuaded them to settle their differences out of court. Later he wrote about this experience:

"Both were happy with this result and both rose in public estimation. My joy was boundless. I had learnt the true practice of law. I had learnt to find out the better side of human nature and to enter men's hearts. I realized that the true function of a lawyer was to unite parties driven asunder. The lesson was so indelibly burnt into me that a large part of my time during my twenty years of practice as a lawyer was occupied in bringing about compromises of hundreds of cases. I lost nothing thereby - not even money, certainly not my soul."

Gandhi was about to return to India after the settlement of the case, but at a farewell party given by Abdullah Seth, he learnt of a bill before the legislature which would deprive Indians in South Africa of their right to vote. He decided to stay and fight against the bill.

Gandhi spent the next twenty years in South Africa, becoming the leader of a struggle for the civil rights of the Indian community. In this struggle he tried ***"...to find the better side of human nature and to enter men's hearts".*** Gandhi's stay in England had given him a glimpse of English liberalism and English faith in just laws. He felt confident that if the general public in England could be made aware of gross injustices in any part of the British Empire, reform would follow. He therefore organized non-violent protests in which the protesters sacrificed themselves so as to show as vividly as possible the injustice of an existing law. For example, when the government ruled that Hindu, Muslim and Parasi marriages had no legal standing, Gandhi and his followers voluntarily went to prison for ignoring the ruling.

Gandhi used two words to describe this form of protest: ***"Satyagraha"*** [the force of truth] and ***"ahimsa"*** [non-violence]. Of these he later wrote:

"I have nothing new to teach the world. Truth and non-violence are as old as the hills. All that I have done is to try experiments in both, on as vast a scale as I could. In so doing, I sometimes erred and learnt by my errors. Life and its problems have thus become to me so many experiments in the practice of truth and non-violence."

Because of his growing fame as the leader of the Indian civil rights movement in South Africa, Gandhi was persuaded to return to India in 1914 and to take up the cause of Indian home rule. In order to reacquaint himself with conditions in India, he traveled tirelessly, always going third class as a matter of principle.

During the next few years, Gandhi worked to reshape the Congress Party into an organization which represented not only India's Anglicized upper middle class but also the millions of uneducated villagers who were surviving under an almost intolerable burden of poverty and disease. In order to identify himself with the poorest of India's people, Gandhi began to wear only a white loincloth made of rough homespun cotton. He traveled to the remotest villages, recruiting new members for the Congress Party, preaching non-violence and ***"firmness in the truth"***, and becoming known for his voluntary poverty and humility. The villagers who flocked to see him began to call him ***"Mahatma"*** [Great Soul].

Gandhi organized demonstrations whose purpose was to show the British public that although the British ***Raj*** gave India many benefits, the toll exacted was too high, not only in terms of money, but also in terms of India's self-respect and self-sufficiency. All of Gandhi's demonstrations were designed to underline this fact. For example, in 1930 Gandhi organized a civil-disobedience campaign against the salt laws. The salt laws gave the Imperial government a monopoly and prevented Indians from making their own salt by evaporating sea water. The majority of Indians were poor farmers who worked long hours in extreme heat and salt were as much a necessity to them as bread. The tax on salt was essentially a tax on the sweat of the farmers.

Before launching his campaign, Gandhi sent a polite letter to the Viceroy, Lord Irwin, explaining his reasons for believing that the salt laws were unjust, and announcing his intention of disregarding them unless they were repealed. Then, on March 12 1930, Gandhi and many of his followers, accompanied by several press correspondents, started on a march to the sea to carry out their intention of turning themselves into law breakers by making salt. Every day, Gandhi led the procession about 12 miles, stopping at villages in the evenings to hold prayer meetings. Many of the villagers joined the march, while others cast flower petals in Gandhi's path or sprinkled water on his path to settle the dust.

On April 5, the marchers arrived at the sea, where they spent the night in prayer on the beach. In the morning they began to make salt by wading into the sea, filling pans with water and letting it evaporate in the sun. Not much salt was made in this way, but Gandhi's action had a strong symbolic power. A wave of non-violent civil disobedience demonstrations swept all over India, so extensive and widespread that the Imperial government, in danger of losing control of the country, decided to arrest as many of the demonstrators as possible. By midsummer, Gandhi and a hundred thousand of his followers were in prison, but nevertheless the civil disobedience demonstrations continued.

In January, 1931, Gandhi was released from prison and invited to the Viceroy's palace to talk with Lord Irwin. They reached a compromise agreement: Gandhi was to call of the demonstrations and would attend a Round Table Conference in London to discuss Indian home rule, while Lord Irwin agreed to release the prisoners and would change the salt laws so that Indians living near to the coast could make their own salt.

The salt march was typical of Gandhi's non-violent methods. Throughout the demonstrations, he tried to maintain a friendly attitude towards his opponents, avoiding escalation of the conflict. Thus at the end of the demonstrations, the atmosphere was one in which a fair compromise solution could be reached. Whenever he was in prison, Gandhi regarded his jailers as his hosts. Once, when he was imprisoned in South Africa, he used the time to make a pair of sandals, which he sent to General Smuts, the leader of the South African government. Thus Gandhi put into practice the Christian principle:

"Love your enemies; do good to them that hate you."

Gandhi's importance lies in the fact that he was a major political leader who sincerely tried to put into practice the ethical principles of religion. In his autobiography Gandhi says:

"I can say without the slightest hesitation, and yet with all humility, that those who say that religion has nothing to do with politics do not know what religion means."

Gandhi believed that human nature is essentially good and that it is our task to find and encourage whatever is good in the character of others. During the period when he practiced as a lawyer, Gandhi's aim was ***"to unite parties raven asunder"***, and this was also his aim as a politician. In order for reconciliation to be possible in politics, it is necessary to avoid escalation of conflicts. Therefore Gandhi used non-violent methods, relying only on the force of truth. ***"It is my firm conviction"***, he wrote, ***"that nothing can be built on violence."***

To the insidious argument that ***"the end justifies the means"***, Gandhi answered firmly:

"They say 'means are after all means'. I would say 'means are after all everything'. As the means, so the end. Indeed the Creator has given us control [and that very limited] over means, none over end... The means may be likened to a seed and the end to a tree; and there is the same inviolable connection between the means and the end as there is between the seed and the tree. Means and end are convertible terms in my philosophy of life."

In other words, a dirty method produces a dirty result; killing produces more killing; hate leads to more hate. But there are positive feedback loops as well as negative ones. A kind act produces a kind response; a generous gesture is returned; hospitality results in reflected hospitality. Hindus and Buddhists call this principle ***"the law of karma"***.

Gandhi believed that the use of violent means, inevitably contaminate the end achieved. Because

Gandhi's methods were based on love, understanding, forgiveness and reconciliation, the non-violent revolution which he led, left very little enmity in its wake. When India finally achieved its independence from England, the two countries parted company without excessive bitterness. India retained many of the good ideas which the English had brought - for example the tradition of parliamentary democracy; and the two countries continued to have close cultural and economic ties.

The Nüremberg Principles

At the end of the Second World War, when the full extent of the atrocities that had been committed by the Nazi's became known, it was decided to prosecute Nazi leaders for crimes against peace, war crimes and crimes against humanity [such as extermination camps]. There was disagreement about how such trials should be held, but after some debate between the Allied countries, it was agreed that 24 Nazi officials and military leaders would be tried by an International Military Tribunal in Nüremberg, Germany, a former center of Nazi politics. There were originally 24 defendants, but two of them committed suicide. One was presumed dead but was nevertheless tried in absentia. Of the twenty-one remaining defendants, eleven were given the death penalty, eight were sentenced to long prison terms and three were acquitted. Similar trials also took place in Japan.

In 1946 the United Nations General Assembly unanimously armed ***"the principles of international law recognized by the Charter of the Nüremberg Tribunal and the judgment of the Tribunal".***

The General Assembly also established an International Law Commission to formalize the

Nüremberg Principles and the result was the following list:

- **Principle I:** Any person who commits an act which constitutes a crime under international law is responsible and therefore liable to punishment.
- **Principle II:** The fact that internal law does not impose a penalty for an act which constitutes a crime under international law does not relieve the person who committed the act from responsibility under international law.
- **Principle III:** The fact that the person who committed an act which constitutes a crime under international law acted as Head of State or responsible government official does not relieve him from responsibility under international law.
- **Principle IV:** The fact that a person acted pursuant to order of his Government or of a superior does not relieve him of responsibility under international law, provided that a moral choice was in fact possible for him.
- **Principle V:** Any person charged with a crime under international law has the right to a fair trial on the facts and law.
- **Principle VI:** The crimes hereinafter set out are punishable as crimes under international law:

  A. Crimes against peace: [i] Planning, preparation, initiation or waging of war of aggression or a war in violation of international treaties, agreements or assurances; [ii] Participation in a common plan or conspiracy for the accomplishment of any of the acts mentioned under [i];

  B. War crimes: Violations of the laws or

customs of war which include, but are not limited to, murder, ill-treatment of prisoners of war or persons on the seas, killing of hostages, plunder of public or private property, wanton destruction of cities, towns or villages, or devastation not justified by military necessity.

C. Crimes against humanity: Atrocities and offenses, including but not limited to, murder, extermination, deportation, imprisonment, torture, rape or other inhumane acts committed against any civilian population or persecutions on political, racial or religious grounds, whether or not in violation of the laws of the country where perpetrated.

- **Principle VII:** Complicity in the commission of a crime against peace, a war crime or a crime against humanity as set forth in Principle VI is a crime under international law.

The Nüremberg Principles are being used today as the basis for the International Criminal Court's trials of individuals accused of genocide and war crimes in Rwanda and in the former Yugoslavia.

The Principles throw an interesting light onto the status of soldiers. According to the Nüremberg Principles, it is not only the right, but also the duty of individuals to make moral and legal judgments concerning wars in which they are asked to fight. If a soldier participates in an illegal war [and all wars, apart from actions of the U. N. Security Council, are now illegal] then the soldier is liable to prosecution for violating international law. The fact that he or she was acting under orders is not an excuse. The training of soldiers is designed to remove the burdens of moral and legal responsibility from a soldier's individual shoulders; but the Nüremberg Principles are designed to put these burdens squarely back where they belong - on the shoulders of the individual.

The International Criminal Court

In 1998, in Rome, representatives of 120 countries signed a statute establishing an International Criminal Court, with jurisdiction over the crime of genocide, crimes against humanity, war crimes, and the crime of aggression. It took four years to gather necessary ratification, but by Thursday, April 11, 2002, 66 nations had ratified the Rome agreement - 6 more than the 60 needed to make the court permanent.

It would be impossible to overstate the importance of the International Criminal Court. At last international law acting on individuals has become a reality! The only elective and just way that international laws can be implemented is to make individuals responsible and punishable, since [in the words of Alexander Hamilton], ***"To coerce states is one of the maddest projects ever devised."*** In an increasingly interdependent world, international law has become a necessity. We cannot have peace and justice without it. But the coercion of states is neither just1 nor feasible, and therefore international laws must act on individuals.

The jurisdiction of the ICC is at present limited to a very narrow class of crimes. In fact, the ICC does not at present act on the crime of aggression, although this crime is listed in the Rome Statute and there are plans for its future inclusion in the ICC's activities. The global community will have a chance to see how the court works in practice and in the future the community will undoubtedly decide to broaden the ICC's range of jurisdiction.

Only 7 nations voted against the Rome Statute of the International Criminal Court in 1998: China,

Iraq, Libya, Yemen, Qatar, Israel and the United States. Despite the negative US vote in 1998, President Clinton signed the Rome Statute on December 31, 2000. However, two years later, the George W. Bush Administration withdrew the US signature and began a comprehensive campaign to undermine the ICC. On August 3, 2002, Bush signed into law the American Service members' Protection Act, which featured a prohibition on U. S. cooperation with the ICC; an "invasion of the Hague" provision, authorizing the President to use military force to free U. S. personnel detained by the ICC; punishment of States that join the ICC; and finally, a prohibition of U. S. participation in peacekeeping activities unless immunity from the ICC is guaranteed for U. S. personnel. Finally, the Bush Administration tried to negotiate a large number of bilateral treaties in which other nations would promise never to hand over U. S. citizens to the International Criminal Court.

The motives behind the Bush Administration's campaign against the ICC are easy to understand. If one wants to maintain an empire, war is a necessity. How else can a powerful nation exert its power? On the other hand, the Nüremberg Principles, the Universal Declaration of Human Rights, the ICC and the United Nations Charter are all aimed at making war illegal and impossible. Especially the Nüremberg Principles and the International Criminal Court aim at placing the responsibility for crimes against peace on individuals. The individual political leader is now responsible. The individual soldier is responsible. Apparently Bush and his colleagues want to continue to start wars and they seem to feel that their nation has become militarily so much powerful that international law no longer serves the US national interests. The other countries of the world will have to decide whether they will allow the United States to place itself outside the law. The American people will have to decide whether they want their nation to be a rogue state.

The Connection

So what is the connection between nuclear weapons, Gandhi's birthday and the Nüremberg Principles? The International Court of Justice has ruled that the use or threat of use of nuclear weapons would generally be contrary to international law. According to Principle VII of the Nüremberg Principles, "Complicity in the commission of a crime against peace, a war crime, or a crime against humanity... is a crime under international law." Therefore all of us have a responsibility, under international law, to oppose the use or threat of use of nuclear weapons. How can we do this? Gandhi's principles of non-violent political protest can perhaps show us how to work in the struggle to rid the world of the terrible threat of nuclear catastrophe.

The Gandhian tradition of non-violent protest played an important role in the movement that ended British colonial rule in India, the struggle against apartheid in South Africa, the black civil rights movement in the U. S. A., in protests against the Vietnam war and the anti-nuclear protests of the 1960's and 1970's. In all these campaigns and protests, the final results were achieved by adherence to Gandhi's principle that good means must be used if good ends are to be achieved. He firmly rejected the proposition that "the end justifies the means." While disagreeing with his opponents, he always maintained a friendly attitude towards them, always searching for the good side in human nature and always believing in the power of truth.

17

Gandhi and Nordic Countries

Holger Terp

Mohandas Gandhi had many friends outside India. This is well known and reflected in his collected works where most of the correspondence between Gandhi and his friends are recorded.

In the Nordic counties Gandhi also had friends and admires.

Some of the people in the Scandinavian countries in the Northern part of Europe did a lot to get to know Gandhi and is it my experience without the recognition by historians or the personalities in the peace movement.

As Gandhi never came to the Nordic Countries, Denmark, Norway, Sweden and Finland though invited many times, the Scandinavians had to travel to India in order to meet him or to write to him. A few Danish missionaries wee in India, so they had the opportunity to meet Gandhi and to learn and discuss with him already during the first world war, when Gandhi were little known in the Vest.

Some of the missionaries are recorded in the Collected Works: Anne Marie Petersen and Esther Færing. Because Christian circles in Denmark financially supported those two missionaries, they published articles about Gandhi and the Indian non-violent struggle for freedom in church publications and church magazines. And the good news from India spread to other parts of the Danish society, especially the folk high schools and from there to the mass media and to the publishers. By the end of the 1930's many of the popular anthologies on Gandhi as well as some parts of his autobiographies were translated published in Denmark and a few of the autobiographies were translated and published in Sweden.

And as the British oppression in India grew during the 1930's the Danish Journalist Ellen Hørup decided that something had to be done about it. Ellen Hørup travelled to India and visited Gandhi and Anne Marie Petersen in 1929-1930. After the visit the established the Danish solidarity groups the Friends of India October 1930. The group also published a magazine with the same name. But that was not enough, for Ellen Hørup moved to Geneva where the International Committee for India and its magazine Indian Press were established. When the fascism of Europe grew, the Indian committee were turned into the news agency Journal des Archives that was closed at the beginning of World War-Two.

Out of the research grew the knowledge that there were many Indian solidarity groups around the world in the 1930's, and that the organised work to support the Indian freedom struggle has had been paid little attention by the historians. I might be mistaken on this matter...

For many years ago I was contacted by the Indian Professor E.S. Reddy who wanted to collect documents relating Scandinavians with Gandhi as he earlier had published volumes on Gandhi and South Africans and Gandhi and Americans.

The hunt for the documentation in newspapers, books, magazines and dusty old files began. And during the research the correspondence between

Mahatma Gandhi and his friends began to surface, some in unexpected places even letters never published before.

Professor Reddy did the research in India and I did the Scandinavian research.

The correspondence between Gandhi and the Scandinavians consist of the main groups:

- Letters to missionaries;
- Letters to publishers; and
- Letters to pacifists and idealists

Some conclusions can be made from the anthology

Gandhi and Anne Marie Petersen were some of the pioneers of the philosophy of liberation.

Also they were pioneers of liberation education.

Anne Marie Petersen believed that the liberation had to start at the bottom of society, making the women economic independent. Thus she established her school at Porto Novo that later were turned into a teachers college. Petersen also had the knowledge and the ability to make the different Caste's work together.

Working with historic documents is important in the present peace work because new aspects of peace and solidarity work can appear. Would the solidarity work of the 1930's be possible today, when a lot of governments have passed laws against terrorism?

International cooperation is most important in order to create peace.

The connections between India and Scandinavia were much broader than hitherto known.

18

Gandhism, Optimism and the Gandhians

Thomas Weber

Introduction

Interestingly, when the current state of the Gandhian legacy is discussed, the examples tend not to come from India. And this appears to be not merely a cultural misappropriation - Indian Gandhians will often say to foreign inquirers that Gandhi has been forgotten in India, that he is being re-imported from the West. In these conversations names such as that of Attenborough and Schumacher loom large. But there are still a great many dedicated Gandhians carrying on the work of the Mahatma in Bharat and in any discussion about the position of Gandhi today it would be instructive to examine their perspective.

The Gandhians do not necessarily speak with one voice. The differences, over and above those of individual characteristics, often depend on the ideology of the individual, whether his or her world view has been coloured more by Vinoba Bhave or Jayaprakash Narayan, and whether they believe that the political situation in the country is deteriorating so rapidly that the ***"need of the hour"*** forces them to compromise on ideals [if not their fundamental principles] in the way that Gandhi often did.

During the mid 1970s, as a result of the Bihar agitation and JP's campaign of Total Revolution which followed, the Gandhian movement split over fundamental philosophical issues. The two leaders of the Gandhian movement, JP and Vinoba, eventually came to differ in their interpretation of the use of ***Satyagraha,*** in the methods to be employed to bring about societal change, the speed at which useful change was possible to achieve, the degree to which Gandhians should be involved in power politics, and the importance of spiritual vs. humanist reasons for acting.

Until then the movement seemed united and appeared to be speaking with the one voice. JP's general deference to Vinoba's leadership finally ceased following JP's frustrating experience of grassroots work in 1970-1 in the villages of Musahari in Bihar. This had two marked consequences: first JP's realization that the results of constructive peace building work in the Vinoban tradition did not justify the effort. This in turn led JP back to his pre-Gandhian roots in political activism, secondly, his emergence from Vinoba's shadow into a position of rival leadership. This led to open differences and to JP taking active control of movement. The result was a split among the Gandhians that has still not quite healed. The lifting of measures aimed at suppressing the Gandhian movement during Mrs. Gandhi's ***"emergency"*** could have heralded a new high point for Gandhian influence in India; however the Janata debacle merely helped to marginalize an already weakened movement.

The Gandhians

Vinoba explained that with the progress of science and the creation of nuclear weapons humanity faced ultimate destruction. In order to neutralize this force of violence and to arouse the world's conscience Gandhi's non-violence had to take on ***"more subtle***

and finer forms." Satyagraha could no longer afford to ***"create agitation or tension in the minds of the opponent,"*** it had to avoid a ***"collision of minds and seek harmony in thought."*** Until change was brought about through understanding and acceptance, rather than through imposition, ***"the seeds of violence, imperialism and world wars would not be rooted out."***

Satyagraha had to progress as the political situation progressed [from imperialist domination to ***"democracy"*** in India] and as science progressed. Consequently, Vinoba declared that Jesus' concept of ***"resist not evil"*** and Gandhi's ***"non-violent resistance"*** were no longer adequate and what now had to take their place was ***"non-violent assistance"*** in right thinking. Without this all that could be achieved was legislative reform, and that could never lead to total revolution. Vinoba saw the use of political structures as a method of solving problems as doomed to failure:

"When one problem appears to be nearing a solution, ten others crop up", and when a solution appears to have been achieved ***"soon it raises its head again."***

In his analysis of the Bihar movement, Shah maintains that Vinoba had long been anxious to discover a new technique because of the traps of the false assumption that once an opposing leader is removed all will be well, and the ***"impassioned tensions"*** of political movements that distract people from their original objectives. With ***Bhoodan***, the land-gift movement, he had already provided the classical example.

The transformation to a ***Sarvodaya*** social order was to be accomplished without directly challenging the legitimacy of the state, for, after all, in a democratic system, power had been entrusted to the state by the people. However, it could not be achieved through the ballot, which Vinoba saw as either a farce that left real power in the hands of the few, or as a formula for disruption. Vinoba's aim was to create conditions, which would ***"do away with the need to use even the power of the State."*** The achievement of this anarchist polity was to come about gradually - he was not anti-state; he hoped to bypass the structures on which the state rested and thus allow it to whither away.

Vinoba was fond of saying that politics disintegrates and spirituality unites. He made it clear that for him there could be no outward revolution without a corresponding internal one, without a change in mental attitude:

"All revolutions which take place, whether they are social or economic, have their roots in spiritual ideas. At first there is a change in spiritual values and later on social, political and economic values undergo change."

Given his activist background, it is not surprising that at the time of this intellectual reassessment, JP's analysis of the political situation and his understanding of ***Satyagraha*** would mature into something substantially different from Vinoba's, that unlike Vinoba he would embrace the position of Gandhi the politician over Gandhi the saint.

While still very much in the shadow of Vinoba, JP saw Bhoodan, bringing about ***"changes of the heart"***, as the vehicle for the establishment of a Sarvodaya social order. If this failed in the first instance, he looked to the experience of Gandhi to provide a path for further action. Subsequent steps were to include an attempt to educate the public to the evil that was being opposed, followed by the launching of movements to place moral pressure on the ***"wrong-doer"*** or ***"mistaken party"*** and finally by resorting to non-cooperation on the assumption that injustice were only possible with cooperation of the wronged party.

In the diary that he wrote while in prison during Mrs. Gandhi's Emergency, JP noted that although Vinoba seemed to hold that ***"systematic change in the political order could be brought about without a struggle, even a peaceful struggle,"*** after twenty years of effort nowhere had success been achieved? He continued pointing out that one of the reasons for this was a lack of atmosphere of struggle:

"It seems to me that in such an atmosphere psychological forces are created that attract men and drive them to accept challenges and to change themselves and others."

While conceding that during the Bhoodan movement through "***Spiritual and moral appeals, the saintly influence of Vinobaji, did bring about some remarkable moral changes in some individuals,"*** he concluded that these could ***"never become a social or psychological force"*** that would be effective in securing a more just society. While Vinoba strove for perfect non-violence, JP spoke of social change through a mass movement of peaceful people's power.

JP's primary concern was the achievement of real democracy and a society devoid of inequalities where all lived in a state of freedom. His concerns, like Vinoba's, were centred on the problems of the human condition - freedom of the human personality, of the mind and of the spirit - but his quest was a political, not a spiritual one. He was searching for the form of social organization, which would provide the masses with the maximum freedom, and the most appropriate way of bringing it about.

JP shared Vinoba's view of a village society and the way that it should be organized. In an open letter to his Praja Socialist comrades, when he finally announced his resignation from the Party in 1957, JP made the point that although he had withdrawn from politics, ***Sarvodaya*** also had its politics - a politics of a different kind. Unlike the politics of party and power, ***Sarvodaya*** politics rested on lokniti [politics of the people] as opposed to rajniti [politics of the state]. He added that ***Sarvodaya*** politics could have ***"no party and no concern with power."*** Its aim was to abolish all centres of power and to achieve a withering away of the state. As this ***"new politics grew"***, JP saw a corresponding diminution of the ***"old politics."***

In his analysis of the relationship of the Gandhian movement to politics at the Thirteenth All India Sarvodaya Conference at Unguturu in 1961, JP noted that, as Gandhians, they did not belong in political parties and should not ***"take part, directly or indirectly, in any political contest for position and power."*** He added, however, that this did not mean that they should be unconcerned with what happened in the political field with the working of democracy. He asked rhetorically whether, if democracy was in peril or if there was danger of political chaos or dictatorship, they should ***"sit back smugly and twiddle our thumbs on the ground that we have nothing to do with politics?"***

JP was for a party less democracy but he saw that there was no alternative to parties in the short term, not until a lengthy process of mass political education had managed to eradicate the distinctions of class and caste. Rather than merely allowing the state to wither away he saw danger for the future if anti-democratic tendencies in power politics were not tackled. During the Bihar Movement he reiterated the party less ideal while organizing a party to oppose Mrs. Gandhi. In his prison diary, in direct contrast to the position of Vinoba, JP wrote:

"No one, at least no one who has no party affiliation and therefore no motivation to exploit every situation for partisan ends, and who is

still anxious to start a peaceful revolutionary movement, i.e. a movement to bring about basic changes in society and in social attitudes, can ever, in the conditions of our country, avoid a confrontation with the kind of government we have."

His rejection of the Vinoba's ***"positive" Satyagraha*** came from his realizations that it was inadequate to produce the psychological climate necessary to bring about the social revolution he desired. And to the charge that his change of direction was politicizing the ***Sarvodaya*** movement he answered that such politicizations ***"should give it immense strength and make it more relevant to contemporary society."***

Both Vinoba and JP knew that the non-violent revolution they desired would only be achieved through the efforts of the people themselves. The differences centred on the means that would be employed by the people to bring this revolution about. Ostergaard makes the point that whereas Western anarchism is ***"immediatist",*** Indian anarchism is ***"gradualist"***. JP was more anarchistic in the Western sense, reverting to active struggle and ***"negative" Satyagraha***. Unlike Vinoba, he was also anti-state, pitting people's power against that of the state. Vinoba, on the other hand, was a gradualist, far more concerned with the purity of the means than with any immediate ends that may be achieved. In this he was following the Gandhian dictum that the ends grew out of the means employed, and echoing Gandhi's statement that even if a Hitler's heart was not ***"melted"*** by the efforts of the pure ***Satyagrahi*** it did not matter because intrinsic values were as important as any instrumental considerations.

The differing approach of the two Gandhian leaders was dependent on their personal convictions, and perhaps even more, on the differences in personality between Vinoba and JP. Vinoba, stressing spiritual values, placed primary consideration on the conversion of the individual so that these individuals could bring about the hoped for changes in society. For him changes in the social structure would not come about without adequate moral development. JP on the other hand, unsurprisingly given his lengthy association with Marxism, saw it as more practical and perhaps more logical that people would change once the environment had been changed.

The perceived failure of Vinoba's approach to bringing about meaningful change led to the more confrontational position of JP. However, given the failure of tackling the government head-on as a way to usher in the non-violent revolution [and in any case the lack of resources to do so], a further re-evaluation was to be expected. That efforts in India are again being concentrated on local peace building as a way of bringing about change, which is a far longer-term project, seems to reflect a return to what may be termed Gandhian basics enabled by the stubborn optimism of the Gandhian fraternity. Perhaps this can be coupled with the simple fact that this approach embodies a more realistic interpretation of the current political circumstances prevailing in the country.

With the passing of the old guard of Gandhian politicians and the alienation of the weakened Gandhian movement from the central authorities, there is very little scope for the toleration of a highly organized group whose avowed aim is to make the state redundant - even if it were possible in some way to recreate the heyday of the Gandhian movement.

The Marginalization of the Gandhian Movement in his landmark work, Asian Drama published in

1968, ***Swedish*** economist Gunnar Myrdal provided an analysis of the social and economic factors affecting India's rate and level of development. There, Myrdal designated the country a ***"soft state",*** that is one where governmental decision making shies away from placing obligations on the populace, and if policies are framed in legislative terms at all, often they are not enforced.

The Indian State bureaucracy did not have the ability to reach into every village, and this, coupled with the Gandhian legacy, including that of resistance to governmental coercion and a philosophical commitment to the proposition ***"that democratic planning requires the people's participation and initiative...in the course of creating the new institutions for self-government and cooperation"*** ensured that a large part would be played by ***Sarvodaya*** workers in the country's path to development. Myrdal believed that ***"rapid development will be exceedingly difficult to engender without an increase in social discipline in all strata and even in the villages."*** And here he means state imposed discipline. In other words for effective ***"development"*** a ***"strong"*** or ***"hard"*** state was a necessity - the Gandhians, however, by very definition, were the champions of an even further ***"softening"*** of the state.

Much has happened since the words of Myrdal were written. During his inaugural presidential address at the half yearly conference of the ***Sarva Seva Sangh***, held at Ernakulam towards the end of 1972, Siddharaj Dhadda stated that:

"The aim of the Sarvodaya movement is to make the people conscious about the reality of the present situation, to diminish their reliance on government, to help them organise their strength and take the management of their affairs in their own hands. We want the

establishment of a real participatory democracy in the place of the present representative one. Representative democracy may have been good in the past when science and technology had not advanced to the extent as to enable the representatives to obtain a stranglehold on the lives of the people through state machinery. The exercise of the power of the Government in the old context was confined to performing its legitimate function of a peace-keeping and coordinating agency...the people were masters of their own lives and destiny, without let or hindrance from outside forces. But the phenomenal advance of science has created a strange paradox. It has made possible and has actually led to an ever increasing concentration of power, political, economic, military, into the hands of an ever diminishing number of people - a smaller and smaller coterie."

In short, India was rapidly losing its status as a ***"soft state".***

With the passing of Nehru and the estrangement between the Gandhian movement and his daughter following JP's call for ***"Total Revolution"***, the ***Sarvodaya*** establishment lost government support for, and was even actively obstructed in, carrying out its voluntary social work activities. As the nation increasingly took on the trappings of a ***"hard state"***, particularly under the regime of Rajiv Gandhi, the Gandhian movement [along with other voluntary agencies] was further pushed to the periphery in terms of the inputs it could provide to the shaping of social organization and development. This trend has been exacerbated by the ever-declining appeal of Gandhian philosophy to the youth of the country with a rapidly swelling middle class desiring an increase in consumer goods, and the absence of a charismatic leader among Gandhians that could counter it.

Perhaps a strong Gandhian movement, as it worked in the 1960s and early 1970s, cannot be tolerated by a state where the political leadership no longer has a philosophical commitment to the values of the ***"Father of the Nation"***, where Gandhian ideas about societal organization are often derided as being utopian and irrelevant as the country moves towards the Twenty-first Century, and where the organization itself is the self-declared vanguard of a revolution aimed at a destruction of the Indian polity as it has evolved in the years since independence. Further, perhaps these types of organizations can only be tolerated where bureaucracy does not permeate all levels of society, where the state does not have the resources to provide its own rapid and adequate intervention in times of social turmoil. As states ***"harden"***, the operation of such groups becomes incompatible with a government that seeks to establish its position as legitimate and sole sovereign.

In 1964, leading Gandhian Narayan Desai was already lamenting that the Sangh's peace brigade, the ***Shanti Sena***, faced two problems that prevented it from being as ***"effective as it should be."*** He named them as a lack of means of quick communication and an extreme lack of finances. The situation for the voluntary sector has deteriorated since. At a time when the ability of the state to move its own functionaries around the country has been aided by the increasing mobility of its armed forces, Gandhian institutions, ever further removed in history from Gandhi himself, are increasingly feeling the economic pinch. And, as the government moves inexorably into areas that were once the domain of Gandhian institutions, people are less willing to donate money to groups that are increasingly seen as costly and amateur parallel organizations.

Erica Linton, an observer of the Sarvodaya movement at the height of its power, made a telling point in this regard. Touring Gandhian pilgrimage sites in Pune with a non-Gandhian chauffeur, at the Samadhi of the Mahatma's late secretary Mahadev Desai in the Agha Khan's palace, she turned to her escort and remarked, ***"You know, I suppose, that Mahadev's son Narayan is the secretary of the Shanti Sena?" "Oh, you mean the American Peace Corps'***, explained the driver. ***"What a sorry state of affairs",*** she commented ***"when foreign volunteers make a greater impact on the community than their own young men."*** It was this realization that led to the setting up of a youth wing of the ***Shanti Sena*** following the Bihar famine of 1966-7. The attempts at Gandhian peace and constructive work, however, never reached the critical mass necessary to make the ignorance of Linton's driver anything other than the norm. And with the decline in, and marginalization of, the Gandhian movement in the years since, there is little evidence that there is any scope for optimism on the part of the Gandhian establishment that there will be any change in this situation in the foreseeable future.

Optimism

Dictionary definitions of optimism mention the inclination to take the most hopeful view of a given situations, the opinion that everything will turn out for the best, that good in the end will triumph over evil. This in turn implies that humans are basically good and therefore can control the evil in them and in society.

Gandhi often wrote of his optimism. He based his optimism on his belief in himself and on his personal expectations. He placed himself among the ***"tribe of Columbus and Stevenson, who hoped against hope in the face of heaviest odds,"*** noting that the ***"days of miracles are not gone."*** And although he claimed to base his optimism ***"on solid facts,"*** the more cynical observers of his life need only to point to the mass killings in his homeland at the end of his long life of preaching the gospel of non-violence to claim that the optimism was misplaced. In the end Gandhi would perhaps have agreed with them, and given what has become the India of his dreams perhaps pessimism is a more realistic attitude to hold.

The opening sentence of a recent book on pessimism informs us, ***"It is now difficult to be optimistic."*** The book, Pessimism, was written just before the end of the Cold War. It gives as the reasons for pessimism a declining faith in progress, the [now at least temporarily diminished] threat of nuclear war, and our destructive treatment of the environment with the resulting problems with feeding the hungry and generating safe energy. Since the heyday of the Gandhian movement, India has experienced increased communal violence, consumerism and centralizing tendencies about which the heirs of the Mahatma have been able to do little.

Bailey, the author of Pessimism, sees new social movements, especially in the fields of ecology, peace and feminism as being the new sources of progressiveness. However, progressiveness and newness, or even popularity and persistence, are not measures of effectiveness. They do not of themselves demonstrate ***"success in shifting the old politics in a more benign direction."*** In his assessment of nuclear disarmament campaigns and ***"green"*** parties, he concludes that given the continuing arms race and exploitation of the environment, ***"there is little sign of encouraging success."*** Bailey sees little possibility of success in situations where the movements cannot win in parliaments. And for social movements this is extremely unlikely - except in the case of the

Gandhian movement, perhaps the archetypical social movement, which ushered in the Janata Government in India. And that lead to perhaps its last great failure.

Those descendants of the ***"irrepressible optimist"*** who threw their lot in with direct political action as the vehicle of change exhibit a noticeable level of pessimism. They saw a long-term view and strategy as inadequate in a rapidly deteriorating world - the ***"need of the hour"*** compelled immediate action. However, this approach also meant short-term defeats. Without a charismatic leader they are unable to capture the imagination of the populace, their message is considered irrelevant in the light of a growing consumerist ethic, people's candidates fail in elections that are dominated by personalities rather than issues; and as the state takes on an increasing number of the functions that were previously the domain of the voluntary sector, and the Gandhians are categorized [or were during the Indira Gandhi government when they were still a force to be reckoned with] as a de facto opposition party, the ***Sarvodaya*** movement has become increasingly marginalized. While they cling to their long-term vision the lack of direct short-term victories dampens their feeling of optimism.

The followers of Vinoba have a different history. To generalize, their optimism appears to be based faith rather than experience and they tend to believe in the intrinsic good, regardless of the apparent instrumental applications, of their philosophy in action.

Conclusion

The walls of almost every Gandhian home or institution are adorned with pictures of Gandhi [who tried political and spiritual, long and short term approaches in his optimists quest to bring about change], and the pictures of both JP and Vinoba [who, perhaps not unrealistically, tended to be polarized in their approaches]. It is possible to see Vinoba's gradualist approach as being ultimately correct in a deep Gandhian sense - while still maintaining a desire for tangible results. The path of ignoring the government, of working outside its structures and letting it wither away ***["worldly" success];*** can only be achieved if enough people follow it through, not merely the odd saint. The result-oriented confrontational approach has a far better chance of mobilizing the masses and seems to have a better chance of at least limited success, and also a greater chance of ultimate failure. Its success cannot make government wither away or achieve the ***"other worldly"*** ideals inherent in ***"pure" Satyagraha***, it can only replace the political structure with a less oppressive one.

Confronting the power structure head-on, however, means that the government cannot ignore its antagonist and ensures that all the forces at its disposal will be directed at crushing any direct opposition. Some opted for the political approach of JP hoping that it could succeed, while maintaining the nagging feeling that in the long run it could not provide the ushering in of the Gandhian ideal. Since the failure of the Total Revolution the conundrum involved in the ***"this-worldly"*** vs. the ***"other-worldly"*** manifestations of ***Satyagraha*** is still being worked through.

Despite the objective reality of their present weakened position in Indian society, the Gandhians are nevertheless generally optimistic about the value of Gandhism as a force to be reckoned with, one which can bring about change for the good. And the most optimistic are the Vinoba supporters, who have not suffered the same tangible defeats as their colleagues who entered the political fray. They see that their message, if not necessarily their movement of old, is one for the ages. They realize that the process will be slow, that there will be setbacks, but are convinced that it will eventually win through, that with a continuation of grassroots work success is assured. By organic means, Gandhi's message will triumph. They firmly believe that all signs point to this outcome - the increasing number of social movements around the world now employing Gandhian methods and the approach of environmental collapse is forcing a re-evaluation of the hegemony of Western lifestyle and consumption patterns in a way that indicates a shift towards a Gandhian outlook.

Although others may see them as anachronistic, and it is reasonable to be pessimistic about the future of the old Gandhians ever again being in the vanguard of a dynamic and influential social movement, they believe that the march of history is now coming the full circle and that they are merely ahead of the times. For life on the planet to continue a simple life is necessary and in order to survive the rest of the world will catch up eventually. It is not a belief in the possibility of miracles, but one that says that humankind is wise enough not to destroy itself or its environment. This self-assured belief in being on the right path leaves no room for pessimism.

19

Some Thoughts on Civil Disobedience: My Duties and Responsibilities

Jeff Knaebel

General Precepts

ALL LIFE IS one. The world is one home. All are members of one family. All creation is one organic whole. No person is independent of that whole. The earth is a sacred gift to be cherished, nurtured, and shared by all.

All human beings are endowed by the Law of Nature [God if you prefer, hereinafter "***Truth***"] with a moral conscience. The highest law of my being is the Law of Truth. The Law of Truth is of a higher order than man-made law. It can also be said that Truth is Love, in the sense that God is Love. Every person is ultimately accountable only to this Higher Law, the working force of which is Ahimsa, non-violence, love.

Man is a social being. It is his duty to live in harmony with the entirety of humanity in accordance with Laws of Truth, without any distinction whatsoever for race, ethnicity, nationality, gender, religion, creed, caste, class, or age. All false appearances belie the actual intrinsic unity of mankind. Our universal language is the language of the heart.

Conflicts must be overcome by great loyalty to humanity, which supersedes all other subordinate loyalties-racial or national. It is the law of Love that rules mankind. Had violence and hatred ruled us, we would long ago have become extinct. Love is what men live by.

The daily prayer of Mahatma Gandhi ***"Lead me from untruth to truth, from darkness to light, from death to immortality"*** declares an evolutionary journey which is the birthright of every human being. Ultimate Truth is the goal of life. Its unimpeded and efficient realization is the natural right of every person. No State possesses moral authority to impede this basic human right of Self-Realization.

The five basic minimum moral precepts of my faith and conscience are

- To abstain from killing any visible living being;
- To abstain from lying;
- To abstain from stealing;
- To abstain from sexual misconduct; and
- To abstain from intoxicants.

It is my duty to adhere to these precepts in my personal actions and also not to support or approve violation of them by others or the State. These responsibilities are intrinsic to my duty to live in harmony with all other human beings.

Freedom of religion means I cannot be required by coercion, force, or threat of force to violate any precepts of my faith, or to support violation of them by the State.

My moral responsibility comprises a universal responsibility for welfare of all beings. My every action affects directly or indirectly the welfare of my fellowmen. The first morality and the first service to others are the same: do no harm. It is my duty to renounce violence in my heart and to employ the power of ***ahimsa*** [non-violence] generated by this great renunciation.

Because non-violence is my most fundamental moral responsibility, it is also my most fundamental human right. This means that I cannot be required to support or approve of the State in breaching the precept of ***ahimsa.***

The scope of non-violence herein includes abstaining from all activities [to the extent humanly possible], which take the life of any visible living being. Economic, ecological and natural resource exploitation of the poor or the weak by the rich or the strong is considered herein an act of violence which it is my duty to resist by non-violent means.

It is my duty to support actions, which promote peace, harmony, and real happiness of human beings everywhere, and to abstain from actions and support of actions by the State inimical to these ends. Greed, hatred, and delusion are the three ***"great poisons"*** which deprive humanity of peace, harmony, and happiness. Therefore it is my duty to abstain from support of actions by the State, which generate or promote these great poisons among human beings.

The end of any action is defined, predicted, and included in the means. Means may be likened to the seed, the end to its tree. They are inseparably linked. A good end cannot arise from immoral means. Man can always have control over the means, but never of the ends. Purity of means is based upon recognition of moral law. The precept of non-violence states that it is quality of means, that is, the intention to suffer for good ends but not to inflict suffering upon others, which provides justification of the ends.

All people are endowed with inalienable rights

to life, liberty, and pursuit of happiness as necessary pre-requisites to enable their achievement of Self-Realization. Other basic human rights are enumerated in the Bill of Rights of the U. S. Constitution, the Charter of the United Nations, and in U. N. Resolutions regarding human rights. The full scope of human rights is not limited to these enumerations. In order to promote the full scope of human rights, it is my duty to resist by non-violent means the forces of evil and violence.

I cannot deny the truth of my perceptions, conscience, and commonsense. To do so would be to deny myself, my capacity to know, my instruments of knowledge, which enable me to learn Truth? I confess that Truth recedes as I approach it, like all highest values. It is like infinity. As a human being, it is extremely difficult to be perfect in truth. Just as the truth of geometry is not denied by an inability to draw a straight line, so my shortfall from Truth does not deny its actuality. If I understand a fact as it is and act on that fact as guided by my conscience, then I have acted according to truth.

My own conscience provides the best understanding for me of Truth in any situation. No other person is endowed by Nature with the ability or right to interpret the guidance of my personal conscience. Certainly no State possesses this power.

Ahimsa and love are one. ***Ahimsa*** means the largest love, the greatest charity. ***Ahimsa***, the active force of love, requires me to dissociate myself from evil-doers, that is, those who employ violence. ***Ahimsa*** is not merely the absence of violence. It is an active engagement in compassion.

Non-violence is the supreme value, the one

cognizable standard by which truth in action can be determined. Suffering deprivation, loss or even injury to one's own person as a substitute for violence to others is the essence of non-violence.

Self-realization as a goal and as a duty herein means complete salvation, total release from cyclic existence of birth-death-rebirth. It is achieved through unswerving pursuit to righteousness of which ***ahimsa*** is the foundation. Since salvation is the ultimate goal of man, his persona, autonomy takes precedence over the State. Self-government is autonomy of the moral self, the moral rule of each man over himself. Duty to one's own conscience and loyalty to Truth [God] are above one's loyalty to State. In matters of individual conscience the rule of majority has no place. Blind submission to social will is not a righteous act. No act, which is not voluntary, can be said to be moral.

An ad performed against the dictates of one's conscience is not a moral act, orders from the State notwithstanding. If a person feels those orders do not conform to reason and moral sensibility, it is his duty to disobey and take upon himself the consequences. It is right to support the actions of State only as long as they are non-violent. When actions of State harm living beings, it is one's duty to withdraw support.

It is blindly ignorant and unrighteous to believe that an act of a majority binds a minority. There are many examples of acts of majorities found to have been wrong and those of minorities to have been right. All reforms have been initiated by minorities in opposition to majorities. So long as the blind belief exists that men should obey unjust laws will their slavery exist? Is a pious man to accept an order to kill his fellowman, tantamount to his own family, on the basis of majority rule? It is contrary to humanity to obey laws repugnant to conscience. Such teaching is opposed to religion and means slavery. Even the government does not expect such a thing front us. It does not say: ***"you must do such and such."*** It says: ***"If you do not do it, we will punish you."***

If man will realize it is unrighteous to obey unjust laws, no tyranny will enslave him. This is crucial to self-rule. Throughout history, men have recognized the God-given right to disobey and to resist government when its tyranny or its inefficiency is great and unendurable.

Individual freedom alone can motivate a person to surrender to service of society. If it is wrested from him, he becomes automation and society is ruined. No society can be built on denial of individual liberty. The moral person is marked by a readiness to suffer and make sacrifice for the highest good. Moreover, the sacrifices must be made and the suffering borne in a spirit of non-violence with malice towards none.

The State does not possess moral sovereignty over the individual and does not inherently possess rights to be granted to individuals. Individuals are endowed. With inalienable natural rights and the State derives its authority from consent of the people. The State cannot grant inalienable rights, it can only impede them up to the limit which people are willing to tolerate.

A righteous person is duty-bound to disobey laws repugnant to conscience, taking upon him the consequences and penalties of civil disobedience, provided, however, that he must never take the law into his own hands. The conscience of the people is ultimate sanction of laws aimed at higher levels of justice and public welfare. It is the righteous person's duty to work towards elevating the social conscience. Rights are not ultimately protected by law, but by the moral conscience of society.

The individual is the supreme consideration. The individual must be a social being who identifies himself with all other living beings. A rational individual recognizes that it is in his own long-term interest not to exploit others or ecology. The good of all beings is the real good of each individual. The good of the individual is included in the good of all. Men, women, and children must be treated as ends in themselves. They cannot be used as agency for others. To achieve self-realization, which is a natural right equals to the right to life itself, is something only free agents can accomplish. It cannot be done by coercion and cannot be derived from power or wealth. All individuals are moral ends in themselves. As they wish to be treated as moral agents, so must they treat others as moral agents.

An act to be moral must transcend all selfishness and egoism. It must be motivated by goodwill for all, since good of individual is contained in the good of the whole. No man can act without affecting welfare of his fellowmen. The moral test of an action is whether or not it is conducive to welfare of all. The great truth is unity of all life and it includes the love and service of all life. Therefore Truth can be realized only through moral, non-violent means.

An organized society presupposes safety, cooperation, and mutual help. These are impossible without non-violence. The logical consequence of violent methods or messages is the increasing brutality of mail. No success is worthy of human effort if it does not ennoble man.

Non-violent civil disobedience is itself a

birthright. There is no volition to overpower the wrong-doer. The aim of the non-violent resister's suffering is to awaken human sympathy in the heart of wrong-doers and convert them from violence to love. Non-violence invokes forgiveness, not vengeance. One must altogether reject even indirect support for a military state. Emigration is an acceptable non-violent action. The main cause of war is exploitation of weaker nations, races, social groups. It is impossible to achieve peace by means of war.

The right to civil disobedience requires habitual and sincere obedience to law. It is a duty to render voluntary obedience to law except when that law fosters untruth. Then it becomes duty to disobey it. Civil disobedience is, in respect of Higher Law, the natural recourse of people when they have no effective voice in their own government.

Power is the central concept of politics. Coercion is embedded in the power of the State. The State represents violence in concentrated and organized form. There is no non-violent State because State means force. The coercive nature of State power goes against the moral value of individual action. Politics divides and separates, in opposition to the unity of all life. George Washington said:

"Government, like fire, is a useful servant but a dangerous master. It is not eloquence, for not justice, it is pure force."

The instruments of State are designed by men to serve their conveniences. They have no intrinsic natural existence. Just as a righteous man dissociates himself from evil acts of other men and does not support or approve them, so must he dissociate himself from or resist evil acts of State. Actions of State are merely the actions of a group of men proceeding according to their perceived self-interest. These actions have no intrinsic moral superiority to the actions of an individual. To the contrary, it is the common human experience that politicians are far away from being a reliable repository of the highest moral and human values. The chance occurrence of my birth on a certain continent in a certain State does not compel me to surrender my moral sovereignty to the political morality of that State. They hold me in thrall by force alone. It is only raw power projected by the State that forces people into acts of mass destruction. No sane individual does these things. My first loyalty is to humanity as one, to the wholeness of the human species, not to a particular State. Nature [God] did not create national boundaries that divide people one from another. Human divisiveness brings death. Unity is life.

A civil society is harmonious. Harmony means brotherhood. Brotherhood must be supported by just law. Law which places property rights above human rights and which creates a judicial I framework for exploitation of the poor by the rich is not moral law. A person must disregard it. A framework of law, which encourages and promotes destruction of our planetary ecosystem on which all life depends, must be resisted by people of conscience. Life-Liberty-Pursuit of Happiness: we declared our independence to enjoy these inalienable rights. Certainly my freedom not to kill and my happiness in non-violence are abrogated by coercive [including penalty of imprisonment] taxation to finance constant preparation for war, marketing of war and implements of war, waging war and the research development-construction of ever more efficient means to kill more and more people in less and less time. Government behind closed doors and concealed in classified documents: how can this be said to be with the consent of the governed? Not only war, but also all forms of secrecy, lies and compulsion inherent in the powers of State are a violation of humanity.

The highest law is the Law of God, the Law of Truth. Love is God. Love does not kill. The first commandment of Christianity is ***"Thou shall not kill."*** The first morality of the Buddha is to abstain from killing. The first precept of the Hindu and the Jain is Ahimsa, non-violence. Non-violence is the highest morality of man. This morality is of a higher order than any state authority. No State has the right to interfere with a person's sincere efforts to pursue the goal of Self-realization through ***ahimsa.***

I will not voluntarily abide by a law of man which violates my understanding of Law of Truth. Nor will I take the law of man into my own hands. I will disobey such laws as are repugnant to my conscience, taking full personal responsibility for acts of civil disobedience and willingly suffering the full consequences and penalties thereunto appertaining. I declare that obedience to any such repugnant law imposed upon me by force makes of me a slave and thereby violates my basic human right to life and liberty. No man, constituted authority or State has the right to make me a slave.

Ahimsa is not merely the absence of violence. It is an active engagement in compassion. Whenever we consume more than we need, we are engaging in violence. We are stealing from others because using resources beyond one's actual needs depletes what is available to meet the need of others, including other species upon whose survival our own ultimately depends. ***Ahimsa*** means not to encroach upon the economic and ecological rights of others, that is, their right to life.

Perceptions of Fact and Moral Conclusions

Actions of the modern nation-state are based upon false or questionable moral premises, some of which are perceived as follows:

- Man lives by greed rather than by love;
- Nature can be freely exploited-that we can destroy and squander billions of years of biological evolution along with interdependent human Cultures without consequence;
- Human institutions can violate the law of Moral Causation;
- Peace and security can be achieved through war;
- Material progress is man's greatest good, even at the expense of the spiritual;
- Denial of interdependence and interconnectedness of all life;
- Denial of man's responsibility to the whole of life;
- Future material progress can be had by mortgaging life itself to present exploitation;
- Human welfare can be achieved by promoting greed;
- The State possesses moral authority over the individual;
- That politics can be divorced from ethics;
- Exploitation of the weak by the strong is permissible;
- Owners of corporations can be absolved of personal accountability for actions of the corporation;
- Corporations can be granted the rights of persons, including political rights, and that they are bona fide participants in the political process;

- That the end justifies the means;
- That the moral code necessary for harmony among individuals does not apply to the State, that is, the lie of the State is permissible;
- That the State has the right to coerce individuals to support its wrong-doings, even to the level of violence which may exterminate millions of human beings and threaten survival of all life on earth;
- That the State is permitted to violate the laws of Truth [God];
- It is morally acceptable for one State to exploit the people and ecology of another, that is, exploitation is an acceptable aim of politics;
- Economic interests of corporations are senior to welfare of individuals;
- An industrial economy is unequivocally a good thing for all humanity;
- That corporations are the best vehicle for human economic action;
- Ever increasing consumption to support an ever-growing economy is a good thing;
- That property rights and investor rights are senior to human rights;
- That the individual is an economic entity and not a moral agency;
- Propaganda rather than truth is an acceptable means of informing the public; and
- That it is permissible to subsidize corporations.

A necessary prerequisite for a non-violent society is justice in all aspects of life: food, shelter, clothing work, education, health, Opportunity for self-realization. Justice means advancing the good of everyone equally, including the weakest. Humanity is one and harmony must be worldwide.

A proper rule of law requires that human rights of all be equally protected. When a body of law is created which tramples the rights of minorities and the weak, such as Bretton Woods agreements, IMF, GATT and WTO, such law is repugnant to the conscience and must be resisted by non-violent means. If we do not find non-violent methods to resist imperialism in all its different forms, including the imperialism of MNCs, the suppressed races of the world appear to have little hope. A prerequisite for peace is radical limitation of corporate power, a re-defining of the corporation as a legal entity, and the rejection of creating artificial needs, the fulfilment of which harms others. Only that economy is good which conduces to the good of all.

The modern science of political economy is false science because it promotes exploitation of man by man. True science is concerned with the welfare and destiny of all men. This is the science taught by the sages: Buddha, Christ, Confucius, Heraclites, Lao Tse, Mahavira, Moses, and Socrates. That economics is untrue which ignores or disregards moral values. An economics which enables the strong to exploit the weak is dismal as well as fake.

In 1981, fifty-three Nobel Prize winners warned Lis of an unprecedented holocaust, encompassing the horrors of mass exterminations and extending the frontiers of barbarism and death. In 1980, while tens of millions of people were on the verge of starvation, the global war machine engaging 60 million people was squandering nearly a million dollars per minute towards our universal extermination. Today the level of violence is even higher. It is incomprehensible.

The most fundamental of human rights is

the right to life. It is morally wrong to support a group of states in their quest for the power to destroy all life. A righteous person, intent upon spiritual evolution, must resist this. Immoral means employed by the State or its corporate licensees result in doing harm and failing to achieve a good end. It is the inevitable result of the Law of Cause and Effect. A perceived success will be only temporary, while the evil will be long-lasting. The lie of the State at war can never lead to Truth; just as war can never lad to peace. Immoral means predict and determine the ends. Modern science and technology have bestowed upon States power beyond limits. This power is being used in a moral vacuum. Increasing power of the soulless state machine and its heartless corporate licensees, large-scale mechanization and automation, concentration of wealth and power all lead to disintegration of individuals, erosion of basic values, and deprivation of man's right to self actualization.

Statistic corporate capitalism has failed because it lacks a moral code based on true human values. We live in a disintegrating culture. That which is best and noblest in humanity is not nourished. The corporate culture does not cultivate generosity, compassion, charity, morality, cooperation, tolerance, wisdom, self-sacrifice, service to others. It does not encourage gentleness and community, mutual support, and harmony. Miller says:

"The capitalist-technocratic-statistic system has become a monstrous destroyer of what loves and life-affirming in the human soul."

In a traditional society, the family and community constituted the basis of morality. Stealing from one's neighbour would be morally shocking. Now, in public institutions, all manner of corruption is expected, and the consequences are huge, because the corruption involves doing violence to entire cultures and millions of people are made to suffer. This radical separation of ethics from politics, foreshadowed in the long-ago writings of Machiavelli, appears to be a generic feature of the corporate statistic structure.

A corporation has no heart, no soul, no conscience, and no morals. It is not a living being. It cannot feel pain, sorrow, remorse, shame, and compassion because it is intrinsically unable to do so. It cannot laugh or cry, enjoy the world, or suffer with it. Most of all, it cannot love. This is because it is a legal fiction; its ***"body"*** is a judicial construct. It is a process, a machine designed for one purpose: to generate maximum revenue at least cost. It is not connected to earth or its creatures, to pleasures, and responsibilities that derive from being human node of earth. When it hurts people or destroys ecology, it feels nothing. It is incapable of feeling. Yet, under law, it is deemed a ***"natural person"*** with all the legal and political rights of a person except for actual voting. This is why corporations are so dangerous: they act in human affairs without feeling and with wholly selfish motives. And they have become very powerful, in some case; more powerful than the host government of which they are a parasite.

Not only does the corporation have the rights of a citizen [such as free speech, right to sue for slander, libel, injury], but it has been granted special protection over property rights. Rate of return on investment has been declared a ***"property"*** immune to interference by citizens or their elected representatives. Under U. S. law they are also granted ***"eminent domain,"*** pursuant to which jury trials were eliminated for determining whether corporate practices cause harm or injury, and if so, the assessment of damages.

The fatal moral flaw which makes these corporations so dangerous to the social body upon which they feed like a cancer is a legal design error. Their owner, the shareholder% is protected by law Koran legal and personal liability for corporate harm to humanity or damage to ecology. It is an attempt by men to create a shield that protects them from consequences of their actions. It is an attempt to violate the Law of Cause and Effect, the law of moral causation. There is no personal accountability of the owners to society. The corporation has no social, responsibility... yet it has legal and political rights by legislative construct. It is a dangerous entity, pursuing only its ***"genetic"*** programme to generate profit without concern for long term consequences to humanity. Can you imagine the outrage that would land on the heads of individuals had they committed some of the crimes of corporations which are as commonplace in the news as to have become routine?

"The special status of corporations has placed them in a position to control vast economic power by which they may dominate not only the economy but also the very heart of our democracy, the electoral process."

"The liberty of democracy is not safe if people tolerate the growth of private power to a point where it becomes stronger than the state it itself. That, in essence, is fascism-ownership of government by an individual, a group, or any controlling private power." [Franklin D. Roosevelt].

President Abraham Lincoln Opined:

"I see a crisis approaching that unnerves me and causes me to tremble for the safety of my country. As a result of the war, corporation

has been enthroned; an era of corruption in high places will follow and the money power of the country will endeavour to prolong its reign by working on the prejudices of the people until wealth is aggregated in a few hands, and the republic is destroyed."

The 500 largest corporations in the world now control 25% of the entire world economic output. The largest 300 corporations own 25% of the world's productive assets. The 50 largest commercial banks and diversified financial companies control nearly 60% of all global capital.

According to Paul Hellyer, Deputy Prime Minister of Canada:

"Globalization is not about trade. It is about power and control. It is reshaping the world into one without borders ruled by a dictatorship of the world's most powerful central banks, commercial banks and multinational companies!"

The prime role of government has been usurped by corporations in order to provide a secure legal environment for profitable transnational investment and competition, that is, security for capital, property, and investors but not for ordinary citizens. The erroneous premise of this role for government is that property rights are senior to human rights, and that the earth and its biological life can be owned and exploited rather than shared and nurtured.

No taxation without Representation: this issue of social justice was at the core of the American Revolution. Beginning with the Bretton Woods international agreements in 194, followed by the Trilateral Commission of David Rockefeller and other efforts organized by elite power-brokers, control of representative government has been systematically transferred from the people to corporations. As shown in the preceding paragraphs, it is not possible for corporations to have an unbiased interest in the public welfare. Documented instances of corporate abuse of the public and the environment are too numerous to list. Campaign contributions and the lobbying arms of huge businesses control elections, legislation and public policy. Powerful men hold in a ***"revolving door"*** rotation high public office and directorships of MNCs, which are members of the military industrial government complex, an unholy and incestuous relationship of regulator and regulated. Reality on the ground is that our ***"democratic government"*** and both of its major political parties are controlled by corporations, not citizens. It is a false moral premise that in a democracy these entities should have political rights and political voice. It is not possible for corporations to represent the will of the people. Thus we the people are de-facto taxed without representation. We have no effective voice in a government controlled by corporations.

Now, through the International Monetary Fund [IMF], World Bank, General Agreement on Trade & Tariffs [GATT], and the World Trade Organization [WTO] at policy level, coordinated through the unholy marriage of governments, central banks and MNCs [multinational corporations] at the operational level, sovereignty of politically constituted governments Ins been usurped by MNCs. The WTO has created an ***"Economic Constitution"*** of the world. Economic exchange is at the core of human action and affects every aspect of life: environment, education, health, labour and political rights, and war. The scale of corporate activity has become so large that it affects the most fundamental right: the right to life itself. Millions of the world's poorest people are deprived of adequate livelihood and health by corporate actions which destroy their ecology and local economies like constitutions, trade agreements set forth rights of their constituents. But these ***"constitutions"*** have been negotiated behind closed doors with input only from corporations. Under W. T. O., only corporations are the beneficiaries of the rights it creates. The interests of others in society are nowhere to be found.

An international agency of corporate constituents has the power to veto parliamentary decisions made by sovereign governments wherever these decisions are ruled ***"trade restrictive."*** At risk are environmental protection, Labour and health law, consumer protection law, control of foreign exchange and massive flows of speculative capital which can so disrupt local economies as to cause the recent Asian economic crisis which did untold damage to the lives of millions of poor people. The agency's proceedings are closed: trade unions, consumer, health and environmental groups are barred. Details of rulings are not published. Members of decision making bodies are not disclosed to the public. Everything is anonymous and there is no public accountability.

These MNCs, which have substantial control over legislation as well as executive branch policy, are hugely subsidized directly and indirectly [that is, global transport and communications infrastructure, R&D, agriculture] with public funds generated through taxation of individuals. Yet they meet in secret, operate clandestinely, and are not accountable to the public. This is truly abusive taxation without representation. Having gained control of political parties and the electoral process, corporations have usurped the government of the people and have created a tyranny. We the people have no effective voice, yet we subsidize these entities with our taxes.

There are other issues with respect to taxation without representation. In 1776 the tyrant was the British King. Today it is an institutionalized structural tyranny of rule by corporations masquerading as democracy. The people vote each 2 to 4 years for, usually [if you ask them], the lesser of two evils both of whom were put in place by corporate money. It is a sham democracy. Corporations are the real power-they forma ***"capitalist junta,"*** a collective dictatorship. The ***"nominees"*** that we elect are not only beholden to the corporations which finance and control the outcome, but sometimes they are shareholders of the same corporations which will come under their regulatory and policy purview. It is incestuous.

Foreign policy is made by people who own banks and corporations which profit from preparing for war, marketing the war machine, and waging war. To find the roots of war, follow the money. War may be couched in terms of freedom, democracy, justice, religion, but if you follow the money, it leads to powerful decision-makers whose constituents in banking and industry profit from war or the exploitation which leads to war. Wars are fought with money borrowed from the public, the employment of which enriches bankers and owners of the military-industrial complex. Only a morally flawed structure permits these owners to influence war decisions.

The recent Afghan situation is one example of many. In India it is widely known that Big Oil, the U. S. G. and Pakistan coordinated early support of Taliban in order to secure access for Big Oil to the fields of Central Asia. Subsequently they destroyed their creation. Now they will rebuild Afghanistan without having lost sight of the original objective: access to oil of Central Asia. It has been reported in the press that families of high

U. S. officials own shares in, among others, Halliburton, Unocal and Carlyle [oil and defence], companies which stand to profit from operations related to the war. No personal allegations are intended herein. I hold malice towards none. The point is that a political structure which permits State decision makers to benefit financially from activities of the State over which they have influence is morally wrong. The set-up is such that MNCs benefit from war while it is being marketed and waged and again profit from post war reconstruction. It is like a meat grinder with human beings the raw feed.

Killing is never justified, but certainly its lowest threshold is self-defence. There can be no justification for killing in the name of some ***"national interest,"*** invariably an economic interest determined by power brokers and not ordinary citizens. No villager is justified in murdering members of another village for their corn. How can USG be justified in murdering for oil? The sheer size and worldwide pervasive presence of the U. S. military establishment, emplaced to protect corporate interests, is attestation to an incomprehensible level of violence. This worldwide projection of power is used to facilitate and expedite economic and ecological exploitation of weaker and poorer people. On the basis of what wisdom has the USG determined that its wasteful, destructive, death-dealing culture is superior to others? True rationality must involve both freedom and foresight. The rationale of unbridled capitalist economics is unable to foresee and calculate future costs in terms of human displacement and disenfranchisement with ensuring class hatred and violence. What gives the U. S. the moral authority to impose this way of life upon others together with the right to defend it at any cost-including nuclear holocaust against the feeble efforts of hapless millions to secure mere survival? Through economic might and leverage we exploit wherever possible. When economic power is insufficient to the purpose, we use armed might.

What was the moral basis for USG's destruction of millions of lives in Vietnam? Under whose code of ethics did USG rain napalm bombs on non-combatant Cambodia, incinerating thatched hut villages along with women anti children, resulting in the destabilization that subsequently spawned the ***"killing fields"***? Whose killing fields are they, really? The list of incomprehensible atrocities could fill a book. It turns the stomach. The human mind has become so brutalized by all-pervasive violence [often gratuitous a, ***"entertainment"*** viewed by small children] that we seem to have become de-sensitized to the point of having lost all sense of moral outrage. We are morally passive in the face of atrocity. The moral scale of society has shrunk to the point that wanton waste of life and destructiveness is ***"normal."***

Tax dollars not only finance directly the military machine, but also through direct and indirect subsidy the life-destroying operations of MNCs. The huge infrastructures of transportation, electric-power, communications media, global-trade, R&D for chemicals, pesticides, agriculture, and biotech are publicly financed. Taxes are subsidizing corporations which stand accused in the judicial system of criminal activities, child abuse, and crimes against humanity [Tobacco and Big Oil]. Taxes subsidize alliances between Big Oil and brutal military regimes in Africa anti Burma. In the 1960s, the USG organized a military overthrow of Brazilian President Jose Goulart. He had instituted capital and land reforms to take back control from MNCs of Brazil's natural resources and had defied the IMF. An alliance of the CIA with US investors and Brazil's landowning elite organized a coup and installed a military junta which overturned Goulart's reforms.

A military infrastructure is needed to keep the structure of globalization in place and to guarantee access to natural resources on which the model depends. The hidden hand of the market will never work without a hidden fist. McDonald's cannot flourish without McDonnell Douglas to build the Stealth Bomber. The hidden fist that keeps the world safe for Silicon Valley's technologies is the U. S. Army, Air Force, Navy, Marine Corps. Keeping the world ***"safe"*** for global corporations does not come cheap: just ensuring the steady supply of oil is costing U. S. taxpayers $57 billion annually. For the targets of military power worldwide, obviously the costs of globalization are much higher." Taxes subsidize increasing international trade which means increasing pollution and destruction. Corporations control the political system which grants these subsidies: they are the driving force behind both the nation-state and globalization. Tax dollars finance crimes against Lie and the same entities which commit the crimes have control of the political system. It is tyranny.

In summary, our planetary ecosystem is being shredded by the violence of greed to fulfil artificial needs, its species genetically engineered, poisoned and displaced, a majority of the world's peoples [the gentlest ones] impoverished, disenfranchised, displaced. Society is devolving into violence and debauchery. Life is being destroyed on all fronts: commercial, military, political, and social. Nowhere is there silence. The key is dirty, the waters poisoned. This vast interconnected killing machine is being financed with tax dollars paid by people who have no effective voice. We have become slaves to an inhuman machine of corporate components-heartless, as Gandhi said, soulless, conscienceless, yet by legal construct ***"natural persons"*** with political rights. We the people created this monster. We the people can peacefully, non-violently, reprogrammed it.

Vie Decision to Resist

Gathering of Elders, Pasquah, Canada: Indigenous Spiritual leaders had come from around the world. The Cree Elder had asked my profession. Upon my response, he said:

"You are like a bank robber. First your people took our animals, then they took our fish, then they took our trees. Then they began breaking even the rocks of Earth herself and taking them. You pushed us from our homelands onto the reserves. Now you are going to flood even the little bat 6 leas to us so that your hydro power project will keep the houses of your big city people cool in summer. You people are like termites eating their own house. What will you do when there is no home left for anyone?"

Chihuahua City [CUU], Mexico, Environmental Conference: The World Bank was financing a project to log the last of old growth forest in Sierra Occidental where the Tarahumara Indians are struggling to survive. The timber is to feed a paper pulp mill. Before an audience of scientists, bureaucrats, environmentalists, and trade officials assembled in University of Chihuahua auditorium stands a Tarahumara Elder. In his hand is a cheap magazine, a transmission of filth. Gazing calmly at the bankers and industrialists, the Tarahumara speaks softly. Holding up the trash magazine, he said:

"You are cutting the last of our trees to

turn them into this. The forest is the life of my people. When you have cut the trees, we will die, and you will read this."

A few miles from the auditorium [***Tarahumara***] women and children are living in burrows dug into mounds of garbage at the city dump. At a small village in the Sierra, a ***Tarahumara*** elder had said:

"I tell my young men riot to fight. I tell them we must be patient, we must wait. The white man will destroy himself."

I had piloted my personal aircraft to CUU to provide volunteer flight service for a conservation organization. The mission was to fly opinion makers for a direct took at logging devastation. But now I knew for sure that my whole lifestyle made me part of the problem. If I sincerely wished to become part of the solution, I must entirely change my way of life.

Man does not lose his freedom except through his own ignorance. The primary ignorance at play in a corporate-statistic society is ignorance of the Law of Cause and Effect, the Law of Moral Causation, and at a deeper level the Truth of Dependent Origination. Freedom and slavery are mental states. First say to ourselves we shall no longer accept the role of slave. Then be willing to act and suffer the consequences. There is no high destiny without self-denial.

Law of ***Ahimsa*** [Law of Love]: Non-violence is the law of the human race and is infinitely greater than and superior to brute force. It requires a living faith and commitment to Truth, which is Love [or God if you prefer]. It is inconsistent with modern imperialism which is based on force for its defence. It protects one's self-respect but not his property. Non-violence can be practiced by all if they have a living faith in Truth and therefore equal love for all mankind. Moral activity on behalf of others is self- realization because humanity is one.

"In order to see face to face the universal and all penetrating Truth, we must be able to love even the least of creatures as we love ourselves. The man who attempts this cannot be indifferent to anything in life. Ahimsa overrides all other forces-it is the only true force in life."

"***Seek ye first the Kingdom of Heaven and all else shall be added unto you. The Kingdom of Heaven is Ahimsa,"*** Gandhi said.

It requires renunciation of violence in the heart with consequent conscious exercise of the power of Ahimsa generated by the renunciation.

The pre-eminence of these principles is made known to me through my personal moral conscience, reason, and life experience. These Laws have been expounded by the great sages of humanity, not notable in my studies of the Buddha, Christ, Lao Tse, and Mahavira. In modern times they have been exemplified by Gandhi, Leo Tolstoy, John Ruskin, and Henry David Thoreau. I have drawn on the inspiration of these and others to organize my thoughts into a plan of action.

Principal axioms of theory and practice of non-violent resistance: Evil is parasitic on good, inhumanity on humanity. No man is entirely devoid of humanity. Suffering, accepted in the spirit of non-violent witness to truth, can restore to a person his lost humanity. All exploitation is based upon cooperation, willing or forced, of the exploited. Non-cooperation and fearlessness go together. The non-violent resister fights with his power of suffering, arouses his opponent's power of sympathy and so restores him to his humanity while restoring to himself justice denied. Non-violent struggle properly conducted, even if it fails, leaves behind no trail of bitterness. Passive resistance is a method of securing rights by personal suffering. It is the reverse of resistance by arms. It involves sacrifice of the self. Sacrifice of the self is superior to sacrifice of others. Civil disobedience serves all, including the tyrant, by teaching him his error. Evil can only be sustained by violence; therefore withdrawal of support for evil requires complete abstention from violence. Non-violence requires voluntary submission to the penalty of non-cooperation with evil. The government itself does not expect our full cooperation. It does not to say: ***"You must do this."*** It says: ***"If you do not do this, we will punish you."*** Sincerity of a moral position requires willingness to accept the costs necessary to see the principles realized. When it violates his moral conscience, no person will submit to the evil of another or group of others except under coercion. The means pre-exist in, predict and determine the end. It is impossible for violent means to achieve moral ends.

Justification for Civil Disobedience: When the injustice is great and morally unendurable, when it is of a nature that can be resolved by non cooperation, when the offence is real to the best of one's knowledge and belief, when administrative recourse is not reasonably available or after thorough examination is deemed to be ineffective, the goal must accord with natural right. The resister must not hate his opponent. The goal must conduce to the good of all.

Certain prerequisites for Civil Disobedience: The following are required in order to earn the moral authority to make a distinction between moral and immoral law. One must have obeyed consistently the law of his country. He must have served society. Must have embarked upon the work of self-purification and be adhering to the five basic moral precepts. Must have met his family obligations and made arrangements for them to be covered in his absence; must be prepared for self-sacrifice, discomfort, possibly hardship. One cannot disobey the law while continuing to live under its protection and with its comforts which are financed by the other citizens who are obeying it. One must strive for harmony of thought-word-deed. To think one thing, say another, and do a third is a lie. One must be prepared to embark upon a programme of constructive service to humanity along with self-sacrifice.

Having, tried hard to understand the ***Law of Ahimsa***, to meet its prerequisites in my personal life, to prepare myself for self-purification and a life of sacrifice and to embark upon a programme of constructive humanitarian service, I committed myself to a personal solo programme of civil disobedience. I hereby declare that I have deliberately disobeyed the tax regulations of my country [but perhaps not the underlying Constitution and Law]. I make distinction between regulation, law, and Constitution because I believe them to be inconsistent and because law and regulation are so complex and permeated with obfuscation as to be incomprehensible to me. The regulations as promulgated in IRS publications seem clear on one point: if a person fails to file and pay taxes due, he is subject to civil and criminal penalties. I hereby serve notice upon authorities of the USG that I have deliberately failed to file tax returns as an act of conscious civil disobedience. I also declare that no taxes are due, as wilt be set forth in the following.

I admit that I have often been unable to act according to the highest moral law, which rules thought as well as word and deed. This does not invalidate the law, it demonstrates the practical difficulties. Geometry is not less true because I may not be able to draw a straight line. I can only take one step at a time. The point of beginning is my capability for non-violence now, to be improved one day at a time. The point of departure for moral practice is prevailing morality, which must be changed, one action at a time towards the goal.

My Personal Programme of Civil Disobedience

As I slowly progressed in self-purification and spiritual growth through meditation practice as taught by the Buddha, the inner moral conflict and despair arising from the knowledge that my labour-through the income tax was being used to kill innocent civilians, women, and children, at many places around the world became unbearable. It became imperative to act in order to save myself from internal disintegration. At first I reacted out of anger and despair at the desecration which was being financed by my labour. As my meditation practice deepened, it became clear that anger was only hurting me and doing nothing to cure the human ignorance, which is the root cause of evil. Gradually I desisted from putting more fuel on the fire of anger. Anger attenuated and was replaced with first forgiveness and then compassion for those people caught in the great MNC killing machine. The call to action metamorphosed into anguished love with malice towards none. Now, my actions are designed with such mindfulness as I can muster to rotate anger at a system gone mad with the violence of its greed into compassion for evil-doers, while dissociating myself from them and from the system. I am doing my best to walk the path pointed by Buddha and Gandhi: self-purification through meditation, renunciation of worldly pleasures and comforts, combined with a constructive programme of humanitarian service. I undertook a moral inventory of my deeds in relation to my government. I served my country across a span of 30 years in a range of voluntary humanitarian and public service. My work received awards and recognition from all levels of citizenship, including local community organizations, a State governor, Secretary of the U. S. Cabinet and the President. As an entrepreneur, I founded companies that created hundreds of jobs and financed a lot of kids through school, paid a lot of taxes. I founded non-profit charitable organizations, co-created a new Montessori school, an adult learning centre and indigenous social programmes. I did significant work in the largest Native American land settlement in history. I obeyed the laws of my country. To this extent I hid earned the moral authority to make my decision.

I examined the possibilities of actual, practical, timely administrative recourse in terms of an individual obtaining permission to cease filing and paying income taxes on the basis of conscience. It is my natural right to act as an individual and not be required to be a member of an ***"authorized"*** organization. No organization has moral sovereignty over my conscience. I have had long personal experience with government at all levels and with the judiciary. They are not bona fide repositories of high moral wisdom. The closer the approach to inner circles of power, the more pervasive are corruption and the lie. I and my companies had been through tax audit with 100% clean marks no adjustments. Some of my acquaintances were not so lucky I am well-informed of the abuse of citizens through tax audits. The invasive procedures of auditors into personal affairs of citizens are an unwarranted violation of the Bill of Rights the power to tax is the power to destroy. The lives of many citizens have been destroyed by IRS abuses. Thee methods keep the public intimidated. Those who request to keep back the ***"war tax"*** portion of their payment on the basis of religion are flagged for special treatment and Subjected to harassment. It is vicious. I studied these matters for long. Based upon my observations and commonsense, it is clear that a citizen acting as an individual has no chance against the government in matters of conscientious objection to the income tax [I note that the destructive activities of the military-industrial-MNC complexes are so systematically embedded that withholding the ***"war portion"*** of a tax is ineffective. It would be like trying to distinguish blood corpuscles which serve the liver from those that serve the lung]. The State has framed the rules. I cannot prevail in a petition brought within the bounds of We self-same rules which my conscience requires me to disobey. I can only act as guided by my conscience in response to my perception of events and my understanding of a civil human society. My choice as a moral being was to take me the path of civil disobedience. These words are not by way of defence, but simply a description so that rational people may have a basis for understanding my actions. I am a simple human being trying to live my ideals. If I run afoul of the State, let it do with me as it wishes.

It is incomprehensible that any government has a moral right to force a person to kill, or through taxation to finance killing and even mass extermination of innocent human beings. How can I support war crimes, human rights violations, crimes against humanity? During the past 50 years the USG has built an inhuman machinery of escalating violence that threatens all life with extinction. The government, having no moral right to require my participation, must rely on brute force to coerce my payment of taxes. Certainly this meets the test of ***"a great and unendurable tyranny."*** If I submit to this, I become a slave I cannot obey the law without violating my conscience and my loyalty to the human race. My choice was to participate as automation in the organized, systematic destruction of life or to withdraw from participation in the corporate-controlled society. The only safe and honourable course for me to keep my self-respect was to disobey and willingly face the penalties.

Having made the decision to cease filing and paying income tax, I undertook a radical reorganization of my life. I would have to emigrate, to become a ***"tax exile."*** It would not be right to benefit from the facilities and protection of my country while not paying my share. Reorganization had to be in gradual steps bemuse of obligations to children. Only when the youngest reached majority could I make the final move. Withdrawing from my businesses, I began devoting myself to a wide range of humanitarian service without pay. I ceased generating income and lived on savings. Personal property of every description was sold to the point of a simple lifestyle. Stocks and securities were sold at substantial losses. Corporate and partnership businesses were divested at large losses. Proceeds were placed in non-interest-bearing accounts so as to generate no income deposits at interest are indiscriminately loaned to government and business involved.

A destruction of life, hence interest ***"earnings"*** are the wages of death. Losses cm asset sales generated a large Net Operating Loss Carry Forward. The needs of My Simple lifestyle could be met out of savings on which taxes had already been paid.

No income tax would be due for remainder of my life. As a tax protestor I cannot in good conscience make a claim for Social Security retirement benefits. The funds I paid to Social Security over a period of more than 40 years are lost to me. It is part of the price of freedom.

When my youngest child reached majority, I moved to India. I ceased filing tax returns. Demands by mail notwithstanding, I believe that filing is not required if the taxpayer has no income. In my circumstances, the demands for information are an unwarranted violence upon my person, my privacy, my right to personal security and to be left alone to pursue my peaceful life. I will not respond. I declare myself to be a free man, no longer a slave to the great MNC-government killing machine.

The path of civil disobedience marked out by Gandhi requires self-sacrifice, self-purification, and a constructive humanitarian programme to run alongside the action of non-cooperation with evil. Here in an Indian village I rent two rooms of stone and mud, take two meals per day of rice-lentils-chapatti, bathe with a bucket of hand-carried cold water and use the same open field toilet as my Indian hosts. My basic cost of living is about Rs.2000 per month [less than $50]. I maintain a serious practice of Buddhist meditation, practice eight precepts [includes complete celibacy] to the extent possible and fast for one day each week. I have helped build two meditation retreat centres and am working towards a third. I tutor English, do voluntary service at meditation centres, help build village schools, establish libraries, sponsor education of refugee children and a tuberculosis programme, and assist in agricultural and reforestation work. I work to contribute to the pool of quietitude and peace in human consciousness, to balm the brutality of Western imperialism, to save our ecosystem from destruction. I organize my life around the ultimate goal of self-realization, the birthright of every human being.

My decision to undertake civil disobedience through emigration and self-imposed exile has entailed some hardship and risk. My wife refused to live in India and found long periods of separation to be unacceptable. She divorced me. The life of an aging foreigner alone and homeless in India is not easy. It is painful to be separated from family, friends, and homeland. There are problems with safe water, food, health, sanitation, and personal security. The cold of snowy winter in unheated rooms is penetrating. Support arrangements are unstable and keep on dissolving. Obstacles of language and culture are daunting. It is a 2-3 day journey by jeep, bus, and train to the nearest bona fide medical doctor. Hospitals of which I have personal knowledge are filthy and septic. Disease is prevalent, civil disturbances are rampant, and war is an ever-present threat. Everywhere I witness poverty, misery, and suffering.

The Ground of Being

High above a mountain village in the ***Himalaya***, on the way towards a place, where I hope to build a meditation hut, I stop to rest at an alpine meadow. A breath-taking visa of Me Grant, "***Himalaya Range stretches for 200 miles. An eagle soars on afternoon thermals as towering thunderheads rise into a Cerulean sky.***"

May remembrance of untrammelled wilderness and a vibrant web of natural life do not vanish from the mind of man? May beauty and the Mystery unlock the latent urge to inquire within ***"Who***

am I? From where have I come? Where am I going? How may I understand, penetrate the cause of birth, old age, decay and death? How shall I live?"

Against this awesome grandeur, one witnesses human wretchedness and realizes the depth of his moral responsibility, a Universal Responsibility towards all beings. My every action affects directly or indirectly the welfare of my fellowmen. The first morality and the first service to others are the same: do no harm.

May I learn from this mountain villager's fewness of wishes and generosity? May I learn to simplify and to use least possible in order that others may live. May I learn to nourish the life-support system of our shared earth? Whatever I have accumulated during my earthly sojourn will remain here upon my demise, so let me learn to share it. Only qualities of heart and mind will accompany me to the next world, there to determine my destiny.

Answering to the war drum becomes unthinkable. The pole star of peace beckons to quiet walks in the woods, or to comforting a child, or communing with a cow [so calm, gentle and nourishing, a cow]. Communing with a cow reminds me of my identity with all that lives.

In a world gone mad with the violence of its greed, a way must be made to the peace and compassion by which alone humanity may survive. Love alone transfigures hatred. ***Ahimsa***, non-violence, is the working force of love.

May the generosity, helpfulness, patience, and forbearance of these mountain villagers inspire all who come here' to renew their connection with others and with Nature. May these villagers and all their visitors be successful! May them all experience real happiness, real peace, and real harmony!

Einstein said: ***"Humanity's problems cannot be solved at the same level of thinking that created them."*** Tolstoy wrote: ***"Love is what men live by,"*** and Gandhi believed: ***"In the midst of death, life persists. In midst of untruth, truth persists. In the midst of darkness, light persists. Hence God is life, truth, love. There is underlying all change a living power that is changeless, holds all together, creates, dissolves, and recreates. This informing power or spirit is God."***

20
Mahatma Gandhi and His Inherent Love for Unity

Mrinalini Sarabhai

Mahatma Gandhi had a deep inherent love for unity, not only amongst human beings but of all life on our planet.

"There is orderliness in the universe. There is an unalterable law governing everything and every being that exists or lives. It is no blind law, for no blind law can govern the conduct of living beings."

Today, when in Gandhiji's Gujarat, violence has spread, violence not only against human beings, but against nature, we wonder how humanity has gone astray. Gandhiji's fundamentals of constructing and conserving an ideal human society always emphasized that every ***"expression of life is interconnected; even nature when exploited beyond limits, revolts, and a host of calamities befall the societies concerned."***

It is imperative that we as citizens of our country strive to eliminate the evils that beset us. Primarily, the elimination of poverty, protection against the abuse of women and exploitation, and environmental degradation, is violence against nature.

He pictured an India continually evolving along the lives best suited to her genius which will have all Indians belonging to different religions, living in perfect friendship. He constantly repeated the words:

"If Hinduism is to live, untouchablity must die." Yet the terrible attacks continue .... ***"Untouchablity poisons Hinduism as a drop of arsenic poisons milk."***

Just outside the Gandhi ***Ashram***, there stood a row of majestic Adusi trees. In spite of protests, they were hacked down. Along the gently flowing river Sabarmati, roads are being constructed. Noise pollution and dirt will soon follow. No citizen can protest. Sadly there is no one to listen. Yet we must persist as Individuals, we must nurture and cherish those values that Gandhiji left for us. We must strive!! As he did!

21

Gandhian Institutions and Unfinished Work of Ba and Bapu: Some Reflections

Rama Rauta

Ba and Bapu are two sides of the same coin. They stand for a culture of Truth and non-violence, i.e. a culture of pursuit of ethical perfection as the ultimate goal of life and pursuit of selfless ethical life of universal love as its means: the essence of Gandhian Philosophy is that Truth is the ultimate goal of life and non-violence is its means. Contrary to the widely accepted view that spirituality belongs to the domain of mysticism, Gandhiji sees clearly that it belongs essentially to the domain of ethics. Unlike for most modern intellectuals, for him ***"to lead a spiritual life"***, and ***"to lead a religious life"*** essentially mean the same as to lead a selfless ethical life of love, and non-violence constitutes the essence of ethics; unlike for them, for him ***"to realize God"***, ***"to realize Truth"***, ***"to realize self"***, ***"to realize liberation"*** essentially mean the same as to realize an enlightened perfect selfless ethical life of love. Unlike them, he sees clearly that the peace and happiness, which involves in a liberated life is not only ever lasting but also of the highest kind

In the beginning of 20^{eth} century in his ***Hind Swaraj***, Gandhiji made a severe condemnation of modern western civilization and articulated an alternative to it involving essentially retelling the basic values of the great teachers and seers of our classical Indian civilization in the context of our present technological age. It was his firm conviction that in the materialization of his vision lay the true freedom of India, and through India of the world at large. He considered the modern western civilization to be essentially an irreligious false civilization in the sense that selfless ethical love, which constitutes the essence of religious life, has no place or only peripheral place in it, and what it considers to be the ultimate goal of life is essentially false. He did not change this view till the end of his life. He sees clearly that the basic values of all great religions are essentially the same.

It is very sad to see that today the modern civilization, which Gandhiji denounced to be a soulless civilization of lust for pleasure and wealth, is spreading like a wild fire throughout the country, and the basic values of our classical Indian civilization, which Gandhi regarded to be essentially a true civilization, are disappearing from the core of our hearts. While various traditional major forms of violence, such as injustice to women, caste and class injustice, communalism, exploitation of rural masses by the urban still continue to exist even 58 years after our independence, a potentially much greater kind of violence in the form of pollution and destruction of forests and wildlife is rapidly growing in the name of development. It is greatly agonizing to see that Gandhians and Gandhian Institutions are hardly doing anything substantial to complete the unfinished work our beloved ***Bapu,*** the apostle of Truth and non-violence of our age.

Let us have a national Gandhian movement to complete the unfinished work of our beloved ***Bapuji,*** a movement to save and purify our civilization, a movement to have a rational culture of truth and non-violence where all religions could grow harmoniously, and where development could take place with loving care of our life sustaining natural systems and their countless kinds of invaluable flora and fauna. Let us transform our Gandhian institutions in to centers of Gandhian thought and action for creating such a movement. Let the Kasturba Gandhi National Memorial Trust [KGNMT], which pays homage to ***MATRISHAKTI***-Mother.

Power-lead such a movement. No lasting Gandhian movement is possible without deep rational conviction about the truth of the Gandhian thought. Hence as a first major step in this direction, every Gandhian institution should have regular formal as well as informal critical study of and reflection over the fundamental aspects of Gandhian thought about various aspects of life- spiritual, moral, social, economical, political, educational, etc. They should have simple ***Dharmashalas*** for participants from the rural side in various meetings/ seminars/ workshops/ conferences, etc to be conducted regularly for rural empowerment with the help of available like-minded persons and institutions. Deliberations over Gandhian thought should be transferred to the masses through a separate TV Channel or through various available religious and cultural TV channels like ***ASTHA, SAMSKAR***, ***Q-T.V***, etc. It is deeply painful to note that even The Gandhi National Memorial & Kasturba Gandhi Trust at Aga khan Palace, Pune, where Kasturba spent her last years with Gandhiji in prison, does not have regular deliberations on Gandhian thought; it does not even have at present a library on Gandhian thought. The same is more or less true in the case of our other Gandhian Institutions.

We must transform our Gandhian institutions in to centers of moral and spiritual awareness and inter-religious dialogue on the one hand, and into centers of rural, women empowerment based on Truth& non-violence on the other hand. Posterity will condemn us and curse us if we allow our Gandhian institutions to die when they could play a great role to build a culture of Truth and non-violence in our great country.

22

Gandhi, Non-Violence and Future of Mankind

C. S. Dharmadhikari

As it is rightly said by the Director of UNICEF, ***"the gulf between the young and adults seems to be growing every day not only in the universities, but in society as a whole. With their needs for absolutes the young are less then ever able to tolerate injustice and disorders of the world".*** Thus, the difference between the capacity of younger and older generations to tolerate injustice and corruption is a real generation gap. There is no use in condemning and criticizing the younger generation, when my generation has failed to reach them the values of life as propagated by Mahatma Gandhi. It is true that on 15th August, 1947, we achieved political independence. But Mahatma Gandhi always used the word ***'Swaraj'*** and not 'independence'. There is a vast difference between independence and freedom. Political independence we did get, but can it be said that we got freedom from inequality or freedom from exploitation of all kinds i.e. economic, religious, social and political? Unless this is achieved, there cannot be peace in the world. When, therefore, the youth or students revolt, though many times wrongly, we have no right to condemn them. As rightly said by Oscar Wilde:

"Disobedience in the eyes of any one who has read history, is man's original virtue; it is through disobedience that progress has been made, through disobedience and rebellion."

The well – known report of the United Nations on human environment tell us that, ***"the emotional attachment to our prized diversity need not interfere with our attempts to develop the global state of mind which will generate the rational loyalty to the planet as a whole. As we enter the global phase of human evolution, it becomes obvious, that each man has two countries, his own, and the planet earth. Now that all habitable parts of the globe are occupied, the careful husbandry of the earth is sine qua non for the survival of the human species and for creation of decent ways of life for all the people of the world".***

But unfortunately even today, people are exploiting nature. The moot question is whether nature is our ally or enemy. The very word 'exploit' is explosive. If we treat nature as our enemy, then man cannot survive on this planet. The last century was a century of conquering nature. I am told, though I am not an expert in the field, that small bird, like sparrows are vanishing because of widespread of mobile phones etc. Modernization has become the latest orthodoxy. We are forgetting that modernization is not necessarily modernity. In this process of modernization, ***'horse power'*** is valued more then ***'man power'***. The 'standard of spending' is equated with the 'standard of living'. Gresham's law that 'bad money drives good money out of the market' is not only prevalent in the market but is also in vogue in social and political circles. I need not speak about Globalization or arm twisting market economy. I hope he will tell us about is. But I must draw your attention to the conclusion reached by the

'Wisdom Bank' of Japan, that Japan is manufacturing artificial wisdom so that men need not use their brains. It is also manufacturing artificial Needs so that greed should become need.

It was on 11th September, 1906, a Movement was started in South Africa, by Mahatma Gandhi, which ultimately came to be known as ***"Satyagraha".*** Initially the name given to this movement was ***"Passive resistance".*** This was resorted by those, who had either no right to Vote or were otherwise, weak. They were not averse to use of arms, if possible, for the attainment of their aims. On the other hand, ***Satyagraha*** is soul force, pure and simple. ***Satyagrahis*** never used physical force, and that too although there were occasions, and when they were in a position to use it effectively. In a sense this was non – violent assistance in the right direction. This year we are celebrating Centenary of this advent of ***Satyagraha***, which started form 11th of Sept. 2005.

We may call it coincidence or destiny; it was on 11th September, that the World Trade Center was demolished. After this demolition US President – George Bush – remembered Gandhiji. After the said tragedy a new Youth Organization has been founded in the United States, named as ***"We want Peace, not War".*** There is another organization known as ***"Seeds of Peace ".***

There is also one more organization of Muslim Youth , who wonders as to whether , it is just and fair to call every Muslim a friend of Bin Laden ? They also observed that it is very easy to live as a Hindu , as a Muslim ,as a Buddhist , as Christian , but it has become very difficult to live as a pure and simple human – being . A point is also raised by these organization that after nine – eleven, though it is difficult to forget the destruction and demolition of the World Trade Center in New York the backlash of hatred can not end terrorism . It is not possible to forget this atrocity, but will it be correct to hate a person whom we did not know , whom we have never seen , about whom we have never heard ? If this hatred is possible , then why it is not possible to love an unseen , unknown and unheard person ? This is a most question , which is relevant even today .

The 20eth Century was the most violent period in human history. More people have suffered and have been killed by organized violence than any other time before. The wars, the genocides, the weapons of mass destruction have created such an enormous mass misery and agony that it is difficult to find any trace of hope. Therefore, Gandhi's teaching of non- violence is most relevant today. This is the reason why amidst report of increasing teenage violence across the United States, a Bill has been introduced in the New Jersey Assembly seeking to include Mahatma Gandhi's teachings of non-violence in the school curriculum. On 12th May, 2000, on Mother's Day in New York , several thousand mothers resolved and demanded a ban on the manufacture of arms, and its use . Therefore, in my view the teaching of Gandhi is not only relevant but also the only alternative. If we follow Gandhi's principle, then it is my belief that this century will be the century of Peace.

Recently, Wolfowitiz, U. S. Deputy Defence Secretary has suggested and advised that Palestinias should adopt Gandhian Principles. He further said:

"If they adopt Gandhian way, they could in fact, make an enormous change very quickly. I believe the power of individuals demonstrating peacefully is enormous."

It is a different thing that U. S. A. is not following this, as the advice is meant for others only. United Nations has declared this decade as the Decade of

Culture of Peace and Non–violence for the children of the world. This declaration pinpoints the basic question before us today and will also help to understand the philosophy of Gandhi.

Gandhi said:

"There is no half – way between truth and non- violence on the one hand and untruth and violence on the other. We may never be strong enough to be entirely non-violent in thought, word and deed. But we must keep non-violence as our goal and make steady progress towards it. The attainment of freedom, whether for a man, a nation or the world, must be in exact proportion to the attainment of non-violence by each".

Elsewhere he stated:

"Non-violence is not a garment to be put on and off at will, its seat is in the heart and it must be inseparable part of our very being".

According to Gandhi, the concept of non-violence is not a negative concept, but it is a positive approach to ***'Life'.*** Gandhi did not resort to non-violent resistance because he was unarmed; he resorted to non-violent resistance, or calls it assistance, because he had shed all fear of arms. Gandhi had also realized the futility of arms. He knew that the best can not be achieved by fear, because ***'feat is a dark room, where only negatives are developed'.*** He also realized that all arms become powerless once the man has shed the fear of arms. This was the concept of non-violence of Mahatma Gandhi which was positive, and dynamic. It provided metaphysical foundation to the concept of morality. Just as we have little reason to expect less violence in a country if all of its citizens are armed with guns, even if they all have the same kind of guns and the same number of bullets, so we have little reason to expect less violence in the world, if all of its nations are armed with weapons of mass destruction, not even if there is some ***'balance'*** or even equality among these weapon. In short, to adopt non-violence is to adopt a new way of coming to terms with our–vulnerability, a new way of dealing with the fear to which we are subject and the fear which we can inspire in others.

Contrary to misconception held by some people, however non-violence is not a matter of substituting non-violent means of defence. Probably even more basic is the transformations of our social and economic institutions so that they are not the source of violence and exploitation, to certain segments of society and they do not create conditions to which violence is the expectable response. The strength of a non-violent society does not lie in weapons of destruction; it lies in the degree to which human values are embodied in its social institutions. These social institutions involve not only the relations of human beings to our natural environment and to other forms of life. If our goal is non-violence, we cannot consume and destroy, destroy and consume, as if it made no difference. For Gandhi, non- violence, in the negative sense is not non-violence. Non-violence is not merely a live and let live formula, but it involves a principle of live and help others to live, and these others should include human beings, animals and nature.

In the present day economy, animals have no place and it is our desire to include animals as members of our family and society. In the Indian Constitution, we have made a solemn declaration that at least one animal, i.e. the cow shall not be killed for any purpose whatsoever. But it must be understood that animals should not be man's toy nor mere pets, because pets and toys are kept as long as they amuse us. The day we chose to regards one animal as sacred and not a mere pet, we took a great stride forward in the direction of cultural progress. Ultimately, what is culture? Culture is the art of living with others, living with nature, with the animal world, and with fellow human beings. The word culture is most important. We want culture of peace or non-violence to be established. Can there be a Culture of Peace of Non-violence, is again a moot question; and what do we mean by culture; such a culture will not be Western or Eastern, but- can be global, only.

The earth is called ***'Vasundhara'*** or ***'Vasumati'***. ***Vasu*** means wealth. We intend to search the wealth, not to exploit it, but to make our lives gratifying and blessed. Therefore, the first article of this revolutionary creed should be that ***'man is the measure of all things'***. And you cannot preserve the dignity of man on charity. The underlying principle is reverence for life . This is true for all lives and that should be our watch – word. The reverence for human life first, then for animals and then for nature. This is known in our ancient lores and ***'Vibhuti Yoga'***– the worship of all, and relationship with everybody that makes life rich. We believe in ***'Advyata'***, i.e. oneness, harmony, co-ordination and mutual co–operation.

I want to ask question to myself, whether Gandhi has become out of date ? There is a misunderstanding about the very concept of Gandhi's non-violence. One armed man can be conquered by 10, 10 x 20, and so on, but not all the armies of the world can not conquer the spirit of one true man. This was Gandhiji's dynamic nonviolence. But today, a question is raised as to whether this instrument of non-violence has got any use? While dealing with a person who does not believe in non-violence, but believers in only race of arms. We are expecting a positive reply from this seminar to this question which is posed today at every corner of the street. It is true that we call our governmental departments dealing with the arms and military as ***'defence department'*** and not ***'offence department'***. Everybody claims that the arms are being manufactured for defence. Is this true and can this create a peace and harmony in the whole world? or will it create war mongering and conflicts ? Is it possible that the ***Shanti Sena*** as envisaged by Mahatma Gandhi could be a solution where people will gather not to kill each – other, but will stake their own lives to establish peace and harmony.

Whether we want ***'Yuddha or Buddha', 'War or Peace? Or peace through war ?'***

In this context, it is worthwhile to note that on 27–09-1984, while addressing the U. N. Assembly the then President of America Ronald Reagan remembered Gandhiji and said that ***"all problems could be peacefully resolved, if adversaries talk to each other on the basis of love and truth . All through history the way of truth and love has always won. This was the belief of Gandhiji and his vision and its remains good and true even today."*** It was true in 1984, but it appears that America feels that it is not true today.

I must remind this august gathering that woman are the silent victims of most of the conflicts and are real targets. We generally talk about empowering women, but do we really mean it , or want it ? In my so called religious country, the birth of the girl child is not welcomed. Further all over the world, atrocities on women are increasing in geometric proportion. Domestic violence is rampant. It was a UNICEF Report which said

"They [Women] already bear and care for the third world's children. They make, wash and mend the third world's clothes. They clean the third world's houses, collect their fuel, cook the third world's food, fetch the third world's water, and look after the third world's sick."

The modernization and mechanization are tending to marginalize women in many sectors. They are either pushed down or are thrown out of the work force. The media has reduced the woman to a commodity. The women all over the world are worried about it. Therefore a movement has started in the name of ***'women against Pornography.'*** They said that ***'it is one thing women can unite upon because we all get raped and we all get beaten'.***

Women are constantly living under the fear of rape. As is rightly said by Brown Miller, ***"Rape is a social and political instrument invented by man to oppress women socially, economically, and politically."***

Noted Parsian Scholar, Elizabeth Bartinder says, ***"Maternal instinct is just a myth invented several years ago to subjugate women. Women gain no glory by being mothers. The instinct is simply oppressive fiction. Therefore, women in Western liberalization movement have gone to the extent of saying that 'paternal instinct is a taboo waiting to be born, criticised and killed.' Therefore, down with motherhood."*** This is an extreme approach but we cannot ignore it , while dealing with the problem of Culture of Peace and Non-violence. Gandhiji spoke about ***'Stri Shakti'***, what exactly does it mean in the present day context ?

United Nations had declared 2001 to 2010 as decade of Culture of Peace and Non-violence for the children of the world. Unfortunately we treat our children as our property. We want them to be our carbon copies or pocket edition. This is nothing but cruelty.

It was Khalil Gibran, who said :

"Your children are not your children.

They are the sons and daughters of Life's longing for itself.

They come through you but not from you.

And though they are with you yet they belong not to you.

You may give them your love but not your thoughts.

For they have their own thoughts

You may house their bodies but not their souls.

For their souls dwell in the house of tomorrows.

Which you can not visit, not even in your dreams.

You may strive to be like them, but seek not

To make them like you.

For life goes not backward nor tarries with yesterday.

You are the bows from which your children as living arrows are sent forth"

The archer sees the mark upon the path of the infinite and he bends you with his might that his arrow may go swift and far.

Let your bending in the Archer's hand be for gladness;

For even as he loves the arrows that flies, so He loves also the bow that is stable.

This view is also expressed by Rabindranath Tagore.

However, it is a moot question as to whether we are living for the children? Are we planning for the next generation? Or we want to grab everything for ourselves, ignoring future generation or their destiny. And, therefore, it appears that United Nations feel that the Culture of non-violence and peace should be for the children of the world, who represent future of the mankind. But they are abused and exploited in every possible sense and way.

Now, though late, there is a realization that there is no other alternative to the principle of non-violence. Otherwise, next Century and Millennium might witness unprecedented, proliferation of violence, because history of wars and human destruction clearly tells us that people have not learnt anything from destruction. Therefore, it should be specifically emphasized that non-violence is to be accepted as the basis of personal life and social life and also as the only feasible and desirable technique of resolving conflicts, and those who advocate peace should practice what they preach.

Future of mankind depends upon its adopting non-violence, as the principle of life on which depends a happy union of science and spirituality. I call it S+G that is Science plus Gandhi.

23
Gandhi, Philosophy and Islam

I. Khan

The beginning of twenty-first century is not much different from the previous one. However, post-11/9 situation has changed the history of the world. Who was responsible for the disaster is not the issue related to any peace lover but the concern as to why at all happened is perhaps the area that an academician or a philosopher wishes to choose for his writings in order that it may help the society to think and change if possible.

Islam has become an important subject of interest even among non-Muslims, especially after the incidence in U. S. A. However, it is unjust to relate the noble concept to something that is related to destruction. Islam has been chosen as literary and philosophical area even by non-Muslim scholars e.g. Mahatma Gandhi, Bernard Shaw, A. J. Arberry, Nicholson, Washington and many Indian writers in English.

It is perhaps the best time to remember a person like Mahatma Gandhi who could teach the lesson of ***ahimsa***, peace, brotherhood, solidarity, unity, togetherness, prosperity, sacrifice, broadmindedness, fraternity, patriotism, spiritualism, humanity and what not. This is indeed the right time that God sends at least one like

Gandhi who could preach good things from each lesson and develop that understanding that is needed for the ultimate survival of the human race.

The term 'Islam' can etymologically be defined as the ***'Religion of Peace'*** as the very word has been derived from the Arabic root, ***'Salaam'*** that means 'Peace'. As a concept, Islam has been used by different people as holy religion that was sent from Allah to people directly by Jibriel [Gabriel], an angle, to the last prophet, Mohammed bin Abdullah.

Islam can also be defined operationally by different people in different self visualized situations. The concept of Islam, according to many people, is highly philosophical. Philosophy is roughly defined as ***'The way of life',*** which is very much related to religion. Besides, if we consider even the technical definition of philosophy as ***'The logical enquiry into the nature of Reality'***, it does not go against Islam. In Qur'an, it has been stated that one should use brain to decide what is right and what is wrong. Moreover, the philosophical dimension of any thought must not make any attempt to contradict the holy concepts related to Islam, Qur'an or prophet Mohammed. Any such queries are not allowed to question for the sake of only questions, but, obviously possible for the purpose of reaching near God or the ultimate ***'Truth'***.

It is imperative here to enlist a few words that are perhaps from the same family of the word ***'salaam'***. ***'Istislam'*** means ***'taking-over'*** or ***'acceptance.'*** Islam also means ***'submission', 'resignation', 'reconciliation'*** [to the will of God]. In Arabic, ***'Al-Islam'*** is the religion that is characterized by a particular belief or faith preached by the last prophet, Mohammed. Further, to talk about the etymological significance of the word ***'Muslim'*** we have to see and understand a few words of the same family like ***'Musalim'*** and ***'Musallam'.*** The former means peaceable, peaceful, peace-loving, mild tempered, lenient, gentle etc. while latter means unimpaired, intact and flawless. Thus, a Muslim [the follower of Islam] etymologically symbolizes peace and submission. In this connection, some names of places can be referred. Baghdad for example, has been historically known as ***'Medina Salaam'*** [city of peace]. It might have been a very peaceful place in the past. Many other examples can be cited. Dar-As salaam [place of peace] symbolizes Paradise. 'Ya salaam' is an exclamation of dismay that means Good Lord! Or Good Heavens! And, ***Assalam-o-Elaikum***, the ordinary salutation of Muslims means ***'peace be with you'.***

It is instructed that a Muslim should say ***'Salaam-o-Elaikum'*** when he goes to or passes by any graveyard because it helps in attaining spiritual peace for those who are buried there. It serves the same purpose of wising peace for a dead or an alive.

'Mayas-salaam' is a greeting of farewell [goodbye], is philosophically based on the idea of peace, safety and security. In addition, peace is the basis of the respected words used for prophets before Mohammed and himself. For prophets before him, people used to say 'Alaihe-As-Salaam [upon him be peace] and for Mohammed ***'Sallallah-u-Alaihe-Wasallam'*** that is a respected word by all which means nothing but peace be upon him.

If one tries to go deeper into all the greetings of Muslims or salutations or the words used to honour and respect, peace [***salaam***] is found common in all. An ordinary Muslim wishes peace for another Muslim, a Muslim greets/wishes or respects prophets including Mohammed by wishing peace. When a Muslim sees/welcomes another Muslim, he wishes peace and when he says ***'good bye'*** to any one he wishes the same. Therefore, it may be said that peace is the ultimate purpose of a Muslim's life; however, it is highly spiritual and philosophical in nature.

Thus, in Islam, the concept ***'Peace'*** bears a great significance. Peace in a society is important from individuals' point of view when he has a physical entity. And, when he departs from here, peace becomes more important for his life hereafter. Therefore, a Muslim who offers ***Salah*** [***Namaz***] or prayer to obey his Almighty's order and tries to fulfill other Islamic requirements so that there exists peace in his grave and he is blessed with Pace in Paradise. Every good Muslim worries about the Day of Judgment. He, therefore, wishes an utmost peaceful place which is none other than ***'paradise'*** that has been promised by Allah for virtuous Muslims. When a Muslim says good bye to this material world a lot of his friends and family members recites holy Qur'an so that the departed soul may further be blessed by Almighty's mercy and there he enjoys complete peace and serenity. Thus, peace is important in either of the situations-here and life here after. Physical comfort in Islam has no importance in any condition. Prophet's life has been an example. He used to sleep on mats and eat ordinary food, and sometimes he passed many sleepless nights without even food. Moreover, he always thanked his Lord for what He gave him, and exercised tolerance and patience for what he could not get because it was not written in his destiny. He has never been aggressive or violent unless it was imperative.

People believe that Islam has been spread by ***Jihad*** [Holy War] through out the universe. It is indeed a misconception. There had been many incidences in the life of prophet Mohammed as a man until 40 years of his age, and after the declaration of Prophethood from 40 years to 63 years. He has forgiven even those who have been very rude to him, however, strictness in his behaviour in whatever amount existed only due to the fact that he wanted to eliminate the wrong deeds from the society. In this connection, the following reference can be made.

Ravindra Kumar [1993] states:

> ***"If we find any thing related to violence during the times of Lord Krishna or Prophet Mohammed its only aim was to establish peace and use of force must have been the only alternative under the given conditions."***

This quotation may be analysed in many ways. Thus, Islam can not be considered a concept or religion that is harsh or rude. On the other hand, Islam is very flexible; however, flexibility depends on a legal and genuine situation.

Pillars of Islam

There are five pillars of Islam: faith, prayer, fasting, Alms and pilgrimage. All five pillars have noble concepts and thoughts. 'Prayer' being the most important pillar for the follower has been emphasized a lot simply because it differentiates between a believer and a non-believer. One can not escape from offering five time prayers, preferably in a group in mosques. But, if one can't go to the mosque for some reasons, he can offer at home or anywhere. However, there are special conditions for passengers/travellers. Prayer obviously symbolizes total surrender before ***'Lord'***.

Similarly, ***'fasting'*** is the pillar next to prayer and mandatory for an adult believer [Muslim]. There is a provision for exception for passengers/ travellers and the sick people. Fasting is an example of tolerance for the sake of Allah.

'Alms' is meant for those who exceed their property/earning from a particular level. Thus, they have to offer a fixed percentage of their property to those who are needy. Therefore, this pillar of Islam is not an obligation on each Muslim. Moreover, this is an embodiment of sacrifice.

'Pilgrimage' is the last pillar of Islam. It is obligatory for a Muslim who is able to travel down to Mecca [Holy Ka'ba] and perform the rites and rituals of Hajj [Pilgrimage]. The entire activity expresses the faith and respect for Allah Almighty and symbolizes commitment and surrender. It also gives an idea of respect towards Prophet Ibrahim and Prophet Mohammed.

The Holy Qur'an

Qur'an is a revealed book. It is holy and the book of Allah. Qur'an itself confirms and validates its authenticity. In the past, many criticism and comments have been made by many non-believers that Islam is not holy or a revealed book. At the time of Prophet Mohamed, some poets claimed it as the work of an Arab poet. As a result, Prophet Mohammed hanged three lines of a verses on the wall of 'Ka'ba' and asked people of Mecca to complete the fourth line to make it a stanza. But, everyone failed. The thoughts, ideas, rules, concepts and forecasts can not be the work of a human being if we look at the way in which the verses and chapters of Qur'an have been sent to the world from time to tie through Jibriel to prophet and from Prophet to the whole world. Qur'an does not require any proof to support its being holy or noble. Many Arabic speaking people have thought and tested its language consequently embraced Islam. The reading of Holy Qur'an gives immense spiritual pleasure that one can't enjoy by reading any other book be of general or spiritual type.

Prophet Mohammed [PBUH]

Prophet Mohammed was sent by Almighty Allah as the last prophet to correct people of Mecca in particular and the world in general. He was born in the family of Abdullah. He became an orphan and his uncle brought him up. Both uncle and nephew worked together for some time.

The Prophet was a different man altogether right from his childhood. He has set himself an example of truth, honestly, equality, tolerance, sacrifice, dedication, surrender before God, politeness, humility, brotherhood, peace, freedom to work, dignity of labour, obedience, faithfulness, love, fraternity, patriotism, human rights, humanity, togetherness, unity and what not. He was first the humble worshiper, a member of family, social being, a leader, a messenger, a prophet. In short, he played different roles in his 63 years life time.

Many people have passed many comments about his personality. But, the perceptions mainly come from those who are non-believers or pseudo-scholars or believers for name sake. Such people can not be considered as critics of Islam or Prophet rather they have only been critical of Islam and Prophet. Criticism should eventually contribute to the issue raised by the critics but critical apprehension sometime leads to a negative effect. Mr. Rushdie's comments don't require to be quoted anywhere because he is an intellectual of that stature who is above all criticism. But, I am sure he is not greater than G.B. Shaw. Mahatma Gandhi respected prophet Mohammed and was even impressed by his noble companions because he had read holy Qur'an and tried to grasp the thoughts and the meaning of important messages that Qur'an and prophet Mohammed tried to give to the suffering humanity for the ultimate betterment.

Prophet Mohammed was the embodiment of tolerance, justice, surrender etc. as referred earlier. One should go through the writings of many great people even by non-Muslims, and not be hostile towards the good aspects of Islam, Qur'an and the last prophet. Gandhiji always respected every religion and Islam as well. He even incorporated many ideas of the Prophet. Once he recalled the time of Hadrat Omer, one of the Caliphs, for restoring justice in the society. Mohammed is the practical side of the Qur'an which is nothing but a book of Fundamentals. It can't be completely understood without the life of Prophet Mohammed.

One may say that Islam emphasises tolerance and proposes acceptance. Had it not been the core idea, the acceptance of all other prophets would not have been the basis of faith for a Muslim. It has been clearly said that one should not speak bad for any religion or the saints or the prophets of other religion for any reasons. Therefore, a Muslim has to respect Christ, Moses or others.

Allah Almighty is the Lord for all and the Lord for the worlds. Qur'an does not declare the Allah's blessings for Muslims only. Rather Allah being the Creator is every body's Lord.

Islam and Related Concepts

There are very many concepts and ideologies that are related to Islam. But, the following are some specific ones that are also related to peace and the betterment of any society.

Jihad and Islam

Jihad as a concept in Islam has been misinterpreted. Every fight or war is not at all holy. A holy war is in defence of holy religion. Unless someone attacks the other a defence is not justified. If an enemy offers compromise a good Muslim has to accept it. A holy war never approves killings of innocent people. Islam always recommends peace by tolerance and patience. This is clearly enjoined in the following verses:

"And for the sake of your Lord be patient". [LXXIV:7]

"Consider the succession of ages,

"Most surely man is in loss,

"Except those who believe, and do good and enjoin, on each other truth, and enjoin on each other patience." [CIII:1, 2, 3]

"Only the patient will be paid back their reward in full without measures". [XXXIX: 10]

"So be careful of your duty to Allah, and set right matters of your difference." [VIII:1]

"And fight in the way of Allah with those who fight with you, and do not exceed the limits, surely Allah does not love those who exceed the limits". [II:190]

"If they find you, they will be your enemies, and will stretch forth towards you their hand, and their tongue with evil, and they ardently desire that you may disbelieve." [LX: 2]

"And if they incline to peace, then incline to it and trust in Allah; surely He is the Hearing and the knowing. [VIII: 61]

There are many other examples that can be cited from the holy verses of Qur'an that support the idea of Peace and patience.

Equality and Justice

One basic element in the value system of Islam is the principle of equality and justice. Equity is also much related to the noble principles of Islam. Qur'an has very clearly stated:

"O mankind, verily We have created you from a single [pair] of male and a female, and made you into nations and tribes, that you may know each other. Verily the most honoured of you in the sight of God is the most righteous." [49:13] Besides, it has also been made clear that there is no difference between an Arab and Ajem [non-Arab].

Community

Community in Islam is very significant. One has to live a normal life in the community and fulfil all the social needs and requirement and the only His prayers and worships get approved by Allah, almighty. Those who escape from the society and go to isolated places even for the sake of remembering the Creator, He is not much pleased.

Qur'an teaches us in this regard:

"Let there be a community [Ummah] among you, advocating what is good, demanding what is right, and eradicating what is wrong. These are indeed the successful." [3:104] and, ***"You are the best community ever raised, you enforce what is right, fight what is wrong, and believe in Allah."*** [3:110]

We should not simply interpret the fight as referred above as the holy war or Jihad. This fight can be referred to even intellectual or philosophical fight against wrong-doers as Mahatma Gandhi fought against vices and bad ideologies through out his life. Similarly a follower of Islam has been instructed to preach his ideologies to those who are not the followers. And if they don't listen to, they are not supposed to be killed. Because on more than one occasion, Allah has commanded to be patient, it requires a great deal of understanding to perceive Islamic teachings.

Morality

Morality in Islam is considered next to the five pillars of Islam. It covers almost all the necessary religious dimensions. But, there are some specific points that can be discussed under the head of religious morality. Such as protection of a man from insanity and degeneration, weakness and indulgence, indecency and temptation. Besides, Islam has also prohibited the followers from certain immoral things related to food, drinking, recreation and sex etc. Among these are:

- All kinds of intoxicating wines, liquors and spirits [Qur'an, 2:219;4:43;5:93-94];
- The meat and products of swine [pork, bacon, ham, lard], of wild animals that use claws or teeth to kill their victims [tigers, wolves, leopards etc.] of all birds of prey [hawks, vultures, crows etc.] of rodents, reptiles, worms and the like, of the dead animals and birds that are not slaughtered and the birds that are not slaughtered properly [Qur'an, 2:172-173;5:4-6];
- All forms of gambling and vain sports [Qur'an, 2:219;5:93-94];
- All sexual relations out of wedlock; and
- Human relations are of high significance in Islam. A forgiver is always a good and great man. He is suitably rewarded by Allah as He promises so.

Allah is the Creator of not a world rather of the universe. Each and every creature is made by Him. Morality is the only principle that can bind us to act human with the rest of the creatures.

Social and International Life

Social life of a true Muslim is based on supreme principle and designed to secure happiness with prosperity for the individual as well as for the society. An individual is nothing without the society and community. Brotherhood and healthy social relations are prescribed by Islam [Qur'an, 4:1;7:189,49:10-13].

In the case of internationalism, Qur'an orders to possess an unshakable belief in the unity of mankind in origin, in human status, and in aims. [Qur'an,4:1;7:189;42:42].

International treaties between one state with the other states should be initiated. In this connection, Qur'an orders to follow the principle. It says: this is the only binding if the other parties remain faithful to their obligations and honour their treaties. Otherwise, there can be no validity of treaties or binding obligations. [Qur'an, 5:1;8:55-56;9:3-4]

No Compulsion in Religion

There is no compulsion in any religion. Thus, being the religion of peace, Islam does not suppress or pressurize any one to do , follow or practice any of its laws or principles. Even once the holy prophet was commanded by Allah not to force any one to embrace Islam rather leave it to him [the follower] and the God [the creator].Qur'an very distinctively presented the concept before us: **"there is no compulsion in religion, truly the right way has become clearly distinct from error; therefore whoever disbelieves in devil and believes in Allah, he indeed has laid hold on the firmest handle, which shall not break off, and Allah is Hearing and Knowing".** On other occasion, Allah says:

> ***"And follow what is revealed to you, and be patient till Allah shall give judgments, and He is the best of the judges."*** [X:109].

The following is the clearest of all the orders to be patient and wait for the results, ***"Therefore be patient; surely the promise of Allah [to make truth triumph] is true."*** [XXX: 60]

Toleration

Intolerance is closely related to pride and arrogance. Both the concept are not allowed in Islam. The one who tolerates is the most powerful man and the one who is humble is very dear to Allah.

There is a clear indication in Islam to respect the apostle who were sent by Allah from time to time to correct the society therefore no follower of any religion has any right to criticize any religion or their leaders. However, one can invite to accept a religion by virtue of its qualities. This can also not be stopped by force or powering slam not less than one lakh and twenty three thousand prophets were sent to this world after Adam who was indeed the first one. Therefore, it is better to keep silence as regard to the greatness of any prophet.

Qur'an says, ***"All nations have had their guides".*** [XIII:7]

"And certainly we raised in every nation an apostle saying: serve Allah and shun the devil". [XVI:136]

Relations with Non-Muslims

Muslims live in a society like India that is characterized by a composite-cultural society. It is imperative to develop goodwill and brotherhood to achieve unity and solidarity for the ultimate target of peace.

Sensing this need, Qur'an states:

"All men are a single nation."

Qur'an's most powerful teaching follows:

"Repel evil by good."

Prophet Mohammed has said quite often, ***"God has sent me to teach good manners and good deeds."*** [Narrated from Jaber]

The holy Prophet also said:

"God is not merciful to him who is not merciful to his creation. Allah has also commanded, and give full measures when you measure out and weigh with a true balance; this is fair and better in the end."

Abu Hurairah, a noble companion and the narrator of the traditions of the holy prophet narrates:

"Do not betray a trust, nor be dishonest even to one who is dishonest to you."

Islam is not a philosophy but it includes many philosophical notions. There is enough emphasis on the following concepts in Islam: Equality, Justice, Truth, Peace etc as referred in the foregoing pages.. Interestingly, the concept of Jihad as present in Islam has been generally misunderstood by many so-called or pseudo-intellectuals of the present time. They are neither believers nor Arabic speaking nor enlightened nor able to interpret things but very much able to poke their nose in the sensitive affairs like this.

Islam focuses on ***'right to live'***. No body should kill any one without any legal and genuine reason. If one attempts to take one's life [given by Allah], the Islamic law would punish his in the same way. This is not meant to punish him but to present as example before society and remind the people of the case that if it happens again, the same punishment will be given for the accused. Thus, the concept of punishment exists is Islam for correction measures.

'Brotherhood' and ***'universality'*** in Islam enjoy a great reputation as holy Qur'an often addresses by calling, ***'O! the people of the world'*** or '***O! People'***. Besides, it also referred at more than one place, to prophet Mohammed that he was sent as ***'blessing'*** [***Rahmat***] for the worlds.

'Neighbourhood' also bears great significance. It is clearly mentioned that food eaten by a neighbour will be ***'Haraam'*** [disallowed] if there is no food to eat in other neighbour's house. It may point towards importance of neighbourhood. There is no reference of caste, creed, race or religion of neighbours. Thus, it is evident that man to man relation; neighbour to neighbour relation is more important because the entire social life is an accord, an agreement and the life is synonymous to peace. There is no concept of life without peace. Besides, peace is also synonymous to agreement or accord.

The concept of ***'justice'*** is closely related to Islam. Without it a peaceful society may appear to be a far fetched concept. In order to promote justice and peace, Islam issued a few very strong recommendations. About a thief, it is legal in Islam to punish him even by chopping off his hand or hands. Similarly, if one kills someone without a reason he will be killed by the judiciary of the Islamic country. However, there is a process that ensures the evidence against the accused whether right, and only if it is proved that he is guilty, the action of legal justice is taken. The action seems to be very cruel but the idea is highly just and noble. People are afraid to commit any crime because of the thought of the action usually taken by Islamic judiciary.

Thus, we may say that at the time of the last Prophet and even now Muslims follow some strict laws that can take life of the sinner or criminal. If it is a matter of religion one may even kill the evil character. Some example of this kind of action may be found during the time of Lord Rama. During the exile period, he had to fight against a very powerful king Ravana who symbolizes ***'evil'*** and in order to teach him a lesson, a battle was fought by Rama. Finally, Rama won the battle because he was right, according to Hindu Philosophy. In this process, he was supported by his brother Lakshmana and many others.

Keeping in view the above-mentioned facts about Islam, the Prophet did not go against the philosophical concept of ahimsa later conceived by Mahatma Gandhi. What Prophet Mohammed, Lord Rama and Lord Krishna did was the need of the time and the only solution to such problems. In fact, ahimsa as well as religion prohibit killing of a living being for no genuine reason. But, if there is a reason, one can aim at eradicating the root of the evil. And, this is the religion. This kind of considerations were the basis of the battle of ***Mahabharata*** and the battle fought by Lord Rama because his opponent symbolized evil.

To be very precise, peace is synonymous to well being, satisfaction, contentment, serenity etc. In Islam, peace has a greater significance. It deals with all the three dimensions of peace-peace in society, peace in grave and peace here after [in Heaven]. The concept of peace is philosophy based. Philosophy is the way of life. One develops a philosophical outlook on the basis of life experiences. Islam is also a way of life adapted by Muslims so it includes a lot from a philosophy. There are many noble ideas in Islam as found in Qur'an and Hadith, reflected through the life activities of the last prophet Mohammed. The following is an example of philosophy of Islam which can be explained as a contribution to the field of Education. ***"Al-Eilm khairan men-al maal"*** [Education is better than money/property]. This sentence indirectly serves a socio-economic purpose of control over people who are greedy and wish to earn and save money and do not want to get education, and prefer saving money. In this context, if we follow the noble sayings of prophet and other noble Islamic personalities, money is considered a material achievement that can give comfort only. It may make an individual highly competitive that may lead to corruptions and evil activities. While, there can be peace of mind even without money and other material achievements. Education can be considered as one of the means of getting satisfaction and peace.

Critics of Islam

Western scholars in general and Orientalists in particular are believed to have contributed to Islamic literature have rather tried in some ways to malign and defame Islam, however, in an artistic manner. The degree may vary from person to person. Muir is found on the top in the case of criticism of Prophet Mohammed and the Holy Qur'an.

There are some soft Orientalists who were bit academic and literary in approach, however, did not contribute to Islam rather to their literary and academic achievements. In this regard, let us look at the statement given by Muir:

"The sword of Mohamed, and the Koran, is the most stubborn enemies of civilization, liberty and the Truth...."

If we analyze the above statement, Mr. Muir has seriously mistaken as most of intellectuals consider holy Koran as a complete guide to Humanity, and the prophet as the saviour, and he considers them a sword.

A German author, Christopher claimed that the original language of Holy Qur'an was not Arabic, but something closer to the Aramaic. Then the question arises who translated the same into Arabic. Was Prophet Mohammed a bilingual or a translator? The so-called critics themselves can seek answer to such questions.

The following are some of the issues that western authors have raised from time to time:

Islam:

- Truth or Myth
- Qur'an being strict for others/non-believers
- Emphasis on Tawheed [monotheism]
- Contradiction [punishment and forgiving]
- Qur'an revealed book or not, and
- Respect for women etc.

The following discussion will include some of the issues:

Islam: Truth or Myth

The question of truth can not be answered or proved by anybody or any thing. Truth is a philosophical and literary concept that can only be felt. Truth has been dealt by many literary figures including John Keats. He said: ***'Beauty is Truth and Truth Beauty'***. Truth belongs to a spiritual world and a man having materialistic outlook may not want to grasp the same because it goes against the temporary, materialistic and physical world in which he lives. ***'Truth'*** is different from ***'Fact'*** or ***'Reality'***. ***'Reality'*** is much closer.

The question whether Islam is ***'Truth'*** can only be answered on certain beliefs, faith etc. The issue of faith seems to be the core of all the question which is raised in the context of all the concepts related to faith in Islam. Is the existence of Allah ***'Truth'***? Is Qur'an Truth? Is heaven or paradise Truth? All these are related to basics of faith and can be proved by Qur'an. But, if one does not have faith in Qur'an, one finds unable to prove as the same can't be attempted to prove as a fact in a laboratory. Neither faith in Islam, nor Allah nor day of judgment nor paradise can be proved. But, one can feel the same. This kind of feeling does not exist only in literature or Islamic field but also in one's daily life, but, the same depends on a person. It differs from individual to individual.

In this connection Bernard Shaw can be quoted:

"I have always held the religion of Mohammed in high estimation because of its wonderful vitality."

Thus, for a progressive scholar or a non-believer, a humble advice can be extended to have a positive outlook by peeping into the facts/concepts like God, equality, justice, brotherhood, charity, love of humanity and nation, respect for parents, duties towards the family, commitment and sincerity for life and faith in the creator.

It is really strange that the creatures have forgotten their creator, Lord or Allah. We are thankless indeed and this sense or feeling exists among many sensible people, poets, thinkers, philosophers and religious scholars.

Islam is a complete system of life that can't be a myth because a myth is narrated only if one is not alive. Islam is presently followed and practised by nearly two billion people all over the world. How can such a notion or religion be a myth? It is indeed truth and people can feel the same. Truth is an eternal, permanent and everlasting but reality is physical, temporary and short lived and a ***'fact'*** is something that can be proved in a laboratory. This very difference can prove itself about the 'truth of the truth' that Islam started 1400 years ago and would surely last till doom day.

Gandhi's statement, ***"No Religion is greater than Truth"*** supports the idea that Truth is equal to ***'Religion'***. In other words, **"Religion' can't be complete without Truth."** Scholars even went on saying that ***'Religion and Truth'*** are synonymous. Thus, Islam as a ***'Religion'*** is nothing but Truth.

Philosophy: The Concept

It has been said that every educationist is a philosopher and every philosopher is an educationist. Mahatma Gandhi was luckily a philosopher-educationist. His philosophical ideas are interwoven in his philosophy and his philosophy is the outcome of his life and education. He once said, ***'my life is my philosophy'***. It meant what he lived was the result of his philosophy and what he professed as philosophy was the outcome of his life. Philosophy and education are the two sides of the same coin and the coin is nothing but the life itself.

It is always believed that philosophy is the backbone of a successful man. Education is the practical side. With out a solid basis of philosophy in general and educational philosophy in particular a person would always lack something in his life that is very essential. One who inculcates the values among the children must good and fruitful philosophical blend of thoughts. Gandhi once stated about education in the following words:

"Education is an all round development of personality".

Value and Human Life

The question of human values has received great significance in the Indian context. Human values seem to be receiving the attention of those who may happen to be the saviours of tomorrow. This involves deeper understanding of human evolution and the limitations of human mind so that the noble principles underlying human values may have the lasting impact necessary for bringing about change in life of a human being.

Spirituality is an important concept related to philosophy, morality, ethics and value system. In the process of his evolution, man has developed certain values as there are always forms of legitimacy and sanction that define the limits of possible behaviour; but there has always been the need to use these values in order that the things can be shaped as per the changing need and requirement of the society is which values can be properly utilised for the ultimate target of the socio-spiritual uplift of the human beings.

Values are nurtured in a particular society and hence are governed by its outlook. A conservative society will develop typical values that suit it while a liberal society will evolve magnanimous value system. Through the ages, ours has been a multiracial, pluro-cultural yet a liberal society. Therefore, the values that this society evolved are also liberal encompassing diverse outlooks of various communities. The values it evolved knows no limits of geography, history or sociology. These are cosmopolitan in the true sense of the word, not meant for citizens of a particular state only, but for human beings as a whole.

The process of education is indeed very subtle as it involves exchange of thoughts and ideas that seem rather intangible. In this sense, it is highly evolved and the most developed phenomenon compared to the processes associated with other sense organs of seeing, hearing, eating etc., which are comparatively more physical in nature.

It is necessary to understand the relationship of man with nature and grasp with distinct clarity the place that he occupies in this universe; it is essential to know the interrelationship between man, and God and the role that man has been assigned to play in society. The very purpose of human life needs a clear-cut definition, so that the goal is all the time in sight. The very structure of this universe of space and matter, their origin and contribution in constituting the visible and invisible nature including the evolution of living beings and man, requires a deep study and revelation. The education that throws light on these basic issues will regulate its knowledge and with discrimination impart the same to man so that he can grow into a mystic or ***Sufi*** rather than a devil.

Man should be educated to further develop these human values, like a tree developing from a seed, so that he may reap the fruits of the human origin and root. He should develop holy nature in which truth dominates falsity and deceit, love overpowers hatred, righteousness and justice over-shadow forces of corruption, and peace eliminates discord and disharmony.

The knowledge that we receive in science and technology does indeed form an important aspect of education. However, an appropriate utilization of resources whatever available and gains brought about by technological advancement education that develops morality and values are perhaps the foremost need of the day. It is the shift of over-emphasis forms the mortal entity to eternity, permanence and immortality.

Education should polish by training the mind. The norms laid down by religions on the appropriate use of the senses should be understood with regard to their real benefit of education. Like everything else in the universe that requires preparation and growth before it is utilised, man too requires development of his highest faculty intellect. Through education he can receive knowledge at home, in society and in schools and colleges for being useful to not only the humans, but other living creatures too. Man cannot play the role of the enjoyer of all that nature has produced and consider gratification of the senses as the ultimate purpose of his life. Man has to practise society prescribed as well as self-imposed discipline in curtailing the sensual impulses as a sacrifice and in exchange to the ability of intellect and discrimination granted to him by nature. Everything in the universe has a purposeful existence of its own and also its utility for the rest. Man too has to abide by this universal principle and must endeavour to fit into the harmonious working of nature. The education that reveals the underlying unity, from which all has emerged, will foster the feelings of love, kinship and brotherhood and strengthen the foundations of human society through generation of fundamental values like honesty, brotherhood, equality, sacrifice, peace, truth, beauty, love, togetherness, solidarity, tolerance etc.

Values not only help a man in self-evaluation, but also in self-drive. An educated man without values has thoughts but the same can never flow into action. Values inculcate significance to life and meaning to death. Without values, life becomes a series of meaningless events, and death of bitter experience.

In sum, it is felt that philosophy in general and ***'Values'*** in particular must be in focus in all spheres of life and Education especially in order to strengthen the society that is becoming valueless. And, the teacher can play a pivotal role in educating the society as a whole, and save the fall of the society.

Gandhian Philosophy: A Summary

Gandhi was a philosopher right from his adulthood. He lived his whole life in a way a philosopher lives. He after his return from Africa completely changed into a political philosopher.

Educational Philosophy

Gandhi's focus on mother- tongue and craft education made him famous as an educational philosopher. He once defined education as a all round development of a personality. He practiced craft education by using his famous ***Charkha*** for cotton as an indigenous product.

Religio-Moral Philosophy

According to Gandhi, religion is a personal matter that should not have a place in politics. For Gandhi, it was a good guide for conduct and not a game for power. He was having a secular mind and concept about it and did not consider a game of power. He believed in ***'Ishwar Allah Tere Naam'***. Besides, his approach was more like a spiritualist-**Sufi** especially in the case of looking at different religions. Morality becomes very important for a person who is really religious. He should behave with a person in a nice and human manner. His whole outlook should be for the uplift of the race and humanity as a whole.

Socio-Political Philosophy

Gandhi's philosophy of peace, tolerance, unity, brotherhood, patriotism and non-violence does not need an introduction and explanation. Even an ordinary citizen of India or an educationalist or a philosopher or a thinker from India or abroad might have studied Gandhi for enriching his thoughts in the field of philosophy and education. His philosophy of ***ahimsa*** is a product of his socio-political philosophy. He believed in a soft and an educational approach. He wanted to teach people to be tolerant than to be aggressive.

Peace Philosophy

Gandhi was a saint in his approach. He wanted an ideal society where peace prevails and people can live a comfortable life. He did not mean by a comfortable life as a luxurious life. Gandhi was the person who fought the entire freedom movement in a peaceful manner and saved the destiny of India during post- independent Indian crisis.

Gandhism and Islam

The greatest Indian saint was influenced by Islam on the whole. But, the most important points and principles of Islam that influenced Gandhi are presented below:

Peace

It is well known to almost every one that Gandhi was a champion of peace. He led the freedom of movement but never allowed any one to follow any kind of violence, though it was badly needed in certain circumstances. Gandhi was much aware of the concept ***'Ohm Shanti Ohm'*** and he tried to practise in his practical life. As a saint he used to be bit away from crowd. It does not mean, he did not like people. He was a very simple man and simplicity is more admired by him. He used to travel in the third class compartments of train and perhaps enjoyed it being with the ordinary Indian public. He believed in the concept preached by Lord Krishna that the path of peace is the path of salvation. Gandhi's role in maintaining peace in post p[partition India is not a secret. He succeeded in his mission of restoring peace even after an emergence of hatred among Hindus and Muslims in 1947. Gandhi was impressed by the concept of peace in Islam. He admired this concept. Gandhi was an open-minded person he believed in Kabir's concept:

"Sadhu aisa chahiey jaisa sup subhay,
Sar-sar ko gahi rahe thothha deyee urhaey."

[A saint should be like a winnower that keeps the essence and discards the husk or useless material].

Justice

Justice as a concept was associated with other philosophical concepts of Gandhi such as Tolerance and Equality. He was a great follower of Justice. He had a great respect for so called lower castes and classes of the then Indian society. Once he remembered the justice of Hadrat Omer, one of the caliphs of Islam in connection with restoring justice in India. This reference has many meanings as:

- He was not satisfied with the level of justice provided to people;
- He was influenced by Islam;
- He respected Islam; and
- Muslims can be also just.

Lastly, Indians can be open-minded and implement some ideas which are found even in other religions in general and in Islam, in particular.

Unity

The partition of India took place because of Jinnah's ***'two nation theory'***. He believed that Muslims and Hindus can not be one nation so there should be two different places to live and govern while Mahatma Gandhi was very much against it. He was a true follower of Unity in Diversity. Perhaps Gandhi was closer to the concept of Islam that 'all men are a single nation'. Religion can't be the only criterion for having a separate country or state. It was proved later in 1971 with the partition of Bangla Desh. The then Pakistan got separated on the basis of culture: linguistic or social. But both East Pakistan and Pakistan were Muslims states. Gandhi always wanted to hold Hindus and Muslims one. And as a matter of reality, Azad like personality always admired him. Perhaps Gandhi was right. Even today the success of Indian constitution and government always lies in the national bond between Hindus and Muslims of India.

Fasting

As we have seen above that 'fasting' is the second most important pillar of Islam. It is obligatory on a Muslim to keep fast during the holy month of Ramadan. But, Prophet Mohammed used to keep fast also on Mondays and Thursdays to earn more virtues. For him, ***'fasting'*** can be used as a tool of tolerance, patience and self- restraint. It has been said that if some one is unable to control his worldly desire he should fast so that he is close to divine principles that will enable him to exercise self control.

Gandhi, on the other hand, practised fasting to revolt against the dirty policies and suppression exercised by the British army. Since he was a precursor of non- violence, he chose this method to raise his voice against the British movement. He proved fasting as the most powerful means of resistance and an example of tolerance.

Sacrifice and Charity

These concepts are found in many religions but very much prescribed in Islam. It is said that one has to give charity in measures depending upon the capabilities of the giver. But, some how or the other, one has to give, however in a little quantity. It assures two things in Islam. First, it shows obedience of God. Second, one is sympathetic towards the poor. Third, one wishes to raise the other's level to at least to survive in the society. This concept was practices by Gandhi to attain equality. He wanted that every Indian should live at least on the level of a prescribed standard. He wanted at least minimum facility of life by which one can eat , dress and educate him and his family as per the need. When he could not do so he sacrificed even his clothes thinking that he did not have any moral right to dress nicely if the fellow Indians are not able to cover even one fourth of their body. And, the whole world is the eye witness of Gandhian principle of equality, justice and sacrifice.

Writing on Gandhi especially on his philosophical outlook is not an easy task. It needs many years to encase some of the glimpses of Gandhi's aspect of philosophy and personality to summarise in certain pages, yet, it is believed that the present attempt to explore Islam, philosophical concepts in Islam and its impact on Gandhi and the Gandhian life style found to be highly relevant in the present society as it badly needs peace and serenity for a peaceful human life. It is really painful to recall the sad assassination of the saint like Gandhi by a so-called Hindu who in my opinion was not a follower of any religion rather the follower of fanaticism, cynicism, extremism and so on. He finished the life of a peace lover who through out preached for ***ahimsa*** that is non-violence.

Let us pray that Gandhi takes birth again to save this society from terrorism and extremism and also pray that no Nathu Ram takes any birth any more and any where in any family in this world.

References

1. Arberry, A. J., The Koran Interpreted, London, OUP, 1964,
2. Bell, Richard, The Qur'an Translated, Edinburgh, Univ. Press, 1953.
3. Dev, R. B., Introduction to Philosophy, Sterling, New Delhi, 1989.
4. Dhiman, O. P., Foundations of Education, Delhi, Atma Ram, 1987.
5. Fazlur Rehman, Major Themes of the Qur'an, Minneapolis, Bibliotheca Islamica, 1980.
6. Hans, Wehr, Dictionary of Modern Arabic [Ed.], New York, SLS, 1976.
7. Hawthing, H.R. & Abdul Kadir A. Shareif, Approaches to the Qur'an [Ed.], London, Routledge, 1993.
8. Khan, I. A. 'Peace Education', Peace Review , Thailand, Vol. 1, No.2, 1998.

9. Khan, I. A. Morality and Twentieth Century Society in Ravindra Kumar [Ed.] Morality and Ethics in Public Life, Mittal Publications, Delhi, 1999.
10. Khan, I. A., Gandhi and Education: Synonymous to Each Other in Ravindra Kumar [Ed.] Mahatma Gandhi at the Close of Twentieth Century, New Delhi, 2004.
11. Khan, I. A., Philosophy: The Essence of Life, Maulana Azad Academy, Journal, Lucknow, Vol.XI, No. 9, Sep.1-30, 1996.
12. Khan, I. A, Maulana Azad, Philosophy and Education, Maulana Azad Academy Journal, Lucknow, September 1-30, 1997.
13. Khan, I. A., Peace: The Ultimate Purpose of Life, Peace Review, Vol. 1, No.2, Thailand, 1998.
14. Khan, I. A., Islam, Philosophy and Peace in Foundations of Education, Delhi, Anmol, 2006.
15. Kumar, Ravindra, Religion and World Peace, Meerut, Sara Publications, 1993.
16. Said, Eward W. Orientalism, London, Routhedge & Kegan Paul, 1978.
17. Rafiq Zakaria, Mohammad and the Qur'an, New Delhi, Penguin, 1991.

24

Understanding the Status of Women Through the Eyes of Gandhi

Faridah Noor Mohammad Noor

Introduction

An old photograph of Gandhi taken upon his return from South Africa in 1915 shows him and his wife, Kasturba, standing side by side.[1] Although her face was solemn, and most probably she was camera shy, standing next to her husband was an indication of her status in her husband's eyes. As a husband, Gandhi had elevated her to his equal status and the proof is the photograph with her standing next to him. Both were still young but the future that awaited them would put Gandhi on the map to change India's future, with her by his side, and to shape the future of Indian women in particular.

Gandhi helped change the path of Indian women through his peaceful yet firm ways. His views on women were modern for his contemporaries so much so that his dedication to fight for the women's causes brought out the women of India who were empowered by his words and actions to take part in freeing India from the British. At the beginning of this new 21st century, this paper intends to capture the status of women, particularly Indian women, through

Gandhi's words spoken and written in early part of the 20th century. It aims to capture the essence of Gandhi's perception of women as individuals, wives and freedom leaders.

Gandhi's Inspiration to Lead Women to Freedom

For Gandhi to fight endlessly for women's equality, he had to be inspired, like many great men, by his mother and wife. His inspiration to lead India's women to a better life came from the first woman in his life and later his beloved wife, namely, his loving mother, and Kasturba, respectively.

His mother and wife were his ***"intimate influences"*** of his life and the relationship he had with these two figures in is life was ***"a most ennobling influence"*** on him.[2] These two women did everything for him: his mother gave him her consent to go to England despite that he could be considered as an outcast for going overseas, and his wife sold most of her jewellery to raise the funds do so.

These two figures inspired him and his understanding of women was through his interaction with them. According to Kapadia, Gandhi credited his wife for his moral strength and personal growth that his wife demonstrated by example. Gandhi's own words confirmed this, ***"My wife made the orbit of all women. In her I studied all women."*** This illustrates how Gandhi respected his wife and his long partnership with her even after 62 years of their marriage.

Trough these two women, who had the most profound impact on his life, he paid his tribute to them, and womankind:

"I have worshipped woman as the living embodiment of the spirit of service and sacrifice."

Gandhi's Hope for Women

When Gandhi wrote to Rajkumari Amrit Kaur from Wardha on 21 October 1931, it was an invitation for women like her to rise up and save themselves from the unfair treatment they received. In his letter, he wanted her and the rest of her womankind to realise that they are just as dignified as the man, and their worth to mankind:

"If you women would only realise your dignity and privilege, and make full use of it for mankind, you will make it much matter than it is. But man has delighted in enslaving you and you have proved willing slaves till the slaves and the slave-holders have become one in the crime of degrading humanity. My special function from childhood, you might say, has been willing to make women realise their dignity."

Gandhi was opposed to the sexist treatment of Indian men towards women and this contributed towards his different image of women during his times. Physically they may differ but that was the only difference he saw:

"To call women the weaker sex is libel; it is man's injustice to women."

Gandhi saw women as man's equal partners. Mahatma Gandhi had said:

"Woman is the companion of man, gifted with equal mental capacities. She has the right to participate in the minutest details in the activities of man, and she has an equal right of freedom and liberty with him."

He spoke of Indian women fleeing from the clutches of the traditional roles of women as wives, child bearers and mothers that hamper their personal growth. This led him to write and speak on child marriage and the position of wives.

Gandhi and Liberating Women from Child Marriages

One of the changes that Gandhi fought for was the abolishment of child marriages. Child marriages hamper the individual growth of the young girls into full spirited women. Many ended as child widows. He encouraged men to boycott child marriages and pressed upon parents to be responsible enough not to give their young daughters to old men for the dowries:

"The least that a parent, who has so abused his trust as to give in marriage an infant to an old man in his dotage or to a boy hardly out of his teens, can do is to purge himself of his sin by remarrying the daughter when she becomes widowed."

Young widows, he urged, should be allowed to remarry if they choose to do so.

Gandhi on Husband-Wife Relationship

In a modern marriage where both spouses work, an understanding where husbands help out with household chores is unquestionable. However, in the early part of the 20th century in traditional colonial India, wives were expected to keep house and serve their husbands and children on hand and foot; or male chauvinistic instincts which tend to undermine what could be a loving and comforting husband-wife relationship. He was openly opposed to the traditional male domination of pushing women to the kitchen part of the house:

"Womanhood is not restricted to the kitchen."

He reminded husbands to give their wives equal treatment, respect their position, be a comrade and allow them the freedom to determine their own lives:

"The wife is not the husband's slave but his companion and his help-mate and an equal

partner in all his joys and sorrows – as free as the husband to choose her own path."

Gandhi was a feminist at heart and he fought for women's liberation during his time. It was reported that he himself helped his wife with the household chores such as the feeding of their baby and also helped his wife himself to deliver since the white midwife refused to show up to help with the deliver.

He saw women as equally competent as man and they were emotionally strong, if not stronger, than man to lead others. Gandhi saw the potential of women of India but he noted that they needed to be first be freed:

"Only when the woman is liberated from slavery of the kitchen that her true spirit may be discovered."

Once freed the women of India were called by Gandhi to work with him on India's independence from the British.

Gandhi's Call for Indian Women's Participation

It was Gandhi's strong belief that women were not less "fit" than men for he included women in his activities to bring about social and political change. In fact, he perceived woman to be stronger than man in terms of their spirits:

"Man can never be woman's equal in the spirit of selfless service with nature has endowed her."

Savita Singh testifies that the socio-political philosophy of Gandhi's is feminist. The non-violent way that he advocated was to encourage women's participation:

". . . the beauty of non-violent war is that women can play the same part in it as men. In a violent war women have no such privilege..."

In fact, Gandhi's faith in woman is such that he declared:

"She can become the leader in Satyagraha ..."

Satyagraha refers to ***"insistence on truth",*** resistance offered to uphold truth (Ravindra Kumar, 2003:87). Therefore, Gandhi was ahead of his Indian contemporaries for even thinking of women to take a lead. When he liberated Indian women out of the backyards and called them out to join in to fight for India's independence. He believed that the women of India needed to shed their traditional roles and partake in the fight for India's independence.

As a result of his conviction and dedicated work in freeing the women of India, thousands of Indian women partook in several of Gandhi's movements. His entourage, including his walk out to the sea known as the ***Dandi March of 1930***, against the Salt Tax imposed by the British Government, included women from all walks of life, Hindus and Muslims included. Although Gandhi had not wanted women to be included in the walk, the women protested as they wanted to be part of the historic event. Such was the strong support from women; all in their appreciation to him for speaking out for them.

Conclusion

The status of woman in Gandhi's eyes was that of equal standing as man. This was clearly indicated through his words and actions. It was through his leadership that more women came into Indian politics, which ultimately produced two women ministers in the first Cabinet of Independent India. Numerous women's groups were formed in India as a result of his act of empowering the women in India. Indian women today have inherited the freedom and dignity; Gandhi had fearlessly fought for in the last century.

His words and ideas remain as strong as they were when he first uttered them. Gandhi, a modern thinker and feminist, spoke for the women of India, and his words can still be heard in the 21st century.

References

1. Locate website on Mahatma Gandhi Album to view the photograph at http://www.kamat.com/mmgandhi/wedding.htm.
2. Refer Kamladevi Chattopadhyay's article on Gandhi titled, "Woman The Comrade", p. 9.

Bibliography

Gandhi Mohandas Karamchand. (1956). An Auto-biography or The Story of My Experiments with Truth. Ahmedabad: Navajivan Publishing House.

Jaya Jaitly,Gandhi and Women's Empowerment. Retrieved on 3/11/05 from http://www.mk.gandhi.org/articles/Jaya%20 Jaitly.htm.

Kamladevi Chattopadhyay. 16 November 2003. Woman the Comrade. Janta Weekly. Retrieved on 14/12/05 from http://www.mkgandhi/articles/ women & comrade.htm.

Kiran Saxena, Gandhi's Feminist Politics, Gender Equity and Patriarchal Values, Retrieved 13/12/05 from http://www.mk.gandhi.org/articles/Kiran%20 Saxena.htm.

Quotes of Mahatama Gandhi. Retrieved on 30/12/05 from http://www.Mahatma.org.in/quotes/quotes.jsp?link=qt

Ravindra Kumar. (2003). *Non-Violence and Its Philosophy*, Meerut: Dynamic, Publications.

Savita Singh. Empowerment of Women: Miles to Go. Retreived on 14/12/05 from http://www.mk.gandhi.org/articles/Gangrade.htm.

Savita Singh, Empowerment of Women: Miles to Go. Retrieved on 14/12/05 from http://www.mk.gandhi.org/articles/Gangrade.htm

Shail Sinha. Mahatma Gandhi: A Crusader of Women's Equality, Retrieved on 14.12.05 from http://www.sinha.com/crusader.htm.

Sita Kapadia, A Tribute to Mahatma Gandhi: His Views on Women and Social Changes retrieved on 12/14/2005 from Gandhi's Views on Women and Social Change.htm)

Sita Kapadia, A Tribute to Mahatma Gandhi: His Views on Women and Social Retrieved on 14/12/05 from Chttp://www.mk.gandhi.org/articles/kapadia.htm.hanges.

25

Culture of Peace: Relevance of Gandhian Concept in the Twenty-First Century

C. Naseema

A notable feature of Mahatma Gandhi's Socio-Political Philosophy was his advocacy of the concepts of peace culture and of non-violence or ***ahimsa***. It may be observed that the concept of ***ahimsa*** was not an original contribution of Mahatma Gandhi and it had been known and practiced in India since ancient times.

Mahatma Gandhi elevated the concepts of peace culture and non violence from the individual plane and applied it to various walks of life such as domestic, institutional, economic, social and political. Mahatma Gandhi's concept of non-violence or ***ahimsa*** was quite extensive and did not merely imply to avoidance of violence. Thus, he considered a harsh speech or thinking bad of others also as a part of violence.

Mahatma Gandhi had said

"I do not like the term 'passive resistance'. It fails to convey all I mean. It describes a method, but gives no hint of the system of which it is only a part. Real beauty–and that is my omit doing good against evil."

Satyagraha is a technique of resisting all that is evil, unjust or untrue by love, self suffering and by appealing to the divine spark in the soul of the opponent. It may be noted that the concept of ***Satyagraha*** differs from passive resistance, in so far as the letter was supposed to be a weapon of the weak and was characterized by hatred.

In passive resistance the violence is abjured on account of weakness. If there is a suitable opportunity, the passive resistor would not mind adoption of violent methods. Hence, it may be observed that passive resistance was a weapon of the weak.

However, ***Satyagraha*** is based on soul force and stands for vindication of truth not by the infliction of suffering on the opponent but on one's own Self. In Mahatma Gandhi's ***Satyagraha*** there is no scope for cowardice.

There are certain common methods like non-cooperation, boycott, strikes etc. in ***Satyagraha*** and passive resistance, but their spirit differs under the two. In passive resistance these methods are used to coerce the opponent to submission whereas in ***Satyagraha*** these instruments are used to exert spiritual influence and Self-suffering.

Another notable feature of Mahatma Gandhi's ***Saty-agraha*** was that it could be resorted to by the individual as well as the community and could be applied to all walks of life.

The concept of ***Satyagraha*** as Mahatma Gandhi had declared:

"It is a force that may be used by individuals as well as communities. It may be used as well in politics as in domestic affairs. Its universal applicability is a demonstration of its permanence and invincibility".

In fact Mahatma Gandhi stood for the practice of ***Satyagraha*** in the domestic and social relations before its adoption in political sphere.

Mahatma Gandhi saw a very close relationship between religion and politics and sought to spiritualize politics and this further strengthened the importance of the concept of peace culture in Mahatma Gandhi's Socio-political philosophy. He condemned politics which was devoid of religion on the ground that it makes man selfish, materialistic and opportunistic.

Mahatma Gandhi highlighted the close relationship between religion and politics and said:

"Those who say that religion has no relationship with politics do not understand the meaning of religion. For me there is no politics without religion. Politics is sub-ordinate to religion. Politics without religion is a death trap because it kills man's soul."

Mahatma Gandhi had also declared that:

"I could not be leading a religious life unless I identified myself with the whole of mankind, and that I could not do unless I took part in politics."

Hence, it may be observed that Mahatma Gandhi saw a close relationship between religion and politics and favoured a religiously dominated politics. Mahatma Gandhi identified religion with morality.

Religious compatibility or incompatibility is not based on purely theological merit; it is rather motivated by considerations other than theological. Religious compatibility cannot be decided at one theological level. What appears to be incompatible at one level may get reconciled at some other level. Thus at a higher philosophical level the

Hindu concept of ***'Advaita'*** and the Islamic concept of ***'Touheed'*** (Unity of God) seem to reconcile.

It can be observed that religion is an organising principle which gives form and shape to societies. Thus religion significantly promotes the concepts of communal harmony, of peaceful co-existence and of peace culture.

Contacts with leaders of various religions and reading of their learned works and the meetings with the ***Sufi*** saints and the saints of the ***Bhakti*** Movement gradually convinced Emperor Akbar that while there were differences of Sect and Creed, all religions had a number of good points which remained obscured due to communal tension between different communities in India.

As a result of this, Emperor Akbar set up a new religion which incorporated the religious philosophies of many existing religions–Islam, Hinduism, Buddhism, Jainism, Christianity and Sikhism.

Thus it can be clearly observed that to promote **Socio-Economic peace culture** in India, it is important to bring about conditions favourable for economic parity, and this economic parity can be maintained and strengthened only by bringing about a social transformation of the existing socio-economic system in India as was also enunciated by the great Mahatma Gandhi.

Mahatma Gandhi was a saint in the tradition of Guru Nanak and Kabir who worked unceasingly for human equality in their respective regions of activity through leading a life of devotion and continuous preaching. Mahatma Gandhi was the greatest advocate of the concepts of communal harmony, of social harmony, of non-violence, of peaceful co-existence, of ***Satyagraha*** and a peace culture in the world and he advocated these concepts in all their forms and manifestations.

The term culture is a highly complex and dynamic concept or reality consisting of many ingredients. It is a total concept or reality inclusive of divergent components. It is symbolic of a way of life, to which accretions are continually being made. The birth and growth of culture was made possible by the freedom and security attained by man through the conquest of nature and the building upon the civil society. Therefore, it is said that agriculture is the best culture whereby man get security. Culture is, the sum total of the activities whereby a person relates himself to the significant aspects of reality, actual or imagined. In brief, culture is a way of life, a way of thinking and a way of worship.

Peace is not merely a state of non-violence or absence of violence. It is something more since it is also a positive state of mind as well as a constructive goal of person, society and mankind. It is true that peace will be achieved by removing all kinds of violence such as war, poverty, starvation, environmental destruction, violation of human rights, cruelty against women and children and so on; yet it has a positive side too.

History bears evidence of the continuity and universality of the quest for peace, both in the mind and life of the in-dividual and the life and commerce of societies and nations.

Peace has both individual and social aspects. Peace at the individual level is the inner peace or peace of mind, a state in which there is perfect harmony among the various psychic forces which otherwise pull in different directions and become a source of conflict and tension. It is a psycho-logical state when mind is free from tension, stress and strain, the different passions and desires and the conflicts that arise from them. It thus signifies a tranquil composure and a peacefulness of temper. At the individual level, it indicates a state in which the sense of being full or complete is experienced when all the faculties of an individual are in full harmony or in total orderly alliance with one another.

At the social level it indicates a harmonious community as peace is the natural or moral condition of man in relationship to others enjoined most intimately in the family, and extended to others by a social bond. Social peace is a state of harmonious relationship between individual as well as groups with varied interests. It is a state of harmony between parts and the whole.

All the great religions of the world have an emphasis on values such as observing truth in thought, words and deeds, living a life of self-restraint, having active love for others etc. It is necessary for a man to develop altruistic qualities which are essential for the promotion of peace as they help in developing a sense of solidarity and identity of interests. If the idea was to be extended to the family of nations, mankind can hope to have peace in the world.

The individual and society are two inseparable aspects of man's life and both influence each other. The individual has to realize his peace as part of the whole which is society and not isolated from it.

Peace, when viewed in the context of social and cosmic interrelationship, also exhibits harmony, wholeness and completeness as the characteristics of the social inter-relationship.

World of Peace

All religions preach peace, but in fact religion has been one of the major source of violent conflict down through the centuries and remains so even today. To facilitate and motivate the people for the study of the essence of all religions, Vinoba Bhave studied the original scriptures of all religions and gleaned the essence of them. He composed three verses in the names of all gods of different religions of the world which is recited during the prayer.

Gandhi says:

> ***"The more we concentrate on the fundamental oneness of humanity, the more do different religions appear as enriching and strengthening one another".***

Science was supposed to help establish peace, but it has created increasingly deadly weapons of mass destruction.

Religious compatibility or incompatibility is not based on purely theological merit; it is rather motivated by considerations other than theological. Religious compatibility cannot be decided at one theological level. What appears to be incompatible at one level may get reconciled at some other level. Thus at a higher philosophical level the Hindu concept of ***'Advaita'*** and the Islamic concept of ***'Touheed'*** [Unity of God] seem to reconcile.

Peace will not be established among men unless men thirst for peace for its own sake. Peace will not come and the world will not be free from violence, until society knows and experiences the greatness and importance of the ***"independent power of peace".***

Peace to be peace in the real sense of the term must be based on a genuine change of heart, when mutual distrust, hatred and enmity must cease for good, giving place to ever-abiding friendship. Peace is unattained by part performance of conditions, even as a chemical combination is impossible without complete fulfillment of the conditions of the attainment thereof.

In brief, peace culture is a relevant theme in all times to be practiced and to be assimilated by every individual.

26

Understanding the Present World Order: Perspectives of Gandhi and Russell

R. K. Kothari

Two consecutive world wars in the first half of the twentieth century and the consequent cold war that survived for about four decades and thereafter the unjust global order that has come into force; all these developments have made us to ponder and chalk out an alternative framework of global order where people allover the globe could live in peace and tranquility with due respect and assured reasonable standard of living. It is in this respect that the frameworks developed by the two distinguished thinkers during the twentieth century, namely, Mahatma Gandhi and Bertrand Arthur William Russell about the establishment of alternative world order models may be considered extremely important and viable.

The fact remains that world history during the twentieth century shall remain incomplete without taking into account the works of Gandhi and Russell. Both were great thinkers, humanist and followers of peace. They would continue to be remembered in future for the simple, unique and unparalleled path they showed to the people for the promotion of world peace. Both are known for their creative thinking and inspiring works for the regeneration of human values towards the promotion of an ideal international society. They had a burning zeal for removing the sorrows, sufferings and misery of the people across the globe. They fought till the end for the well being of human society. In this article, a very modest attempt has been made to understand the present world order from the perspectives of Gandhi and Russell.

In this context, it is necessary to define the scope of world order. The world is a relatively large network of activities and interactions among people with having geographical boundaries properly demarcated in which the sovereign states function independently or in communities. The sovereign states are not the geographical entities alone; they are socially and historically linked together. World order in fact constitutes a complex network of human beings on the one hand and of sovereign states on the other. It is a product of ideas and ideologies pertaining to various aspects of life-political, economic, cultural, ecological and so on. It is not necessarily confined to a group of states or a particular continent; it may be multi-continental and global in spread. However, it is difficult to define the concept in specific terms because its meaning is culture specific and deeply rooted in the geopolitical realities of time and space.

International System and the Present World Order

It was much anticipated by the scholars and policy makers that the rise of the nation-state system during the seventeenth century after the treaty of Westphalia would solve most of the problems of the world and more particularly it would be able to reduce the possibilities of wars to a significant level and thereby to strengthen physical and human security. However, without any hesitation one may conclude that the nation-state system failed to achieve its desired goals and consequently there is complete anarchy and disorder in the present international system. The recurring wars and the destructions that have been taking place since the establishment of nation state system convinced the people that the concept of sovereign nation states was no longer a safety valve against wars. Consequently, the movement towards formation of world govt. started in the early part of 20th century that resulted in the formation of the world government named as the League of Nations. It envisaged voluntary surrender or limitations of national sovereignty. But the League failed to emerge as a responsible international organization and consequently it lost its relevance. The collapse of the international order within the framework of the League of Nations by 1938, forced the major powers to form another world govt. and as a result the United Nations came into existence in 1945 with certain specific objectives in mind.

For long, almost till the middle of twentieth century, the world order in vogue was Euro-centric. However, gradually the Russians rejected the imperial order enforced under the hegemony of the United States. It challenged the Euro-centric world order and tried to present a suitable alternative. The cold war period that lasted for about four decades, after the end of the Second World War, was dominated by Soviet and American style of socialist and capitalist orders. However, the disintegration of the Soviet Union in the early 1990s paved the way for a uni-polar world characterized by the dominance of the only superpower the U. S. A. By virtue of its military and economic strength, it continues to shape the destiny of world politics to promote its own foreign policy objectives and national interests. The U S intervention in Iraq and Afghanistan are the two recent examples to corroborate this stand. Some powers like Germany, France and Russia attempted in vein to dissuade the U S from enforcing its will. Thus, in the present international context the U S hegemony remains unchallenged.

United Nations which was supposed to emerge as the truly multilateral body to effectively deal with various crises in the international system has not been able to pay much attention to that. Some commentators say that the United Nations has been totally hijacked or monopolized by the U. S. A. Therefore, the objective to promote a new global order keeping in mind the interests of the states in general, particularly the developing world, has remained unfulfilled. Without entering into any debate, it may be pointed out that the United Nations has failed to live up to the expectations of the common people across the world. Moreover, today the very survival of the United Nations depends upon the mercy of the big powers, particularly the U. S. A.

The existing world order suits the interests of the imperialist powers which prefer to maintain status quo. It does not support any type of revolutionary transformation & change in the present international situation. The people who support the present world order are minority. Majority of the people are deprived from the access to global resources. A large section of the people in Asia and Africa suffers from malnutrition and lives below the poverty line. They are forced to live even without two meals a day. Such unjust system must be changed.

The pursuit of peace through development has added a new dimension to the notion of world peace. It is felt that economic development of the third world countries is a major precondition for the promotion of peace. With the establishment of the United Nations, peace has been progressively linked with development. Previously any such linkage was unthinkable. The convergence of all parties on the need for development is yet to emerge.

Alternative Models of World Order

Mahatma Gandhi did not concern himself much about global problems. However, the occasional remarks he made on international affairs together with an extension of the implications of his utterances in the domestic context will reveal a fairly clear world order he has projected. Russell, in contrast, although being a pure mathematician, developed keen interest in philosophy. His concise book, **The Problems of Philosophy**, appeared in 1912 and gradually, he paid much attention towards developing an alternative model of world order.

Russell was deeply disturbed by the developments that took during the First World War. At the outbreak of the war, he was an outspoken pacifist. In July 1914, he collected signatures from fellow professors for a statement urging England to remain neutral in the imminent war. The concept of parochial nationalism that promoted mass murder and large scale violence was criticized by Russell. To him, militarism is caused by ***"cowardice, love of dominion, and lust for blood."*** During the Second World War Russell, however, abandoned his pacifism. He explained that the use of force is justifiable when it is ordered according to law by a neutral authority for the general good but not when it is primarily for the interest of one of the parties in the quarrel. Similarly Mahatma Gandhi was also extremely pained at heart to have witnessed the sufferings of the people caused by the two world wars.

Russell provided two alternative suggestions: one solution was for the creation of an international organization backed up by force to keep the peace; another solution, he suggested, was passive resistance as suggested by Gandhi. According to him, if this was intelligently adopted by the whole nation the national life could be better protected. Gandhi, in contrast, not only discouraged the use of force but also opposed any types of stockpiles of weapons to resolve any conflict.

During the war, Russell published several books on politics, war, and peace. **Principles of Social Reconstruction** was released in America as **Why Men Fight**. In this work he argued that the passions of war must be controlled, not by thought alone, but by the passion and desire to think clearly. To him, wars could be prevented if the great powers firmly determine that peace shall be preserved. Peace could be permanently maintained by a world federation with the civil functions of a state legislative, administrative, and judicial and an international military force. This authority would legislate, adjudicate and enforce international laws, but would not interfere with the internal affairs of nations. In **Political Ideals** Russell discussed the need for an international government to secure peace in the world by means of effective international law. The benefit of having law rather than international anarchy will give the international government a respected authority so that states will no longer feel free to use aggression. Under the circumstances, a large international force will become unnecessary.

The world order framework developed by Gandhi essentially aims at developing a culture of peace, whereby man would be able to curb his aggressiveness and prepared to follow a policy of peaceful coexistence or at least a policy of non-military global competition. Gandhi considered war as the creation of minority, who tries to impose their will upon the majority. Human beings by nature are non-violent. If they were violent, as projected by some political thinkers, then it would have been difficult for them to survive till date. The very fact that so many people live in this world today implies that man is more non-violent than violent. Gandhi saw human beings as divine.

Despite the fact that war has been the common feature of the international system in the past as well as present, human beings, according to Gandhi, have always thought in terms of establishing peace at the local, regional and global levels. To say that violence is part of human nature is to deny the difference between animals and humans. In fact, Gandhi stressed upon the unilateral rejection of the use of violence in any form in any human relation particularly in international relations. He prescribed moral means to settle all disputes – interpersonal or international. During the Second World War, Gandhi advised England not to fight Hitler with arms and show to the world the use of Satyagraha in international relations. Thus while Gandhi spoke in favor of moral means, Russell kept both the options open, i.e. the use of force as well as passive resistance for the promotion of world peace and physical human security.

For Gandhi, violence breeds violence. He firmly believed that violence could not be removed by violence; it could only be removed by non-violence.

As fire can not extinguish fire, war cannot abolish war. But how can a country follow non-violent path when it knows that it is encircled by enemies. In Gandhian vocabulary, there is no enemy; only there can be adversaries who could be won over by soul force, not by brute force.

From Gandhian perspective, such condition could be met only by changing the minds and hearts of the people because the seeds of war lie in the minds of the people. Gandhi emphasized on changing the mindset of man for developing a culture of peace. It is through this method that the world would be prepared to negotiate a policy peaceful coexistence at the global level. Gautama Buddha and Lord Mahavira preached the message of Ahimsa and compassion. Ashoka one of the greatest emperors had followed Buddha's teachings in giving up wars and to follow the path of peace after the Kalinga episode. Jesus Christ preached the message of love, forgiveness and peace. In contemporary times, Gandhi has voiced the efficacy of non-violence against violence.

Gandhi prescribed moral means to settle international disputes. He made this experiment in South Africa and India with the hope that the example he presented would inspire the whole world to follow suit. Gandhiji's conception of India's independence had global relevance in the sense that he wanted free India to be an instrument for human welfare and global peace. As stated earlier, Russell advocated moral means to settle disputes; however, the option to use force was also open before him, although under special circumstances.

Diagnosis of World Problems and Remedial Measures

Russell pointed out that capitalism is the root cause of major problems in the international system. It has the utmost desire to exploit the resources of underdeveloped countries which gives rise to conflict and contradiction in the international system. He recommended the abolition of private ownership of land and capital as one necessary step towards peace. However, he did not advocate the abolition of capitalism as a means to peace. Gandhi, in contrast, supported private ownership and advocated the promotion of trusteeship system where every individual including the capitalists would voluntarily contribute a part of their income to the trust for the well-being of the common people.

Gandhi viewed man as essentially good. He saw human beings as divine. It is the quality of self restraint which distinguished man from brute. The divine element is present in all men and hence all are equally endowed with the capacity to develop non-violence. Gandhian non-violence postulates a positive relationship between man and man, man and nature, man and society, and among different societies.

It is necessary to end exploitation of man by man for the sake of promotion of social justice and equality. Human values are to be promoted and nurtured so as to develop the feeling among the people that they are not resident of a particular country, rather resident of the world. ***"Jai Jagat"*** [vctory of the world] was the slogan raised by Gandhi, who has been described as an apostle of peace. He strove and died for peace. For Gandhi peace is integrally related to justice. Peace is not mere a cessation of hostilities. The precondition for peace, according to him, was freedom from exploitation. According to him, only non-violent and just peace could ensure lasting peace. Gandhi wrote in ***Harijan Patrika*** [March 22, 1946]:

"Peace will never come until the great powers courageously decide to disarm themselves.

Exploitation and domination of one nation over another can have no place in a world striving to put an end to all wars—I have no doubt that unless big nations shed their desire of exploitation and the sprit of which war is the natural expression and atom bomb the inevitable consequence, there is no hope for peace in the world."

It is important to note that Russell also held the big powers responsible for the lack of peace in the international system.

Russell supported the idea of the League of Nations and world govt. for the promotion of international peace and security. He also advocated the idea of national disarmament. In 1936 he published **Which Way to Peace?** In this book he criticized isolationism and encouraged international law and world govt. with an international armed force to prevent war. Whereas for Gandhi, arbitration, world govt. international organization, disarmament and defense force etc. were not the ideal solutions. He had reservations about the efficacy of international law as an instrument for the solution of inter-state disputes. Gandhi prescribed for a world federation of free and independent states. His concept of world govt. transcended the traditional thinking. According to him, the international organization could not satisfy the conditions for bringing genuine peace. He argued that peace would not be established through mere conferences. He was not hopeful about League of Nations and the United Nations because both these organizations lacked the spirit of non-violence and failed to promote world peace and security.

The development of nuclear weapons caused Russell deep concern. In November 1945, he gave a speech in the House of Lords and recommended that nuclear weapons be brought under international control. He believed that world government was the only alternative to avoid the disaster of nuclear war. People and nations must become willing to submit to international law. Russell suggested that all fissionable raw materials be owned by an international authority. International inspectors must ensure that no nation or individual has access to fissionable raw material. But for Gandhi the absence of war or weapons does not mean the presence of peace. He believed that the doctrine of non-violence should guide relations between states. He therefore argued for total disarmament. He was optimistic enough to advocate unilateral disarmament. If one great nation opts for disarmament many others would follow suit. Gandhi stated that with the establishment of a democratic world federation, universal disarmament would be practicable. As a messiah of peace and non-violence, Gandhi focused on the supremacy of moral force over physical force.

Gandhi believed that complete disarmament was possible only through following the path of non-violence. In this regard, he stated that India would be the first country to provide leadership to other nations for the promotion of world peace. However, the precondition for disarmament was to end exploitation of one state by another. Therefore, the Gandhian way claims to stand for non-violent and non-exploitative social order which alone could ensure just and enduring peace. If individuals could preach non-violence, the whole nation could also do so.

Gandhi was of the firm opinion that war could never end wars. Violence breeds only violence but can never end violence. War is destructive and peace is constructive. They are opposite to each other. Peace is a positive force of cementing people. The search for peace, according to Gandhi, should be in the way of non-violence alone.

For Russell, the steps toward peace include the abolition of nuclear tests, the solving of differences without the threat of war, bringing fissionable materials for the production of nuclear weapons under international control and a reduction of conventional forces, appointment of a Conciliation Committee with representatives from the major powers and neutrals, the prohibition of foreign troops on any territory, and the establishment of a Federal International Authority with armed force to prevent war. Russell advocated that the armed force be kept under the command of officers from neutral countries.

Russell supported the idea of an international court which would enjoy the same authority as national courts. He advocated that there would be more freedom in the world under effective law & it would be easier to maintain civilian control over the military. The scientific and technological advancements have not only made international anarchy more dangerous, but also the facility of world cooperation is now more available. He further argued that for the sake of a stable international system greater economic equality & opportunity must be granted to the poorer peoples of the world. He emphasized the role of education for the promotion of peace and justice. He stated that education ought to be global in scope and perspective. He also highlighted the need for peace movements across the globe despite having differences among nations on various issues.

Gandhi, in contrast, stated that despite the fact that nations have become independent, there is still ideological imperialism and also economic domination of one nation over others. Such dependencies must disappear and it has to pave the way for the complete independence and equality of nations. Today we live in a violent world but men fundamentally desire peace. It is recognized by all that no just and social order or stable peace can flow from violence, war and repression. Good means alone can lead us to ever lasting peace. If peace is established by violence it will be of no use. Thus neither Gandhi had imposed faith neither on international organizations nor on the effectiveness of international laws as proposed by Russell.

Mahatma Gandhi said:

"I would not like to live in the world if it is not an integral one."

He also said:

"My patriotism is not exclusive, but embraces the whole world. I am against the patriotism that seeks to develop one's own country by ways of making other nations suffer or exploiting other nations."

He viewed the world as one single unit. Gandhi and Russell both spoke in favour of a stable international system based upon the values of peace and social justice.

Russell pleaded:

"There lies before us, if we choose, continued progress in happiness, knowledge and wisdom. Shall we instead choose death because we cannot forget our quarrels? I appeal as a human being to human beings. Remember your humanity and forget the rest. If you can do so the way lies open to a new Paradise; if you cannot, nothing lies before you but universal death."

On the question of modern civilization, Gandhi and Rawls differed significantly. Gandhi denounced the modern industrial western civilization. He renounced western materialism and modern technology like telegraph, telephone and even railways. He considered the advent of technology and industrialization as the basic cause of human misery in modern society. Although Gandhi recognized the immense increase in productivity and consequent rise of living standard in the West, he denied that industrialization promotes happiness and well-being of the common people. Gandhi also rejected modern economic order because it was based on economic inequality; it dehumanized man and ignored his personality. Throughout the West the prevailing aim of governments, political parties, and the public generally is maximum incomes and maximum production and consumption of goods and services. The outcome is a persistent demand for higher incomes, more markets for bigger exports of goods in order to import large quantities of food, raw materials and luxuries, increasing social tensions at home, and dangerous international tensions arising from the intensive competition among nations for markets and supplies. Russell, in contrast, extended his support and sympathy towards modern western culture and civilization.

Assessment

In the final analysis, the inference that could be drawn from the above is that although Gandhi and Russell had differed on the paths to be followed towards the promotion of new global order, they had a common objective in mind that is the utmost desire to achieve world peace and thereby making lives of the human beings safe and secure.

Both Russell and Gandhi were political activists. Through out his life Gandhi actively participated in political campaign against the British rule in India. He also expressed deep concern on many international issues including his campaign in South Africa against the policy of apartheid. Russell also from 1950 till death was extremely active in political campaigning. He established the Bertrand Russell Peace Foundation in 1964. He supported the Jews in Russia and the Arabs in Palestine and condemned the Vietnam War. Last twenty years of his life were primarily devoted to warnings about nuclear danger and protesting about policies of war.

Russell discouraged the use of force to the extent possible. He suggested that happiness depends on harmony with other people. War, according to him, was inevitable as long as big powers have pride of patriotism which promotes mass murder. Russell stated that passions of war must be controlled. Wars could only be prevented by a positive life of passion. Impulse must not be weakened but directed "towards life and growth rather than towards death and decay." Gandhi, on the contrary, was thoroughly opposed to the use of force in any form and thereby opposed the concept of war.

However, the common ground between the two has been that Gandhi and Russell, both, fought against the unethical and unjust order in favour of an international system based upon the principles of equality and self respect among nations as well as among citizens across the globe.

References

1. Bandyopadhyaya, Jayantunaja, *Social and Political Thought of Gandhi*, [Howrah: Manuscript India, 2000]
2. Brown, Chris, *Understanding International Relations*, [London: Macmillan, 1997], pp.22-24.
3. Gandhi, M. K., *Harijan*, March 22, 1946.
4. John, M. S., "Gandhian Concept of World Order: An Evaluation" in Ramjee Singh and S. Sundaram, [Ed.], *Gandhi and the World Order* [New Delhi: APH Publishing Corporation, 1996]

5. Maharajan, M., *Mahatma Gandhi and the New Millennium*, [New Delhi: Discovery Publishing House, 2001]
6. Mishra, Suresh [Ed.], *Gandhian Alternative*, [New Delhi: Concept Publishing Co., 2005]
7. Mukherjee, Subrata and Ramaswamty, Sushila [Eds.], *Political Ideas of Mahatma Gandhi*, [New Delhi: Deep and Deep, 1998].
8. *Perspectives of Peace Research*, Peace research Centre, Gujarat Vidyapith, Ahmedabad, August 1972.
9. Shuying, Wang, "Gandhi's Economic Thinking and His Internationalism" in Ramjee Singh, [Ed.], *Gandhi and the Future of Humanity*, [Varanasi: Manak Publications, 1997]

Refer websites

www.humanities.mcmaster.ca/~**russell**

en.wikipedia.org/wiki/**Bertrand_Russell**

www.quotationspage.com/quotes/**Bertrand_Russell**

www.mcmaster.ca/russdocs/**russell**.htm

27
Peace, Non-violence and Democracy in Burma: Voices from India of Buddha and Gandhi

Sulak Sivaraksa

I can share my thoughts with you but also to understand the unique circumstances of the struggle for democracy in Burma which is being fought both within and outside Burma today. Here I express my deepest concerns relating to the crisis of substance. This is afflicting every walk of our life and more evident in our attitude to religion as we are attracted by the rituals than the substance. There are many people who are corrupt and societies which are at war with each other yet they all want to purify themselves. They may belong to any religion but it is the weakness of the institution that has permitted the spread of this consciousness. This is also true of the institution founded by Lord Buddha and this applies to Mahatma Gandhi as well. There are Buddhists who worship Lord Buddha but do not consider the need to follow his teachings. This is also true of the followers of Mahatma Gandhi. At times Gandhi is over praised. There are many people here who think that Gandhi is great but do not consider the need to follow him. Gandhi for me is like the Buddha. He made all of us to become a little better human being. If we can become Buddha even for two to three minutes I would consider that as a great blessing. We need to be aware, mindful and kind to other beings.

India is a big country with its culture and civilization spread all over Asia. But the Indians do not want to recognize this reality about their own culture and civilization. They like to learn from the West. I think it should be the other way. The West should learn from Asia. We also have to learn from the Indians. The Thais ignore Indians and readily admire the Japanese and the Americans. Development is a new religion that everyone wants to worship and follow without any respect for values of traditions. Everyone wants a greater share and materialism is the driving force behind this motive. There is little concern for the poor and marginalized people in the world. There is little respect for nature and cultural traditions of the people. The spiritual basis of the relationship between man, nature and development has been overlooked for the sake of economic growth and material progress. The Assembly of Poor in Thailand has been struggling to change this attitude of the government and the people at large. In America there is a wonderful group of people who really take Buddha much more seriously than we Buddhists do in Asia. They take Buddha seriously and sometimes for their own end. We need to remind them constantly about the meaning of the life and teachings of Buddha.

We need to overcome our greed and selfishness. There are changes taking place in the world. The socially engaged Buddhism is spreading in the world today. I do think what His Holiness the Dalai Lama had said is very important. He observed that 'religion is only secondary and what is more important is spirituality.' Spirituality has been killed by the West in the name of enlightenment.

The West also used to be spiritual not so long ago. The spirituality suffers when the Church becomes powerful and the priest turns more powerful than the rest. What we need today is the spirituality. To be spiritual is to breathe properly. We begin to breathe right from the time when we are in our mother's womb and continue breathing until we depart from this life. We do not yet take good care of our breathing except for those who practice ***Yoga*** and other forms of body and mind activities. If we concentrate on our breathing it will help us enhance our intellectual power, become more humble and we can even learn the mystery of next life.

Mahatma Gandhi has said that we are not important but what we do mindfully becomes very important. When we fight for democracy in Burma and we must also fight for Tibetan freedom and elsewhere in the world. I am quite certain that your despair in Burma could soon be converted into a hopeful condition. Your struggle and experiences would serve as an example as well as inspire the younger generations in future. The younger people will become more enthusiastic and inspired. I am always hopeful. I find younger people as more inspiring and educative. They teach us a lot. I come from the upper middle class background but I continue to learn so much from the poor. You grow when you are prepared to learn from others and with this growth we can overcome hurdles and the challenges facing our lives. The multinational corporations have the latest technology and the best qualified people to serve their interests. What they lack badly is the spiritual dimension to progress. Hence they are always short of moral legitimacy. Spirituality and moral legitimacy do not constitute as Puritanism. It is good to lead a more simple and normal life. We should care for spiritual values and show our concern for the poor and suffering people in the world. I think all these steps would help us move in the correct path in life. I am a Buddhist and I try to learn from my own struggles. We have to be careful in understanding the purpose of our action. We sometime undertake a task to satisfy our ego or seek recognition. We should therefore become more aware of ourselves. Meditation and spiritual practices are so important in this regard.

We must learn to respect and show our concern for others. If we meet people from Burma outside their own country the best thing to do is to try to be their friend. You should know and understand that the people from Burma are living here and elsewhere in the world in exile. We should listen than preaching to them. They may not have solutions to their own problems. We do not have answers to all our questions either. What they need most is our understanding and friendship. The Burmese possess their own positive and negative national characteristics. If I may say so the Burmese are sometimes very arrogant. I admire them for many positive traits. We cannot change them and we only need to understand them better. The ethnic divide and conflict inside Burma has to be seen from the context of colonial British rule and the oppressive native rule. The basic trust and goodwill among the common people suffers due to secrecy and lack of democracy within a system. It is highly important to remain open, honest and democratic. These are very important qualities along with our continuous struggle to become more humble and a better human being. We shall overcome.

28
Problems Before Present Education: Some Remedial Suggestions Through Gandhian Approach

Ravindra Kumar

Six years ago we have kept pace in 21st Century. There are more than six hundred *crores* of persons in the whole world now. The population of our country, India, is more than one hundred *crore*. A big number of people all over the world are facing many challenges and problems in the current century of which unemployment is the foremost problem being faced. Estimatedly, more than one hundred *crore* people that are approximately 1/6 of the population are in the clutches of the problem all over the world. It is not an easy task to control this problem expeditiously, thereby ensuring employment to all. We can very well perceive that human society is badly affected owing to this. It causes many foul resultants. Although it is not a topic of analysis here, yet it can be conveniently grasped that one, who does not have source of income and cannot earn in accordance with one's requirements, can go to any extent: we can guess all such vivid problems of serious nature. In such circumstances, only well-directed education, equipped with flexible methods according to the needs and the demands of the time can be capable of resolving the problems. This alone, can be a ground for our optimism. We can expect from it a way leading to the fulfillment of aim of human life, subsequently for freedom from varied problems.

In every age and time, there has been immense importance of education and its methods in accordance with national and regional circumstances. It has accorded a base of life full of pleasure, fulfillment and peace to human beings along with making them self-dependent. However, education and its method prevalent in the circumstances prevailing one hundred, five hundred, one thousand or two thousand years before cannot be as significant today as it was then. It is noteworthy that there has been an effect and action in every era to make education humanly fit according to the time and circumstances. Needless to say, this was the need of the time.

In our country, it is being said regarding education since ancient times, ***"Sa Vidyaya Vimuktaye"***. It signifies that the aim or/and objective of education is to make a man self-dependent in every field. It has this very end within its fold. Merely writing, reading or alphabetic knowledge does not amount to getting any benefit from education. Getting education in real sense means sharpening the intellect, or getting rid of day-to-day problems and to bring about complete harmonious development of personality based on equal opportunity. That's why Mahatma Gandhi, a true representative of the people of his time too talked of education capable of all round development of humans to enable them to lead a righteous life becoming self-reliant.

Population in the world has increased rapidly. At the time of independence, that is exactly 59 years ago, India had 33 *crores* of people. Now this is more than 100 *crores*. Primary and higher secondary schools increased in proportion to the increase in population. Colleges and universities, imparting higher education, also increased. Number of universities or similar institutions is 250 in India alone. Literary knowledge increased tremendously on the world level. It is cent percent in many nations. The day is not far away when everyone will be literate. Number of degree holders is also on the increase. We are all observing significant progress that has been and is continuing in the field of computer due to advancement in science and technology. In spite of achieving all this, we do not see a decrease in economic and social problems pertaining to humankind. Dreadful problem of unemployment has emerged with the increase in population, which rendered man non-peaceful at social and economic planes.

How has all this happened? Literacy increased. There has been much increase in number of degree holders. There have been research accomplishments. Education developed remarkably not only at basic and secondary levels but also at higher level. Then, why there is no peace among human beings? The straightforward and simple answer to this query is that the direction of education is not adequate. Educational method today is full of several flaws. This condition prevails, more or less, in all countries of the world. It is not only in context of India alone. I have been to many nations of Asia and Europe during the last one decade. All are, more or less, under pressure of the problem of unemployment. They are also perplexed while pondering about future. I would like to quote an example of The Netherlands. I have been there a few years back. It is a beautiful and developed country. Population there is not very much. However, I found that hundreds of young men and women were worried about their future after getting education up to the highest degree conferred by a university. The Government of Netherlands provides allowance for fulfillment of basic necessities [meals, clothes, housing, medical facility, etc.] to unemployed young men and women. This suffices towards their subsistence anyhow but their future life remains in dark indeed. They cannot build a golden future while being unemployed and depending upon unemployment allowance only. They are unable to carry out all sided-development of personality. They cannot keep pace with others in the society. It is in this perspective that when I asked a young man, going to complete his Ph. D. thesis, about his future planning, he replied, "The biggest problem before me is regarding getting an employment. I shall be nowhere if I do not get it within a year.... I want employment, whatever it may be".

What is apt to say for an educational system when a person is in perplexity even though he is going to get doctorate degree and is the citizen of a developed nation. I again asked this young person, "You get unemployment allowances in your country: why are you so worried?" He answered, "Yes, it is true that an unemployment allowance exists. There are many joyful on this accord...but, is it a life?"

Not all the nations provide unemployment allowance to their citizens. However, where it is prevalent, it is not a permanent panacea of the problem. Let us then deliberate as to what the students achieved after getting higher education. What could they gain after getting education up to 20, 22 or 25 years of life at varied levels? This is a problem oriented question before the system, educationists and social scientists as well as before the students. In fact, it is the sole responsibility of the system, educationists and social scientists to make education humanly fit according to the time and the circumstances. They cannot avoid this responsibility. It was in this context that 2500 years ago, Plato, the Greek philosopher expressed and gave to the society his views on aims and methods of education. He told about gradually making it practical. His views have significance to some extent even today.

Not long ago, Mahatma Gandhi called upon adopting a method with basic/fundamental education in which knowledge is not given for the sake of knowledge. It has its practical aspect because of preparing student for self reliance and to lead a life with work. His call was important and happens to be so even today. It is antagonistic that we did not adopt it. The loss caused to us on this accord cannot be estimated easily.

In Indian circumstances, there was absolute necessity of adopting an employment-oriented educational system according to Mahatma Gandhi's views. He was rightly of the opinion that the Indian education system can be effective only when it is well disposed towards the circumstances or situation and is modified according to time and space. Even today, the guidelines suggested by him are relevant to a great extent.

We are attached to a hundred years old system and that has become completely fruitless today. It has become difficult today for a Ph.D. degree holder to the get job of a clerk. I mean to say that non-attention towards above-mentioned responsibility for so many years has resulted in education not becoming successful in accomplishing its aims and objectives. Especially, it has not been successful in solving the problem of unemployment. As such, it is now quite essential that this system should be made practical and effective as per the demands of time and suggestions made by Gandhiji. It should be made collaborative in toto to human values as desired by him.

In this context, it is the demand of the time that technical knowledge, for which Mahatma Gandhi has used the term ***buniyadi***, must be recognized as a compulsory part of education. It should be admitted that this knowledge should be akin to conditions prevailing in the country, resources available, etc. Subsequently, it should be gradually developed in further education of a student according to his capabilities, interests and attributes. I have two examples to clarify my above-mentioned statement. I was a student of sixth or seventh class when two men came to my school to demonstrate how to make Lifebuoy soap. The Principal ordered all students to assemble in the playground. Both the men taught the students how to make the soap. Next day, a student brought such an exquisite Lifebuoy soap made by him that it surpassed even the soap of the company. The boy went to the Principal and presented the same to him. He praised the student very much. This definitely stimulated the courage of the student. The Principal presented this work of student before all in the school and asked to derive inspiration from that. This further inspired that student. The boy became interested in technical knowledge. He was virtuous. Accordingly, he continued to make Lifebuoy soap off and on at his home by *ghee*. The father of the boy was very angry at this. He used to come to the Principal so often to say, "You invited the persons who told how to make soap indigenously. My son has been constantly increasing the household expenses".

The father did not encourage his son. Even then, the son continued to take interest in soap making. Today, he is approximately 47 or 48 yeas of age and is the General Manager of an international soap manufacturing company. The soap of this company is famous all over the world for its remarkable quality. The son had to wait for 30 years to achieve a place but even then he did praise worthy job because of his virtue, interest and capability. He could have achieved this distinction within 25 or 20 years in case he had encouragement from his father.

The second example relates to the period of my higher education. There was a girl student in my college. Her father was an ordinary farmer but was immensely interested in sugarcane and resultant products. He had gained considerable knowledge of these.

His daughter, the student of this very accord, also took keen interest in performance relating to agriculture. The student passed B.Sc. in first division. Her father wished her to be a candidate at Civil Service and to go for M.A. by faculty change. The girl did not want this but respecting her father's wishes, she changed the faculty and passed M.A., securing third division. She was under rebellion against her father now. She further worked very hard for two years and passed M. Sc. [Ag.] obtaining first division. She undertook research assignment subsequently and today she is an eminent scientist. It is a fact that the girl had to waste quite a significant time of two years but she presented a good example before others as per her virtue, interest and capability. An encouragement from her father at the prior stage could have been better.

I intended to say by all this that a student should come out with a certain mind from the education that the degree earned by him is apt towards an employment unto him. This is possible only when he possesses technical knowledge also in the specific field: notwithstanding that, he may have a degree in science, commerce or arts. A graduate can proceed on the way of life only after getting an employment. It is definite that education with technical knowledge makes employment an easy task. While doing so the graduate will not face difficulties in thenceforth developing his personality, keeping pace with others in the society or moving ahead at socio-economic level. Ultimately, this technical knowledge and education paves way to social, national or international welfare. We shall now have to achieve real aim of education through it.

India, amongst countries of South and South-East Asia etc., even today, is based in respect of agriculture and economy related to industries linked with it. These can be the root source of employment in our nation. In this very stream, in certain other countries including that of Europe, there are also industries linked with livestock, fishery or forestry and to so many sources of employment as well. It is our duty now to develop technical education based on above-mentioned foremost sources in accordance with the national circumstances and need of the time. Further, it should be made compulsory in educational syllabi pertaining to our nation. We should remember that if we do not take steps in this direction in right earnest and do not accord employment orientation to education, 1/5 part of our population in 21st century, i.e., 20 crore people will be badly effected by unemployment. It will have evil impact on economic and social fields indirectly as well as directly.

Our system of education is faulty. We stressed in by-gone years on opening more schools; having new schools, colleges and universities. It was essential too. This cannot be termed an unfair step. But as per the suggestions of the great Mahatma we did not put stress on changing the educational system according to the need of the time while doing so. It is owing to that, that education today is not capable of providing employment. I have observed some fulfillment in this direction in Thailand, Philippines, Malaysia and many European countries. It is, however, voluntary and exists at higher level. This will have to be accorded with compulsiveness. We should work in a planned way. Only then we can get rid of the problems in the present century. It is this very expectation that we now have from education.

Glossary of Indian Terms

Ahimsa	:	Non-violence
Ashram	:	Hermitage; abode of spiritual teacher; place for disciplined community; one of the four stages in the life of Hindus
Charit	:	Composed by
Dalit	:	One belonging to depressed class
Dharma	:	Religious injunction; religion; duty
Gurudeva	:	A great teacher; a title bestowed on Rabindranath Tagore
Harijan	:	One belonging to untouchable class; a weekly started by Mahatma Gandhi early in the fourth decade of twentieth century
Himalayan	:	Of Himalaya- a house of ice
Khadi	:	Handspun handwoven cloth
Mahatma	:	Literally high-souled person, a title bestowed on Mohandas Karamchand Gandhi
Manas	:	A man
Naam	:	Name
Rajya	:	A state; a province; rule or kingdom
Ramayana	:	Hindu epic narrating the story of the abduction of Sita, wife of Lord Rama, the Prince of Ayodhya, by Ravana, demon-king of Lanka, and her rescue after the conquest of Lanka by the army lead by Rama

		and the death of Ravana at Rama's hand
Sadhana	:	To achieve by work or devotion; to study; to accomplish; to learn
Sanyasi	:	One who renounces the world; an ascetic
Sari	:	A cloth worn round the lower body by Indian women
Satya	:	Truth
Satyagraha	:	Insistence on truth, resistance offered to uphold truth [a weapon made popular by Mahatma Gandhi during the Indian freedom struggle]
Swami	:	An owner; proprietor; master; lord; king; a title of the supreme being
Swarajya	:	Self-rule
Vande	:	Praising; praise; salutation; adoration; homage; reverential greeting
Vedas	:	The sacred early Hindu scriptures, four in number
Vishva	:	The world; the universe

Index

A

Abdul Qadir Khan, 161-62, 166
Abu Hurairah, 268
Adhyatmik Shakti, 23
Advaita, 296, 299
Afghanistan, 220
Africa, 222
African
  Cotton Farmers, 65
  Countries, 65
Agha Khan Palace, 196, 241
Ahimsa, 20, 24, 76-77, 88, 201, 203-05, 210, 225-26, 228, 235, 255, 270, 282, 293, 308
Akbar, 296
Alcoholism, 66
All India Sarvodaya Conference, 190
America, 92, 94
American
  Peace Corpse, 196
  Revolution, 217
Anti-Ballistic Missile (ABM), 162
Apartheid (South Africa), 179
Apology of Plato, 44
Arabs in Pakistan, 319
Arberry, A.J., 255
Arjun, 109-12, 142
Armament Industry, 45
Arms Race, 197
Artificial Wisdom, 245
ASEAN Block Countries, 81
Ashok, 308
Ashram, 145
Asia, 318, 323
Asia and Africa, 304
Asian Economic Crisis, 217
Asiatic Law Amendment Ordinance, 1906, 148
Atomic Bombs, 166
Atrocities, 152
Aung Kyaw, 79
Aung San Suu Kyi, 79-81

B

Baghdad, 257
Bangladesh, 280
Banking and Industry, 220
Battle of Kurukshetra, 109, 111
Bhagvad Gita, 109-11, 114-20, 139-40, 142
Bhakti Movement, 296
Bhakti Yoga, 110, 112, 116
Bhan Singh, 51
Bhartiya Kisan Union, 60
Bhave, Vinobha, 185-89, 191-92, 198-99
Bhoodan Movement, 188-89

Bhutto, Zulfikar Ali, 161
Bible, 21
Bihar Agitation, 186
Bihar, 62
Bihar Famina, 196
Bihar Movement, 187, 190
Bill of Rights, 204, 231
Bin Laden, 245
Bio-Piracy, 54
Biotechnology, 54, 57, 59
Biotechnology Industry, 61
Black Civil Rights Movement, 179
Black Marketing, 99
Boar War, 23, 43
Bose, Subhas Chandra, 114, 154
Brazil and China, 65
Bretton Woods Agreements, 213, 217
Britain, 41
British
  Army, 281
  Colonial Rule, 79, 179
  Empire, 170
  Imperialism, 155
  Movement, 281
  Raj, 171
  Rule India, 314
  Rule, 42, 44-45, 96, 320
  Rulers, 104
  Textile Industry, 56
Bt. Cotton, 62
Buddha, 87, 89, 140, 210, 213, 226
Buddhism 91, 308, 318
Bunyadi, 326
Burkino—Mali, 65
Burma, 79-82, 222, 319-20
Burmese
  Groups, 80
  Social Programme Party, 79
  Struggle, 80
Bush, George W., 245
  Administration, 163-64, 178
  Administrative Policies, 159

C

Calogero, Francisco, Italian Nuclear Physicists, 167
Cambodia, 222
Cancun Negotiations, 65
Capitalism, 214
Cargill and Monsanto, 64
Central Asia, 220
Champaran, Bihar, 149
Charkha, 55-57, 88, 278
Charter of UN, 204
Chemical Fertilizers, 100
Child Marriage, 287-88
China, 100, 161
China US, 177
China and Taiwan, 163
Chinese, 47
Christ, Jesus, 213, 226, 262, 308
Christian Anarchism, 140
Christian Bomb, 161
Christianity, 91
Civil Disobedience, 79, 172, 201, 207-08, 210, 227-229, 233
Campaign, 171
  Movement, 119, 152-54

Civil Rights, 169
Civil War, 79
Civilization,
  Indian, 240
  Modern, 240, 313
  Western, 240
Clinton, Bill, 178
Co-existence, 107
Colonial Exploitation, 45
Colonialism, 56
Commercial Banks, 217
Communal Violence, 94
Conciliation Committee, 312
Confucius, 213
Congress Party, 170
Congress Working Committee, 155
Consumer Protection Law, 217
Consumerism, 72, 197
Cottage Industries, 35
Crimean War, 135
CTBT (Comprehensive Test Ban Treaty), 162-63
Cuban Missile Crisis, 159
Culture and Society, 136

D

Dada Abdullah Seth, 169
Dalai Lama, 318
Dalits, 137
Dandi, 77
Dandi March (1930), 152-53, 290
Danish
  Missionaries, 181
  Solidarity Groups, 182
Das, Ram Mangal, 88
Day of Judgement, 258
Deccan Riots, 67
Decision Making, 219
Democracy, 194
  In Burma, 317
  Participatory, 194
  Representative, 194
Democratic Planning, 193
Denmark, 181-82
Desai, Jeevanlal, 145
Desai, Mahadev, 196
Desai, Narayan, 195
Deshpande, Nirmala, 80
Dhaddha, Siddhara, 193
Dhyanyoga, 112
Digitalization of Information, 71
Disarmament, 311
Discriminating Policies, 42
Disobedience, 244 see Civil Disobedience, 79

E

Economic
  Conflict, 128
  Crisis, 49
  Development, 305
  Policies, 151
Economy, 64, 99, 216, 248
Ecosystem, 62, 234
Education, 31-35, 37, 118, 146, 212, 271, 274-77, 312, 321-26
Formal, 36
  Higher, 36
Religious, 33

Result Oriented, 37
Technical (Bunyadi Basic), 34-35
Educational
Development, 32
System, 32, 36
Elimination of Poverty, 237
England, 168-69, 174, 286, 305, 307
Environmental
Conference, 224
Degradation, 237
Equality and Justice, 263
Ethics, 215
Ethnic Divide in Burma, 320
European Union, 81

F

Family Planning, 100
Farm
Suicide, 67
Suicides in India, 64
Farmers
Rights, 60
Movement, 59
Suicide, 66
Farming Communities, 58
Father of Nations, 195
Federal International Authority, 312
Feudalism, 67
Finland, 181
First World War, 135, 151
Fissile Material Cuto Treaty, 162
Flora and Fauna, 241
France, 160
Free Trade, 54, 58, 60, 65
Free Trade Policies of WTO, 64
Freedom Movement of India, 98

G

G-22 Alliance, 65
Gandhian, Institutions, 195, 239
Gandhi and Russell, 301
Gandhi National Memorial, 241
Gandhi Peace Foundation, 80
Gandhi, M.K., 17, 104, 129, 202, 293
Application of Scientific Methods, 124
Ashram, 129
Basic Moral Concepts, 202
Believer of Sarvodaya, 119
Champion of Peace, 279
Charismatic Leader, 104, 106
Concept of Non-Violence, 293
Daily Prayer, 202
Father of Nation, 97
Husband Wife Relationship, 288
Influence of Bhagvad Gita, 109
Inspiration of-, 139
Kesar-e-Hind, 151
Legacy, 133
Methodology for Truth and Non-Violence, 128
Movement, 290

Non-Violence, 203
Perspectives, 121, 128
Philanthropist, 104
Philosopher & Nationalist, 274
Political Indoctrination, 107
Pollock, 142
Socio-Political Philosophy, 293, 295
Spiritual Master, 140
Status of Women, 285, 290
Strecher Bearer, 135
Struggle for Freedom in India, 122
True Nationalist, 31
Tolstoy's Disciple, 140
Gandhi's
Fundamentals of-, 237
Gujarat, 237
Legacy, 69
Non-Violence, 168, 186
Philosophy, 68
Philosophy of Life, 17
Satya, 18, 20
Satyagraha, 75-76, 78
Special Wheel, 56, 58
Vaishnava Family, 17
Value Education, 31
Gandhian
Basics, 192
Educational Philosophy, 277
Establishment, 196
Fraternity, 192
Ideals, 199
Institutions, 240-42
Leaders, 191
Legacy, 185, 193
Method, 98
Movement, 186, 190, 192-93, 195-98, 241
Non-Violence, 309
Peace Philosophy, 278
Perspectives, 308
Philosophy, 25, 99, 194, 239, 277,
Politicians, 192
Principles, 246
Religio-Moral Philosophy, 278
Social and Political Philosophy, 278
Struggle, 98
Vocabulary, 308
Gandhism, 96
GATT, 54, 57, 60, 213, 218
Gautam Buddha, 24
Gene Banks, 59
Genocide, 176, 177, 246
George W. Bush Administration, 178
Germany, 174
Girl Child, 250
Gita, 20-21, 23
Global Markets, 63
Global War Machine, 213
Globalization, 53, 60-61, 63-64, 66, 217, 223, 244
Glossary of Indian Terms, 331-32
Godhra (Gujarat), 49
Godse, Nathu Ram, 94, 282
Gokhale, Gopal Krishan, 101, 139
Gospel of Renunciation, 133-34, 137

Goulart, Jose, 222
Goulart's Reforms, 223
Govt. of India Act, 1935, 154
Greater East India War, 76
Green Revolution, 57, 67
Grey, Colin S., 165
Gujarat, 17, 145
Gun Factories, 141
Guru Nanak, 296

H

Harishchandra, King, 17
Hate Groups, 48
Heraclitus, 213
Hind Swaraj, 45-46, 55
Hindi Muslim Unity, 149
Hind Swaraj, 240
Hindu
  and Muslims, 157, 279-80, 290
  Bomb, 161
  Muslim
  Riots, 50
  Muslim Violence, 50
  Philosophy, 140
  Scriptures, 18
  Votes, 94
Hinduism, 21, 140, 238
Hiroshima and Nagasaki, 98, 162-63
Hitler, 48, 191, 307
Hitler and Mussolini, 47
Human Rights, 61, 81, 213, 217, 261
  Violations, 231
Hunter Commission, 152

I

Imperialism, 54, 56
Indentured Labourers, 42
India and China, 41, 81, 148
India and Pakistan, 156
India's
  Freedom, 76, 97
Independence Movement, 55
Indian
  Anarchism, 191
  and Pakistani Nuclear Bomb Test, 161
  Civil Rights Movement, 170
  Community, 42, 169
  Farmers, 69
  Freedom Struggle, 182
  Gandhi Champion, 80
  Gandhians, 185
  Home Rule, 170
  Merchant Community, 42
  National Congress, 87, 101, 105, 154
  National Movement, 149
  Nationalism, 140
  Peasantry, 63
  Politics, 105
  Women, 285, 290
  Sexist Treatment, 287
  Women's Participation, 289
Indira Gandhi Govt., 198
Industrial Disputes, 98
Industrial Relations, 97
Industrialization, 45, 55-56, 141, 314

Inner Temple London, 168
Intellectual Property
  Crimes, 54, 61
  Rights, 57, 59
  Rights Laws, 69
  Rights Protection, 59
  International
  Atomic Energy Agency (IAEA), 167
  Committee for India, 182
  Court of Justice Hague, 164
  Criminal Court, (ICC), 176-78
  Law, 160, 163, 177, 179, 306, 311
  Law Commission, 174
  Military Tribunal (Nuremberg), 174
  Missionary Conference, 47
  Monetary Fund, 22, 213, 218
  System, 302-04, 309-11
  Trade, 223
  Welfare, 47
Iran, 162, 168
Iraq, 94, 178
IRS Abuses, 231
Islam, 91, 255-56, 263, 268-72, 280
  Brotherhood and Universality in-, 268
  Morality in-, 265
Islamic Judiciary, 269
Islam—Sikhism, 296
Israel, 93, 178
Israel, India, Pakistan and Cuba, 160

J

Jainism and Christianity, 147
Jallianwala Bagh, 151-52
Japan, 76, 141
Japanese, 47
Japanese and American, 318
Japanese Army, 154
Jatak Stories, 88
Jesus Christ, 24
Jewish Bomb, 161
Jews in Russia, 315
Jihad, 258, 262, 268
Jinnah's Two Nation Theory, 280
Jnana Yoga, 110
Johannesburg, 43, 148
Johannesburg to Durban, 142
JP, 198, 199 see Narayan Jayaprakash
JP's Campaign of Total Revolution, 186
Judiciary, 230, 269
Judiciary System, 81, 88

K

Kabir's Rebirth, 88
Kaira (Gujarat), 149
Kaira and Bardoli, 99
Kalinga Episode, 308
Karma and Dharma, 109
Karmyoga, 110, 111
Karnataka
Land Reform Act, 66

Rajya Ryot Sangha (KKRS), 60
Kashmir, 161
Kasturba, 285
Kasturba Gandhi National Memorial Trust (KGNMT), 241
Kaur, Rajkumari Amrit, 287
Khem Karan, 51
Kochrab (Paldi), 145
Koran, 21, see under Quran also
Kriya Yoga, 20

L

Labour and Health Law, 219
Lahore, 51
Land Gift Movement, 187
Land Revenue, 99
Lao Tse, 213
Law Courts, 45
Law of Truth, 201
League of Nations, 303, 310
Leo, Tolstoy, 226
Libya, 162, 178
Linguistic Groups, 42
Literacy, 323
London Vegetarian Society, 135
Lord Buddha, 114, 317-18
Lord Irwin, 153, 171-72
Lord Krishna, 20, 23, 109, 111-14, 118, 140, 142, 259, 270
Lord Mahavir, 24, 114, 213, 226, 308

M

Mahabharata, 18, 290
Majumdar, Gangaben, 55
Mandela, Nelson, 104
Marxism, 192
Mass Media, 182
Mass Production Factories, 44
Materialism, 24-25
Mecca, 260
Meditation, 229-30
  Buddhist, 233
  Centres, 233
Mesa (Arizona), 48
Middle East, 94, 163
Middle Eastern Oil, 93
Military Industrial Government Complexes, 218, 220, 231
Minority(ies), 47, 93
Modern
  Economic Order, 314
  Industrial System, 45
  Welfare, 47
Modernization, 244, 251
Mohammed Bin Abdullah, 140, 256, 258-62, 268, 270-71, 280
Mono-cultures in Agriculture, 62
Monopoly Rights, 60
Monsanto Corporation, 62-63
Morality and Ethics, 32-34
Moses, 213, 262
Munltinational Corporations, (MNCs), 213, 217-19, 221-22, 229, 231, 233, 319

Muslim
Camp, 51
League, 155
Minority in India, 94
Muslims and Christians, 94

N

Nag, Kalidasa, 76
Napalm Bombs, 222
Narayan, Japaprakash, 185-86, 188-92
Natal (South Africa), 42-43
National
Identity, 42
League for Democracy (NLD), 79-82
Liberation Movement, 31
Nationalism, 45
Nature Cure, 135
Navdanya, 57-59
Nawab Bibi, 51
Nazi, 174
Negroes, 44
Nehru, Pt. Jawaharlal, 136, 153, 194
Neo-Nazi Group, 48
Netherlands, 323-24
Neutron Bombs, 160
New International Economic Order, 128
NGOs, 50
Noakhali (West Bengal), 86
Non-Cooperation, 60, 98, 104, 119, 233
Non-Cooperation Movement, 23, 151-52
Non-Nuclear Weapons States, 160
Non-Violence, 45, 47-50, 77, 80, 83, 91-96, 107, 109, 117, 122-28, 133, 135-36, 141, 145, 147, 157, 170, 189, 197, 201, 203-05, 208-10, 225-27, 229-30, 239-43, 245, 247-51, 253, 296-97, 309, 311, 317
Policy, 49
Society, 129
Nordic Countries, 181
North Korea, 162-63, 168
North West Frontier Provinces, (NWFP), 156
Norway, 181
NPT Review Conference, 162
Nuclear
Arms, 164
Bomb, 122, 167
Disarmament, 160, 162-63, 165, 197
Energy, 160
Non-Proliferation Treaty (NPT), 160, 162-64
Posture Review Paper, 163-64
Proliferation, 167
Reactions, 167
Secrets, 162
Terrorism, 167
Weapon State, 162
Weapons, 159-63, 179, 310
Nuremberg, 164-65, 168-69
Nuremberg Principles, 159, 174-79

O

O'Dyer, Michael, 152

P

Pacifism, 305
Pakistan, 51, 94, 105, 136, 156, 161, 166, 168, 220, 280
Pakistan's Nuclear Weapons, 162
Palestinians, 246
Partition of India, 23, 156
Patel, Vallabhbhai, 149
Patent, 54
  Act, 68
  Monopolies, 57
  Rights, 63
Peace and Security, 310
Peace Cultures, 293
Peaceful Co-Existence, 127, 296
Peasant Organization, 67
Pietermaritzburg Station, 42
Planetary Ecosystem, 209, 223
Plato, 325
Political
  Economy, 213
Parties, 50, 190
Rights, 218
Population Control, 97
Porbander, 168
Praja Socialist Comrades, 189
Pretoria (South Africa), 168
Prison Diary, 190
Property Rights, 217
Punjab, 152
Puritanism, 319

Q

Qatar, 178
Quit India Movement, 154-55
Quran, 256, 258, 260-66, 270-72
Quran and Hadith, 270

R

Race of Arms, 250
Racial Law, 43
Raj Chanderbhai, 139-40
Rajkot (Gujarat), 41
Rajoguna, 110, 113-14
Ram Charit Manas, 84-85
  Rama, 22, 24, 83-87
  Kalpavriksha, 86-87
Ramakrishna Order, 75
Raman, Maharishi, 23
Ramayana, 21-22, 83-85
  Ramrajya, 22, 86
  Concept of-, 85
Reagan, Ronald, American Pres., 250
Rebirth and Salvation, 21
Reforms in Indian Administration, 153
Refugee Camps, 49
Religious Doctrine, 92
Religious Morality, 265
River Ganges, 107
River Sabarmati, 238
Rockefeller, David, 217
Rogue, Frank Silva, 49
Rome, 269-70
Rome Agreement, 177

Rome Statute, 177-78
Round Table Conference, London, 154, 172
Rowlatt Act, 151-52
Rural Empowerment, 241
Rural India, 50
Ruskin, John, 134, 139, 142, 226
Russel, Bertrant Arthur William, 301, 305-08, 310, 312-15
Russia—North Korea, 163
Rwanda, 176

S

Sabarmati Ashram, 145, 147, 149
Sabarmati Express, 49
Sabarmati River, 145
Salt
  Acts, 154
  Laws, 68
  March, 172
Salt, Henry, 135
Salvation, 32-33, 205, 279
Salvation Army, 148
Sangha Parivar, 94
Sarva Seva Sangh, 193
Sarvodaya, 44, 136, 142, 190-91, 193
  Movement, 191, 193, 196, 198
Social Order, 187, 188
Satoguna, 110, 113-14
Satya, 17, 18, 20
Satya/Ahimsa, 149
Satyagraha, 23, 43, 68, 75-76, 78, 92, 95, 120, 140, 144, 148, 150, 157, 170, 186-88, 191, 199, 245, 290, 294-96, 407
  Ashram Sabarmati, 55
  In South Africa, 140
  Movement, 149
  Philosophy of-, 148
  Techniques, 294
  Tax, 290
Scandinavian Countries, 181-82
Science and Technology, 214, 323
  Development, 56
Second World War, 98, 154, 174, 182, 303, 307
Seed
  Corporation, 58
  Freedom, 58
  Monopolies, 61-64
Service and Britishhood, 99
Seth Tayeb, 164
Sevagram, 47
Shanti Sena, 195-96, 250
Shaw, Bernard, 255, 261
  Shrimadbhagvad Gita, 18, 44
Sierra Occidental, 224
Silicon Valley's Technologies, 223
Simon, Sir John, 153
Sir Cripps, 154
Slavery, 31, 68, 206
Smuts, Jan, 148
Social
  and Economic Institutions, 246
  Justice, 75, 309
  Movement, 197-98, 200

Order, 100
Revolution, 191
Security, 97, 233
Socialism, 129, 148
Socialist/Capitalist Order, 303
Society(ies), 24, 33-34, 53, 61, 72-73, 97, 99, 133, 136-37, 183, 189, 196, 199, 206-07, 223, 228, 231-32, 259, 262, 265, 267, 269-70, 275-77, 281, 296-98, 302, 309
Danish, 182
Indian, 199, 279
Non-Violent, 212, 248
Traditional, 214, 216
Socrates, 140, 213
Sodhi, Balbir Singh, 49
Soil Conservation Programme, 59
South Africa, 42-45, 104, 136, 142, 145, 147, 169, 172, 245, 285
and India, 308
Boar War, 135
Resistance Movement, 46
South Africans, 182
South Korea, 163
Soviet Union, 303
Spinning Wheel, 55, 56
Spiritualism, 33
Spirituality, 274, 319
Status of Women, 285, 290
Stealth Bombs, 223
Stri Shakti, 252
Suicide
Bombing, 94-95
Bombs, 94
Economics, 63, 68
Suicides, 64-66
Swadeshi, 129
and Swaraj, 69
Swaraj Satyagraha and Sarvodaya, 68
Swami Satyananda Puri, 75-76
Swaraj, 44, 243
Sweden, 181
Syhgenta, 64

T

Tagore and Gandhi, 133-37
Tagore, Rabindranath, 23, 76
Taliban, 220
Tamoguna, 110, 113-14
Terrorism, 245
Terrorist, 166, 167
Textile
Labour Association, 147
Mills Britain, 67
Mills Workers, 147
Workers, 98
Thai Society, 49-50
Thai-Bharat Cultural Lodge, 76
Thailand, 76, 318
Third World Countries, 305
Thoreau, Henry David, 226
Tibetan Freedom, 319
Tolstoy Farm, 143-45, 150
Tolstoy, Leo, 133-136, 140, 148
Philosopher of Russia, 140
Philosophy, 141
Total Revolution, 199
Totalitarianism, 54

Touring Gandhian Pilgrimage, 195
Trade
Agreements, 219
Liberalization, 64
Related International Property Rights (TRIPs), 54, 68
Treaty, 54
Unions, 50, 219
Trade, Technology and Property Rights, 53
Treaty of Westphalia, 302
Trilateral Commissions, 217
Tula (Russia), 134
Tulsidasa, 21-22, 84
TV Channels, 241

U

UN, 81, 167, 244, 246, 250-51, 303-05, 310
Charter, 178
General Assembly, 164, 174
Resolution of Human Rights, 204
Security Council, 176
UNESCO, 127
UNICEF, 243, 250
Universal Declaration of Human Rights, 178
University of Bombay, 41
Untouchability, 48, 129
Upanishads, 72-73, 84, 109, 140
Uranium, 161, 165, 167
US, 48, 65, 161, 163, 166, 178-79, 221, 230, 245-46, 255, 303-04
Army, 223
Constitution, 204
Intervention in Iraq and Afghanistan, 304
Investors, 223
Law, 215
Military Establishment, 221
Nuclear Weapons, 163
Soya Farmers, 65

V

Value Education, 31-32, 34, 37
Vedas, 21, 72, 85, 109, 140
Vedic Scriptures, 84
Vegetarian Ethics, 134-35
Vibhuti Yoga, 249
Vietnam, 222
Vietnam War, 179, 315
Vijapur (Baroda), 55
Village Handicrafts, 35
Violence, 45, 47-48, 91-96, 99, 122, 124-25, 157
Communal, 197
Israeli and American-, 95
Physical, 91
Retaliatory, 94-95
Victims of-, 95
Voting Rights, 45

W

War Crimes, 176-77, 231
War Tax, 231
Warangal (AP), 62

Wardha Ashram, 21
Weapons of Mass Destruction (WMD), 246, 248
Wisdom Bank of Japan, 245
Women Liberation, 289
World Bank, (WB), 218, 224
  Structural Policies, 64
World Health Organization, (WHO), 164
World Order, 301-02, 304-05, 307
  Euro-Centric, 303
World Peace Movement Trust, 80
World Trade Organization, (WTO), 54, 65, 213, 218-19

Y

Yemen, 178
Yoga, 319
Yogananda Parmahansa, 21
Yugoslavia, 176

Z

Zend Avesta, 21, 150
Zulu Rebellion, (South Africa), 23, 43, 135